The
DEVIL'S
Dinner

ALSO BY STUART WALTON

*In the Realm of the Senses: A Materialist
Theory of Seeing and Feeling*

A Natural History of Human Emotions

Out of It: A Cultural History of Intoxication

The
DEVIL'S
Dinner

A GASTRONOMIC and CULTURAL HISTORY of CHILI PEPPERS

STUART WALTON

St. Martin's Press ❧ New York

THE DEVIL'S DINNER. Copyright © 2018 by Stuart Walton.
All rights reserved. Printed in the United States of America.
For information, address St. Martin's Press, 175 Fifth Avenue,
New York, N.Y. 10010.

www.stmartins.com

Designed by Steven Seighman

Library of Congress Cataloging-in-Publication Data

Names: Walton, Stuart, author.
Title: The devil's dinner : a gastronomic and cultural history
    of chili peppers / Stuart Walton.
Description: First edition. | New York : St. Martin's Press,
    [2018] | Includes bibliographical references and index.
Identifiers: LCCN 2018022094| ISBN 9781250163202
    (hardcover) | ISBN 9781250163219 (ebook)
Subjects: LCSH: Hot peppers—History. | Cooking (Hot
    peppers)—History. | Food habits—History.
Classification: LCC SB307.P4 W35 2018 | DDC
    633.8/4—dc23
LC record available at https://lccn.loc.gov/2018022094

Our books may be purchased in bulk for promotional,
educational, or business use. Please contact your local
bookseller or the Macmillan Corporate and Premium Sales
Department at 1-800-221-7945, extension 5442, or by email at
MacmillanSpecialMarkets@macmillan.com.

First Edition: October 2018

10 9 8 7 6 5 4 3 2 1

In memoriam Rosemary Stark

Contents

Introduction   ix

A Note on Spelling   xxiii

Part One: Biology

1   Our Favorite Spice—All About Chili   3

2   Apaches, Vipers, and Dragons—Types of Chili   32

Part Two: History

3   Spice of America—The Chili in Its Homelands   73

4   Three Ships Come Sailing—The Columbian Exchange   91

5   Blazing a Trail—Chili's Journey Through Asia and Africa   104

6   "Red and Incredibly Beautiful"—Chili Goes to China   122

7   From Piri Piri to Paprika—European Variations   135

8   Bowls o' Red and Chili Queens—An American Affair   152

9   Pepper Sauce—A Global Obsession   170

10   Taste and Touch—How Chili Peppers Work   185

Part Three: Culture

11   The Devil's Dinner—Discovering the Dark Side of Chili   197

12   Hot Stuff—Chilies and Sex   213

13   Fighting Talk—Weaponized Chili   224

14   Superhots and Chiliheads—The Cult of Chili   232

15   Man Food—How Chili Became a Guy Thing   245

16   The Globalization of Taste—Can Chili Save Us?   258

Acknowledgments   271

Notes   273

Select Bibliography   283

Index   287

Introduction

At the time of this writing, Smokin' Ed's Carolina Reaper, grown by the PuckerButt Pepper Company in South Carolina, is officially the world's hottest pepper.[1] On the Scoville heat unit (SHU) scale used throughout most of the last hundred years to measure the hotness of chilies (and which measures the McIlhenny Company's Tabasco sauce at somewhere in the range of 2,500–5,000 SHU), tests at Winthrop University have calibrated the Reaper at 1,569,300 SHU. In other words, you would have to dilute the ground pepper in sugar solution more than 1.5 million times before you could no longer detect its heat. And if you don't dilute it at all, you may well detect its heat 1.5 million lifetimes after introducing it to your tongue.

The cute little Carolina Reaper is emergency-room red, with a delicate, wrinkly body tapering to a little point like a hornet stinger. Its squarish shape is not unlike that of a miniature bell pepper, but there the resemblance ends. Swallowing one Reaper can set your whole soul on fire; the SHU reading of a bell pepper is zero. When bell peppers began appearing in groceries in northern Europe in the 1960s, many consumers were convinced that they would be hot and spicy, a misapprehension that obstinately outlasted the first taste for many who dared to try them. They were red peppers, and red pepper was what went into hot sauces like Tabasco, or what turned up in little jars labeled cayenne, for deviling up your eggs or adding a warmish luster to your first attempts at goulash.

Whole chili peppers were only available in these formative times from Asian and West Indian groceries, into which only their respective Chinese, Indian, and Caribbean constituencies ventured. Now chilies are on most supermarket shelves. Everybody knows that you can't cook Mexican or Thai or Indian food without them, although people still cling to certain potently persistent chili myths, such as that the smallest ones are hottest, the red ones are the hottest, or that all the hotness is contained in the seeds.

In contrast to these early, nervous encounters, an enthusiastic hot pepper movement has sprung up in the modern era, extending deep roots not just into the southern United States but across the length and width of the nation, spawning festivals and academic colloquia and broadening the range of hot sauce products available everywhere from specialist delicatessens to menus at fast-food franchises. In the United Kingdom, too, a hot sauce movement has coalesced around a perennial calendar of fiery-food festivals, hives of devotional activities that often include a chili-eating contest, over which a small coterie of intrepid maniacs exercises the same dominance as does an exclusive band of elite players over the international tennis circuit.

Chili, which was once terrifying to the Anglo-American imagination, is now big business—and big culture, too. The pepper has generated its own study institute at New Mexico State University, responsible in 2006 for identifying what was then the world's hottest pepper, the bhut jolokia, a hybrid variety of Eastern India that is about two-thirds the strength of Pucker-Butt's finest. Annual conferences and research programs for plant breeding supplement the institute's dedicated work of situating hot peppers in the cultural and gastronomic imaginary of chefs and consumers, a labor of assimilation that has turned the one blaring signal that chili peppers developed at the origin of their evolution—a warning to mammals to stay well away from them—into just what is most attractive about them.

Hot pepper culture is a triumph of alimentary defiance over biological instinct. Like many a potent intoxicant, the chili promises immediate sensual pleasure as well as an aftermath of pain, and a rather instant aftermath at that. There are ecstasies of regret to be had

from tasting even a tiny fragment of chopped hot pepper, and infernal miseries for those who, soon after the
chopping, carelessly rub their eyes, put in their iPod
earbuds, or visit the bathroom. (Among the suggestions
an online forum offered to sufferers in that last category were to apply yogurt to the affected organ, or—more
enterprisingly, if less effectively—to run outside and
expose it to the air.) Yet none of this is sufficient to
deter hardcore chili aficionados. Rather, pain only
encourages them.

Chili has undergone a transition from a food—
whether a simple spice, an ingredient, or the emblematic dish known across the Western world as chili con
carne—to a way of life, the structuring principle of encounters with food that have long left behind the idea
of simple sustenance or nourishment and turned into a
transformative experience. In cultures ambivalently
torn between individual liberty and social subversion in
the matter of controlled substances, the hot pepper
movement has become gastronomy's own version of a
drug subculture. Nothing involved in the movement is
illegal, as long as what's involved are the peppers themselves and not their pure alkaloid capsaicin, which was
banned as a food additive in the European Union in
January 2011 on the grounds that an extremely high
intake of it could be carcinogenic. But the culture sur-
rounding chilies is one of willingly incurred risk to
one's soft tissue and overall gastric harmony, while the
race to produce ever more concentrated, searing heat

in each new variety reflects the trend toward increasing intensity in the synthetic compounds targeted at users of street drugs. Some scientific researchers even claim that a taste for chilies is in itself a species of addiction, with its own cognate pattern of initial rejection followed by the gradual development of tolerance and then the eventual craving for more of the stuff in hotter versions once the old ones no longer cut it.

Much of this would doubtless bemuse those cultures where the raging fire of chili has been gastronomically indispensable for centuries. A Thai banquet that opens with a bowl of tom yum soup locks the taste buds in an immediate wrestling hold from which it mercilessly won't relinquish them: the salty pungency of *nam pla* (fish sauce) and the unapologetic sour sting of lime juice, lemongrass, and tomato are undergirded by roaring waves of white-hot fury from a fistful of finely minced red chili. What subsequent dishes can the tenderized palate possibly register in the aftermath of such an assault? Only ones sizzling with more chili.

In the tiny Himalayan kingdom of Bhutan, sometimes known as the world's last Shangri-la, chilies are no mere spice ingredient, but are pure sustenance in themselves, eaten as the principal item in curry dishes that might include supporting bulk from soft cheese (as in the national dish, *ema datshi*), and as the condiment—chili pickle—that adds relish to a whole repast. Chilies came to Bhutan via India, probably in the eighteenth century, and were adopted more wholeheartedly there than anywhere else on earth, such that a standard purchase of a kilo (2.2 pounds) of whole peppers, the local variety known as sha ema, is the minimum weekly requirement for a small family.

Bhutanese people of all ages thrive on this diet, tears of apparent contrition streaming down their faces as they eat. The delicate infant palate becomes habituated to peppers early. Chili pervades its consumers' bodies with a radiant inner heat, a potential lifesaver during winters at high altitude, and the perspiration it provokes efficiently eliminates toxins. More than anything else, say the Bhutanese (as well as every hothead from Veracruz to Sichuan), spicy food gives you energy. It lights you up with interior heat and releases waves of happiness. Isn't that, more than leaving you overstuffed, what good food should do? In the rarefied air of Thimphu, nestled in its river valley at the world's apex, anything blander would speak of the misery of scarcity.

In the Western context, the hot pepper movement has become very much a guy thing, like running the barbecue or ironing your own shirt. Competitive tasting appeals to the pugilistic instinct that may have diminished with advancing middle age or the expanding waistline, and eating something that is so transparently dangerous has some of the sheer daredevilry, not to mention the thrill, of extreme sports. There are women competitors at some of the chili-eating contests, but they are greatly outnumbered by men, and it is worth asking why this is. Perhaps women generally don't see the point of it, in which case to a certain male mind-set, a man's readiness to surrender his organism to fifty shades of sizzling might still be a marker of perceived virility.

Certainly the claims made for each new contender in the superhot stakes don't exactly come with the rapturous ring of most gourmet talk. English farmer Gerald Fowler's candid description of the naga viper (1,382,118 SHU), which he improbably bred in 2011 on his small farm in the rainy northern county of Cumbria, is typical: "It's hot enough to strip paint," he commented affably. Tasting a Carolina Reaper for an article in *Maxim* magazine, journalist Steven Leckart's analogy was that it was like "being face-fucked by Satan"[2] (". . . presumably," he forgot to add). What, after all, can you do with peppers that pack over 1.5 million SHUs into their little, shriveled purses? The same thing you do with all the others, suggests its breeder, PuckerButt's Ed Currie: make it the foundation of hot sauces and salsas. And may God have mercy on your tongue.

The chili pepper's rapid progress around the world from the days of Columbus onward has been one of food history's enduring testaments to globalization, an extraordinary enough thought for an ingredient that seems to have only one warning to consumers: nil by mouth. To imagine world cuisine without the chili is like imagining it without sugar, which was also once the cultivated taste of a gastronomic minority that grew maniacal for it. Whereas sugar was initially the marker of elite taste only, its systematic production soon generating one of human history's monstrous tragedies in the expanding slave trade, hot peppers made their way around their world on their own improbable merits, rooting themselves in indigenous cuisines and peasants' diets with incendiary spice and fortifying nutrition. If peppers' fiery ardor would eventually be somewhat tamed in the slowly simmering casseroles and soups of the Austro-Hungarian empire, it still glowed incandescently in Mogul cooking, relieved the austerity of the Orthodox monastic diet of imperial Russia, and fired up the newly awakened senses at the crack of dawn in Chinese congee and Vietnamese chao. For those so inclined, chilies added another kind of heat to the potency of vodka and schnapps in bitter northern climes. Today, there are chili whiskies, chili beers, and chili liqueurs for the hottest shots and shooters. Chili air fresheners will add kaboom to your living room or car. Thierry Mugler's A*Men, a fragrance for a man intent on making a lasting impression, contains red chili amid the more obviously seductive notes of coffee and vanilla to assure you that, whatever the smoothness of his exterior, he's hot stuff where it counts.

Transported to Europe after the first exploration of the Americas, the chili, probably a variety of *Capsicum annuum*, was found to be a versatile creature. It could be preserved in oil, vinegar, or salt for using whole, or it could be dried and ground into a spice powder, as with paprika or Spanish *pimentón*, and used as a hot seasoning in soups and slow-cooked dishes. The adoption of chili overturned the established historical trajectory of migrant food ingredients, whereby a social elite develops a fashionable craving for it and thus inflates its market value until it is eventually disseminated among poorer classes as an everyday, affordable staple. The European elites did not widely accept chili for culinary use until around the mid-eighteenth century, only after much of its fire had been tamed. In this almost neutered form, it became a minor ingredient in the spice mixtures of effete French gastronomy. In Italy, careful breeding drew the searing sting from the chili and produced the widespread, inoffensive bell pepper, standby of Italian *peperonata,* Basque *piperade,* Provençal ratatouille, and some variants of Sicilian *caponata.*

Not the least attractive attribute of the chili pepper, particularly the red that most varieties attain when ripe, is its color, which does not dull in cooking, and which brings a welcome, vivid flash to the garnishing of otherwise neutral-looking food such as rice dishes. Before the arrival of chilies, there were no bright red vegetables in Europe. The nearest thing was the beetroot, more an indelible inky purple than a flaming scarlet. There were red fruits (and a fruit is what the chili pepper is), but there was nothing used in the vegetable context that had anything like the pepper's striking hue. Since ancient times Europeans have associated red with fire, peril, anger, and blood, with spiritual danger and mortal wounding, and the color's cultural meanings have allowed chilies to become emblematic of hot-bloodedness, a choleric disposition, and a potentially hazardous sexual allure. There was some dispute about precisely how chilies fit within late Hippocratic-Galenic humoral theory: some dietetic authorities insisted, since chilies were used as a spice, they were a hot food and thus to be avoided by fiery-tempered people. Others argued that, since they were actually a fruit, chilies were therefore cold and should be shunned by melancholic or phlegmatic types. The question was eventually decided in favor of the former definition, as indeed it was in the shamanic medicinal systems of the chili's native lands, as explained by Thomas J. Ibach, a researcher among the Nahua peoples of Mexico. "Medicinal agents, whether traditional or modern, are sometimes classified by their color, and/or the sensation they cause in reference to taste or feeling. Medicinal agents that are red or pink in color, or that have a burning or stimulating feeling, are generally classified as 'hot.'"[3]

Indigenous customs, to which European colonialists were not inclined to defer, classified chili peppers as an aphrodisiac. The Aztec peoples mixed them with cacao and vanilla to compound a reliably potent love philter, and already in the sixteenth century, Europeans theorized that hot peppers were a stimulus to sexual appetite, and indeed performance, in men. As late as the nineteenth century, Spanish priests still occasionally condemned chili-spiced dishes as the food of carnal temptation, a warning that doubtless did the pepper's domestic reputation no harm at all. Their occasionally phallic or testicular shape, depending on the variety, along with their frequent use to spice sausages, made chilies quintessential man food from the earliest times, nature's Viagra. If chilies might excite the venereal instinct among the young and hormonal, they were by the same token prescribed to cure frigidity, and in later times they would be burned at Basque wedding ceremonies to ensure a fruitful marriage. An Indian brand of condom flavored with *achaar* (sizzling hot pickle) should ignite that someone special, while the present-day sadomasochistic practice of coating a condom in chili oil, a considerably more atrocious recourse than molten candle wax or electric jumper cables, speaks as eloquently of the hot pepper's association with hot sex as it does of the unbreakable sensual compact of pain and pleasure.[4]

While I confess I, or indeed some enterprising partner I haven't yet met, have that last enjoyment still to look forward to, something of its arduous ecstasy may be imagined from the oral consumption of chili. I have before me a Caribbean hot pepper sauce (65 percent of its volume is comprised of a mash of Scotch bonnet and habanero chili peppers) with an SHU reading of around 10,000. That's about five times the intensity of Tabasco. One can use it straight up as a condiment or a dip or include it as a cooking ingredient or an element of a marinade.

Here goes a teaspoonful. The initial impression is a delicious fruitiness, the juicy ripeness of tropical fruits, which rapidly gives way to a lightning-quick burn that travels across the front of my tongue and along the sides and then hits the back of my throat as I swallow. There is, as is traditional with Caribbean sauces, a fair bit of mustard in it, which gives it a slightly acrid vinegar kick, but the overwhelming impression is of having poured some scalding hot liquid into my mouth. After I swallow, the searing feeling on the front half of my tongue gets gradually stronger rather than fading, to the extent that, about three minutes after I taste it, it's a severe, active irritation, something that needs treating and cannot be ignored. The hotness in my throat has subsided, a little of it has spread to the inner edges of my lips, but it's my tongue that feels most abraded. If I try to move it around my mouth, the pain flares up in excruciating little flashes. Five minutes and it still hasn't begun to ease, but now my nose is running and my breath is a little gaspy. The front part of my tongue looks a little redder, but I could be imagining it. The burn, which I can mitigate only by drawing air over the inflamed tongue, finally starts dissipating about ten minutes after that one spoonful, but only very slowly and reluctantly.

To analyze the effect of a product like this is not just a matter of taste. It does have a taste, a combination of hot and sour and fruity, but it is also very much a feeling, a haptic sensation in the mouth. Added to the side of a plate for dipping other ingredients into, it transforms those other foods into something else. They retain their flavor, but their intrinsic essence has been subjected to a more dominant range of sensory impressions. A hot sauce is at once a seasoning and an experience. And, unlike many another favorite food experience, it delivers every time.

This book is an investigation of the botanical identity, culinary history, and cultural meanings of the world's most versatile and most widely loved spice.

A Note on Spelling

There are three spellings of chili currently in English use. "Chili" is the predominant American version, "chilli" the British and other Anglophone style. "Chile" is preferred in the southwestern states for its Hispanic authenticity and is the spelling used throughout Spanish-speaking Central and South America. Since the word originated in Nahuatl, a pre-Columbian pictographic language scratched out on animal hides, none of these spellings has any preeminent claim on correctness. I have used "chili" throughout this book, except in quotations or the names of organizations such as the Chile Pepper Institute.

Part
ONE

BIOLOGY

I

Our Favorite Spice—
All About Chili

The chili pepper plant is a many-branched herbaceous perennial that grows up to around twenty-four to thirty-six inches tall. Often having a luxuriant, shrubby look, it is a member of the *Solonaceae* family, which includes nightshades, potatoes, tomatoes, and eggplants. It has smooth leaves that sprout alternately along each side of its stems and are oval or lanceolate (shaped like spearheads with tapered ends). At flowering, the plant produces bell-shaped white or pale purple blooms containing five stamens, and its fruits are seamless pods that vary in form from round berries to the more characteristic long, thin cases, with a central placenta to which the numerous seeds are attached. Depending on the variety, the fruit ripens to green, yellow, orange, red, violet, or dark brown. Cultivated in temperate rather than tropical climates, it may yield no more than a single crop annually, while some varieties are grown for ornamental purposes only.

Exactly where the wild chili plant first developed

remains shrouded in mystery. From residues identified in primeval refuse dumps and in ceramic artifacts, we know that wild chilies were being gathered and used in cooking in Mexico as far back as 7000 B.C.E. The earliest evidence of the chili's domesticated use by humans, which dates back to around 5000 B.C.E., places it in an area of southeast Mexico that extends over sections of the present-day provinces of Puebla, Oaxaca, and Veracruz. These domesticated plants were descendants of the wild capsicums first encountered by nomadic Mongol peoples who had migrated into the Americas during the last Ice Age, when there was a northern land bridge across the Bering Strait between Asia and North America. As these peoples moved southward into the subtropical and then tropical zones of the continent, they came upon a whole array of wild plant foods, which they began incorporating into their own hunter-gatherer diets.

The fact that settled agricultural communities in Central America eventually began the cultivation of chili peppers, and much else besides, does not mean, however, that this was the chili's original home. Paleobotanists now think that chilies were carried to this region from the South American interior (most likely the vast tropical savanna zone of central Brazil known as the Cerrado) through a process of natural dispersion, principally by birds that would have consumed them in their regions of origin and then excreted the seeds as they flew north. By this means, the natural habitats of the chili plant expanded gradually into Central America. Unlike mammals, birds are not sensitive to the heat of chilies and do not grind up the seeds when eating them, so they pass whole through the avian digestive system.

There is evidence of the dispersal of cultivated chili peppers across a wide area of northern South America, as well as sites in Panama and across the Caribbean Sea in the Bahamas. Archaeological findings published in the journal *Science* in February 2007 by a team from the Smithsonian Institute's National Museum of Natural History, led by Linda Perry, revealed that chilies were being systematically grown and used in cooking as early as around 4100 B.C.E., in sites far distant from the original area of cultivation. Already, then, at this early stage, migrant peoples were transporting their expertise in growing the plant from one area to another and probably also trading the peppers. In many of the residues studied, chili was present alongside maize deposits, suggesting that an early food system combining the processing of cereal grains and chilies had arisen among these ancient peoples.

Four particular strains of the wild capsicum genus had been domesticated in this early era, and to this day most varieties of hot pepper belong to one or another of these four groups. The most widely cultivated is *Capsicum annuum,* the species that includes the jalapeño, cayenne, and poblano varieties but also the innocuous bell peppers of Mediterranean cuisine. All of these are distantly related to the original wild bird pepper of the

Americas, which still grows naturally in the Caribbean, Mexico, and Colombia. After *C. annuum* comes *C. frutescens*, which includes the staple Thai pepper variety, the tabasco, the piri piri, the malagueta, the kambuzi pepper of Malawi, the Indonesian cabai rawit, and the xiaomila, one of the foremost varieties in Chinese cooking, grown in the southwest province of Yunnan. *C. chinense*, a probable descendant of *C. frutescens*, despite having a Latin name that translates as "Chinese pepper," originates, as all chilies do, in the Americas. (This misattribution was the slipup of an eighteenth-century Dutch botanist, Nikolaus von Jacquin, who thought chilies were native to China because of their widespread use there. In fact, they had originally been transported to China by European merchants and explorers in the sixteenth century.) Members of the species *C. chinense* are also known collectively as the bonnet peppers and include the fearsome Scotch bonnet of the Caribbean islands, the Trinidad moruga scorpion, the yellow lantern, the habanero, and India's bhut jolokia. *C. baccatum* encompasses the widely used aji variety, as well as lesser-known exotica such as the lemon drop and Brazilian starfish.

A fifth domesticated strain, *C. pubescens*, is by far the least widely disseminated, and is the only one that was probably not known to the ancient Native Americans. So named for its hairy leaves, it exists only as a cultivated species, having never been wild, and is quite distinct from its relatives. Grown in Peru, Bolivia, and Mexico, it is known respectively as rocoto, locoto, or manzano—the last, meaning "apple," given the shape of the pepper's mature fruit.

As well as being a staple food, the chili pepper was likely also put to other uses in ancient times. The acrid fumes it produces when burned, especially in bunches, made this practice a known means of fumigating domestic dwellings in Aztec and Mayan civilizations (bloodsucking insects don't like smoke), and chili also became an indispensable tool in the pharmacopoeia of the Mesoamerican region. The efficacy of hot spice in clearing blocked sinuses is an experience known to many diners in Thai and Indian restaurants. Long before the modern science of dietetics established the nutritional value of the chili, though, simple observation showed that people who fed on it thrived. We now know it contains significant concentrations of iron, potassium, and magnesium, as well as vitamin A, many of the vitamin B complexes (especially B_6), and plenty of vitamin C. It seems likely that the chili found a place in the regional diet because it was one of the few crops that grew reliably at high altitudes, and the fruits retained their pungency when preserved through drying into the winter months. A fascinating aspect of the archaeological study of chilies is that trace elements of the plant have been found in a broad range of cooking vessels, suggesting that chilies were already subjected to a versatile repertoire of culinary uses very early on. Their presence in a vessel known as a spouted jar—essentially a form of decanter for transferring liquids to smaller containers—

indicates that they were being used in drinks of one sort or another, as well as in condiments or relishes into which other food items, such as chunks of meat, could be dipped.

The chili plant is versatile enough to have adapted to a wide range of growing climates, and its domestication in various regions was determined by indigenous peoples by the establishment of which strains were best suited to which conditions. Around 1000 B.C.E., when the people known as the Arawak began their millennium-long migration from the northeastern zones of South America to the Caribbean islands—Trinidad, the Lesser Antilles, and Hispaniola (modern-day Haiti and the Dominican Republic)—they brought with them the tropical species of chili that had thrived in the torrid hinterlands of the southern Americas. This was the chili variety widely known as *aji* among the South American and West Indian peoples, probably C. *baccatum*. At some later stage—we don't know precisely when—a second chili species was transported to the West Indies from Central America, this one better equipped for thriving in more temperate climatic zones. It went by a name derived from the language of the indigenous Mexican Nahuatl (Aztec) people, and this is the term that has been in widespread use throughout the Western world ever since: *chili*. (Nahuatl would in time donate several other food names to European languages, via Spanish, including tomato, avocado, and chocolate.)

What would the chili pepper have looked like at the

earliest phase of its domestication? An educated guess can be made in light of the fact that plant historians think that the C. *annuum* variety known as chiltepin, or chiltecpin, is probably the ancient ancestor of all domestic cultivars. Chiltepin chilies still grow wild across a broad swath of Central and South America, and even in the southern United States. Gathering wild chilies in Sonora Province in northwest Mexico and in the mountainous parts of the southern Arizona desert is an intensive activity that takes place in the fall and winter each year. The chiltepin chili has small round or slightly oval fruits that ripen to orange-red, and it is a hot variety. Its name also derives from the Nahuatl and has its root in *tepin,* the word for "flea," indicating something of its tiny dimensions. Despite its modest size, the chiltepin has the same intensity as a fleabite, registering up to around 100,000 on the SHU scale (see pages 18–20 for a full explanation of the heat-measuring systems for chilies). How hot the pepper is when it comes to be eaten depends on the stage at which it is processed: the unripe, green fruit is the mildest and is generally eaten as a condiment pickled in vinegar; the ripened, red, just-picked fruit has distinctly more attack on the palate; the dried, whole version more again; the fieriest of all comes in the form of the dried fruit with its seeds scraped out. Mexican people describe the action of the chiltepin as *arrebatado,* an adjective that connotes the sense of something snapped up hastily or impulsively, indicative of the fact that while the heat of the chili is certainly scorching enough, it tends to fade quite quickly rather than leaving a prolonged smolder in the mouth.

In some regions, chilies appear to have been reserved for tribal elites, the exclusive delicacy of chiefs and elders rather than the staple food of the common people. Archaeologists in northwest Mexico and the southwestern United States have unearthed charred chili seeds in the presence of luxurious items of jewelry made from copper, turquoise, and crystal, which finding does not necessarily mean that subaltern folk didn't eat them, too, but does suggest that chilies were an indispensable element of the lifestyle of the privileged. However, these areas probably began to produce domesticated chilies on a significant scale only after the arrival of Spanish colonialists in the early sixteenth century, so perhaps the chilies that appear in the much older garbage deposits in the Chihuahua province of Mexico were the product of a very restricted pre-Hispanic cultivation for the upper echelons of society only.

The fact that, in certain areas, chilies had become the food of elites anticipates the role they would come to play in the cosmologies of indigenous peoples, which we shall look at in greater detail in part 2. Whereas the chili pepper became a currency in simple barter economies, it took on a more exalted role in the myths of the Aztec, Toltec, Mayan, and Incan peoples over the centuries. Searching for the explanation in the distant prehistory of chili cultivation, we need only imagine the effect that these pungent, fiery little pods might have had on palates that had not encountered anything like them before. The standard diet of much of pre-Columbian America consisted of maize, beans, and squash. Against the background of these nutritious but essentially very bland ingredients—grains, pulses, and fleshy gourds— the sizzling heat of chilies transformed the eating experience into something else entirely. They have a digestive effect as well: the saliva produced by eating chilies is rich in the enzyme amylase, which helps to break down the sugars in starchy foods into more assimilable glucose. Chilies were, and are, a quintessential seasoning, a gift from the gods as indispensable as salt, and the grisly prospect of a life without them elevated them at an early historical stage to the status of the sacred.

The pugnacious flavor of chilies made them well-suited to perform combat and defense roles in indigenous mythologies. They were used not only to ward off evil spirits and more terrestrial pests, but also in counter-magical rituals to guard against the effects of the "evil eye," the maleficent intentions of enemies. Protective strings of dried chilies known in Spanish as *ristras* were draped on the external walls of houses or worn as necklaces, a kind of spiritual armor against the attentions of demons and vampires that anticipated the symbolic role that garlic—another pungently enlivening food seasoning—would play in many European cultures.

The wide range of culinary and symbolic uses to

which people have put chilies remains quite strange when set against one rather obvious fact: The chili pepper's biological makeup is telling humans, and other mammals, that it does not want to be eaten by them. So how did it come to develop such an aggressive nature, and how did humans manage to overcome its aversive signals?

How the Chili Came to Be Hot

The heat in chili peppers comes from a naturally occurring substance called capsaicin. On the tissue of many mammals, including human beings, capsaicin produces a burning sensation that gives the impression that some level of damage is occurring. It has this effect because mammals are equipped with a sensory pathway known as the transient receptor potential (TRP) channel. On contact, capsaicin binds with this channel and activates an alert signal that deceptively convinces the organism that it is being burned, typically at around 108°F (42°C). We'll look at the biology of this effect in more detail in the next section, but for now, the question arises as to why and how the chili plant developed this defense mechanism.

The most obvious advantage of capsaicin is that it deters mammals with grinding molars from eating the pepper plant and destroying its seeds or reducing them to a state where they are no longer capable of germinating.

Birds, which lack the TRP channel and are consequently not sensitive to the searing heat of chilies, will feast on the ripe fruits to their stomachs' content, in due course dispersing and propagating the unharmed seeds in their excreta. This process is how the chili pepper spread northward from its original home in South America. But an interesting question remains: What influences some plants to produce hot chilies while others remain devoid of spice?

In 2001, a team led by Professor Joshua Tewksbury conducted a pathbreaking study in southeastern Bolivia, the wild chili's original heartland.[1] What influences the development of capsaicin in wild chilies is not necessarily the behavior of either rodents or birds, but that of an order of insects belonging to the *Hemiptera* family known as the true bugs (cicadas, aphids, leafhoppers and their relatives). These insects also feed on wild chilies, using their pin-sharp proboscises to pierce the fruit of the pepper and ingest the juice inside. It appears, however, that these insects are as sensitive to capsaicin as mammals are, since after initial investigation they will reject those chilies that are hot. Tewksbury's team found an obvious correlation between the highest incidence of insect puncture marks and a lack of spiciness in those particular chilies. So what might the significance of that conclusion be?

When chilies are punctured in this way, the humid conditions prevalent throughout these tropical zones allow airborne fungi to enter and infect the plant. Molds form on the seeds and gradually kill them—unless, that is, the plant can manufacture its own defense against the fungus. That is where capsaicin comes in. The fungal growth cannot withstand attack by capsaicin, as Tewksbury's team confirmed when they replicated this process in the laboratory. As more capsaicin was progressively introduced, the molds had less chance of surviving. In drier areas, where there is naturally less humidity and smaller insect populations, there are more non-spicy chilies because the plants do not have to defend themselves from molds to the same degree. By contrast, in the more humid regions, where there are more insects creating more damage and allowing the pepper plants to become infected with fungus, there are more naturally occurring hot varieties.

What this means is that, even before birds and mammals entered the equation, a combination of local climatic conditions, insects, and naturally occurring fungi had already begun to determine which plants produced spicy fruits. And it seems likely that ancient native peoples discovered that those plants that showed the fewest puncture holes would be the spicy ones, and so they began gathering, then cultivating, those varieties as part of their diet.

What led humans to develop a taste for the spiciest peppers, though? Could it be that these primordial palates were as discerning in their food preferences as that of any modern-day restaurant critic? Against that rather fanciful hypothesis, a far more practical explanation suggests itself. What attracted early Americans to the spicier plants was their observation that the hotter varieties contained less or no fungus. In other words, they came with their very own built-in food preserver. Long before temperature-controlled food preservation was possible, the spicy chili's antimicrobial properties helped to preserve not just the pepper itself, but any food mixed with it. This quality makes chilies practically useful for storing food in leaner times, but it also has a medicinal implication. Microbial infection in food was a common cause of serious illness, even death, in primeval cultures, and it can still be deadly where preservation technologies are sorely lacking. Since capsaicin in chilies was a powerful counteragent to such infection, humans may have adapted as they evolved to develop a taste for spicy hotness. If this is true, as Tewksbury's team proposed, then the domestication and eventual spread of chili peppers is a prime example of humans' and plants' evolutionary developments marching in step with each other.

Capsaicin

The primary compound in chili peppers that produces the burning sensation is capsaicin. It is the hottest and most prevalent of a half-dozen related components in chilies, known collectively as capsaicinoids. Around 70 percent of the heat in hot peppers comes from capsaicin. In its pure form, capsaicin is about one hundred times hotter than the average scorching habanero chili, if such a thing can be imagined—about sixteen million SHU.

Attempts to isolate the active component in chili peppers progressed rapidly in the early nineteenth century. In 1816, a Swiss researcher, Christian Bucholz, partly isolated an impure form of capsaicin from dried Spanish chilies and proposed naming it capsicin after the plant genus *Capsicum*. Scientists in Germany, France, Denmark, and Britain made further progress in analyzing the component through the 1820s, but it was not until 1876 that capsaicin was extracted in its almost pure state by a British chemist, John Clough Thresh, and given its present name. The absolutely pure form was finally isolated in 1898 by German scientist Karl Micko, whose findings appeared in a publication invitingly entitled the *Journal for the Investigation of Necessities and Luxuries*. A full understanding of the chemical composition and structure of capsaicin began to be formulated in 1919 by American chemist E. K. Nelson, following which his compatriot Stephen Foster Darling, in conjunction with an Austrian researcher, Ernst Späth, first prepared synthetic forms of it in 1930. The other, related capsaicinoids were discovered only in 1961, by a team of Japanese scientists.

According to a persistent popular myth, most of the capsaicin is in the seeds of chili peppers, which is why Western chefs often roughly chop chilies and add the lot—seeds and all—to the dish they are cooking. Jalapeño slices bristling with seeds are a common sight among pizza toppings. In fact, the seeds contribute very little, other than looking a bit messy. They can be scraped away once the chili is split without any loss of heat. The greater part of the capsaicin is instead concentrated in the pith, or the white membrane that holds the seeds in place. Since the seeds are obviously in contact with that, they will pick up some of the membrane's heat, so recipes that tell you to avoid scraping out the seeds in the interest of maintaining heat are not entirely misguided. It's tricky to get rid of the seeds without also getting rid of the pith, but not impossible. On the other hand, the common instruction to remove the seeds if you want to diminish the heat of the chili is all but pointless. The reason that the heat is concentrated in the membrane is explained by the plant's evolutionary biology. When chilies developed capsaicin as a method of combating fungus, they concentrated it in the very part of the fruit where the mold was most likely to develop. There is also some heat in the flesh of the chili itself, as you will discover when you put a tiny snippet on your tongue to test it. If that's all the pepper going into your recipe, you will still get lots of heat in the finished dish. For that extra kick, though, include at least some of the pith.

In its pure state, capsaicin is a partly crystalline compound that is colorless, odorless, and either oily or waxy. While it is legal to buy on both sides of the Atlantic in either liquid or crystalline form, the European Union banned capsaicin from use as a food additive in January

2011, although essential oils in which it occurs have not been proscribed. As the packaging will sternly inform you, capsaicin should be handled only with protective gloves and with something to shield your eyes, too. Adding it in droplets to your cooking is a high-risk venture, but what else are you going to do with it?

Measuring Capsaicin

Because the range of heat in chili peppers—cultivated varieties as well as those growing wild—is so variable, a biological trait scientifically known as polymorphism, it was inevitable that, sooner or later, somebody would devise a measurement system for calibrating it. The first such system, and one that is still in use today, was devised by Wilbur Lincoln Scoville, an American pharmacist born in Bridgeport, Connecticut, in 1865. It was while working at the Parke-Davis pharmaceutical company of Detroit in 1912 that he formulated what became known as the Scoville Organoleptic Test, a method for determining relative levels of spice potency in different types of chili peppers.

What is interesting about the Scoville scale is that it relies on a fundamentally subjective act of judgment. To establish the heat level of a pepper, it is first dried and then infused in alcohol to extract its capsaicinoids. These are then diluted in a sugar solution in decreasing concentrations, and the resulting preparations are then tasted by a panel that usually consists of five tasters. The dilution of capsaicin carries on until a majority of the tasters—at least three—can no longer detect any heat. Whatever level of dilution is necessary to reach that state is then expressed as a numerical value: For example, dry pepper extract that has to be diluted with half a million times the quantity of solution would be given a reading of 500,000 SHU.

It isn't difficult to see possible objections to such a procedure. First, one person's "pretty hot" might be another's "fairly mild," so some means of standardizing the tasters' own judgment criteria needs to be established first. Second, individual tasters have widely different concentrations of heat receptors on their tongues. Some people are just naturally more sensitive to chili hotness than others.

Since the palate rapidly becomes desensitized to levels of chili heat over an intensive period of tasting, the system subjects tasters to only one pepper sample at a time. That last point might be familiar to anybody who has gone from stall to stall at a chili fair, tasted the different products, and found fairly quickly that they can no longer distinguish the average hot from the sizzling hot. There is another possible flaw in this procedure, though. Given that the Scoville test involves trying to detect smaller and smaller concentrations of capsaicin in solution, many tasters' palates would likely become desensitized to levels of capsaicin that they would readily pick up if they were tasting the solutions completely fresh.

Despite its many imprecisions, however, the Scoville scale endured through most of the twentieth century in the absence of any more reliable system. Developed in the 1980s, a technique called high-performance liquid chromatography offers a more objective way of assessing relative heat. By a process of pressurizing the capsaicin solution through a column containing a solid, adsorbent surface, the various components in the solution are separated and analyzed for their intrinsic heat capacities. It's the same process used to test for performance-enhancing drugs in the urine samples of athletes. The measurements are expressed in pungency units defined by the American Spice Trade Association (ASTA). One ASTA unit is equivalent to about 16 SHU. So a Tabasco pepper with a rating of 32,000 SHU would convert to roughly 2,000 ASTA pungency units. Any conversion table between the two scales will be imprecise, though, to the degree that the Scoville system itself is imprecise.

That said, SHU readings are still what the hot pepper industry prefers for measuring the hotness of its products, from raw peppers to chili pastes and relishes, and so, notwithstanding the caveats expressed above, that is the system I use in this book.

How Capsaicin Works

The reason that contact with chilies produces painful sensations in tissue is, as explained above, that capsaicin effectively tricks the organism into thinking it is being burned. It does this by binding to a receptor in our sensory neurons known in the scientific shorthand as TRPV1, or transient receptor potential vanilloid type 1. (Capsaicin is a member of the vanilloid group that also includes the primary component of vanilla beans.) This group of receptors is principally what enables the body to detect extremes of temperature, the contact of acidic or corrosive substances, or the effect of any kind of abrasion or chafing. That message, when transmitted to the brain via TRPV1, persuades the neural system that the organism is undergoing damage and alerts it to avoid the source of harm. It's the reason you jerk your hand away in a split second when it accidentally makes contact with a hot surface. Although it seems hard to believe when your mouth is on fire, no direct tissue damage results from eating chilies or hot dishes spiced with them. In every other respect, though, the brain is fooled into reacting as it does to intense heat: with sweating, facial flushing, and the dilation or widening of blood vessels, resulting in reddening of the tongue. While these properties have been enough to deter other mammals, reptiles, and insects from eating hot peppers, humans with their highly evolved intelligence began to see through the delusive effect in ancient times.

The fact that chilies were domesticated in five separate zones, resulting in the five principal species of *Capsicum*, is evidence that, long before the science was understood, human beings had learned systematically to disregard the aversive signals that the chili plant was sending out.

For some people, it should be made clear, the distress caused by eating or just coming into contact with chilies is all too real. It is possible to be allergic to them, so that consuming them may result in skin rashes and other forms of dermatitis. People working with chilies in large-scale food processing without skin protection have often developed a painful dermal inflammation known as Hunan hand syndrome: the condition is named for the spicy cuisine of the Chinese province, since it was first identified among Chinese restaurant workers tasked with rubbing the skins off roasted chili peppers. An excess of chili heat can also produce gastric disturbance—anything from a persistent attack of hiccups to vomiting and diarrhea. Only trial and error will establish where your own personal limits lie, and in some cases avoiding chilies altogether may well be the safest option.

The immediate antidote to the flaming pain of hot chili in the mouth is anything containing dairy fat. Cold milk, yogurt, or—best of all—ice cream soothe the burn because capsaicin is soluble in fats, and the milk protein casein, which is present in all dairy products, acts like an extinguisher on the fiery compound. Oils can also do the trick, and so can alcohol, counterintuitively, because capsaicin is soluble in ethanol. A mouthful or two of cold white wine can be just as effective as milk, and a nibble of bread makes a good absorbent material, mopping up capsaicin from the mucous membranes. What doesn't work, as so many have discovered to their frustration, is water, since capsaicin is hydrophobic and not soluble in water. If the water is iced or very cold, holding it in your mouth may briefly seem to soothe the burning, but it returns in full force as soon as you swallow. Milk is the way.

The burning sensation of chili may be an excitement or a torment, depending on your attitude toward acute gustatory discomfort, but capsaicin also appears to have beneficial effects on the human organism, too. In response to the painful stimulus, the brain releases a flood of biochemicals called endorphins, which are its natural painkillers. They work by inhibiting the ability of nerves to transmit pain signals to the brain, and like many pharmaceutical pain relievers—primarily opiates— they thereby produce a sense of tremendous satisfaction and even pleasure. This has led to the suggestion that people who eat a lot of hot, spicy food are in pursuit of what has been called, drawing on the language of illicit substances, the "chili high." Could it be that people who claim to have developed a chili habit are actually seeking the endorphin high that capsaicin provokes?

When you factor in the evidence that capsaicin consumption also releases another potent neurotransmitter, dopamine, responsible for feelings of well-being and general contentment, it becomes a little easier to understand some people's apparently masochistic devotion to setting their mouths on fire. We shall return to these questions in detail in part 3.

The only problem with the endorphin and dopamine effect is that it operates according to the law of diminishing returns. When serious chiliheads constantly seek out the next hottest thing on the market, or when they intensify the chili pepper quotient a little more every time they cook themselves a batch of chili con carne, they may well be trying to re-create the power of the original experience as it progressively diminishes. This is what Shakespeare's Sonnet 52 characterizes as "blunting the fine point of seldom pleasure." Enjoy it too much, and it becomes gradually less enjoyable, so that more is required to achieve the same effect, thereby progressively devaluing the original pleasure.

On the other hand, there is no need to worry that a serious chili habit will blunt your receptivity to pleasure-triggering brain chemicals. It isn't just pain that triggers endorphins. Vigorous physical exercise, sexual activity, and even laughter are also known to produce the pleasurable response, and only a Grinch would recommend limiting those.

Chilies and Health

In the twenty-first century, inflated claims about the various positive and negative links between diet and health are par for the course. Those who are concerned about eating right are bombarded almost daily with extravagant theories about this or that ingredient, often the basis for entire outlandish dietary systems promising to add years to our lives and shave inches off our waistlines in the process. Such diets come and go with the tides of fashion, and yesterday's cure-all regimen is today's hocus-pocus. Is anybody still on the grapefruit diet? What we can establish about the health benefits of eating chilies, and spice-rich food in general, should be treated with due caution, and even now, much of it awaits further dietetic evaluation.

What we can say with certainty is that chilies contain many beneficial nutrients. As we saw above, a typical raw, red chili, being a plant food, is a good source of dietary fiber, and it contains high concentrations of vitamins B_1 (thiamin), B_2 (riboflavin), B_3 (niacin), and B_9 (folate), as well as excellent levels of vitamins A, B_6 (pyridoxine), C, and K. As for minerals, the chili has useful amounts of iron, magnesium, phosphorus, and copper, and is a very good source of potassium and manganese. All of these vitamins and minerals have essential roles to play in the human diet, and their high concentrations are what helped our distant ancestors to thrive. Chili peppers are low in sodium and contain zero cholesterol, though a ripe fruit does contain about five percent sugars. One standard pepper, weighing about 1.5 ounces (42 grams), contains around 18 calories.

On the strength of this nutritional data, we can say with confidence that a chili-rich diet can assist with fighting infections, create and maintain collagen to keep hair and skin looking radiant (through antioxidant vitamin C), regenerate cells throughout the body, and promote the formation of red blood cells in particular (iron and copper). It helps maintain healthy eyesight and guards against age-related macular degeneration (vitamin A), decreases blood pressure and regulates healthy blood circulation through the relaxation of blood vessels (vitamin B_9 and potassium), and promotes the production of good, high-density cholesterol in the body, boosting cardiovascular health by helping to break down the bad, low-density type (vitamin B_3).

Considering all of these factors, research teams all over the world have in recent years been conducting experiments to assess the health and life expectancy of populations that eat plenty of chili. According to a study published in the *British Medical Journal* in August 2015, a team at the Chinese Academy of Medical Sciences, working with a study group of 500,000 subjects over seven years, found that regular consumption of chili peppers prolongs life expectancy proportionately with frequency of ingestion.[2] The team found that people in the observational target group were less at risk of premature mortality from the big worldwide killers—

heart disease, stroke, cancer, diabetes, and respiratory system disorders—if they regularly ate spicy food than if they didn't. The risk was 10 percent less for those who ate spicy dishes once or twice a week, 14 percent less among those who ate them most days or every day. The results were equal between men and women. An editorial accompanying this report noted that more work was needed to establish whether there are consistent pathways between these medical factors and the consumption of chili, but that the observational data looked very encouraging.

As we saw earlier, capsaicin has strong antimicrobial properties, inhibiting the growth of fungus within fruits that have been punctured by insects, but also helping to preserve other foods that have been spiced with chilies. It gives chili-rich food an antibacterial advantage, protecting the consumer from infection and also inhibiting the spoilage of other food. Capsaicin is known to be lethal to around 75 percent of all food-borne pathogens, making food poisoning from spicy dishes considerably less likely than from nonspicy ones.

Two studies in 2015 gave sustenance to the long-held hypothesis that chili is a preventive factor in obesity. A team of biophysicists at the University of Wyoming found that the capsaicin molecule increased metabolic activity in mammals, causing their systems to consume more energy and preventing weight gain even in cases of relatively high-fat diets.[3] (The mammals tested, it should be added, were mice.) Perhaps even more pertinently, research at the University of Adelaide, Australia, established that capsaicin binds to receptors in the stomach lining to produce the feeling of satiety.[4] We can all, perhaps anecdotally, attest that very hot food seems to exhaust the appetite sooner than blander food does. The Adelaide findings suggest that this sensation is accounted for by more than just the effect of the burning sensation on the tongue and palate.

In 2012, a team working at the Chinese University of Hong Kong found that capsaicin breaks down bad cholesterol by promoting the good variety and helps to dilate blood vessels to improve blood flow.[5] At the time of this writing, the most encouraging recent findings have come from a pair of researchers at the Robert Larner, M.D. College of Medicine at the University of Vermont, Mustafa Chopan and Benjamin Littenberg. Reported in January 2017 in the multidisciplinary scientific journal *PLOS ONE*, their survey of more than sixteen thousand adults in the United States corroborated the Chinese findings reported two years earlier in the *British Medical Journal*. That is, risk of untimely death, both from specific causes and from any cause at all, was reduced by a factor of about 13 percent in those who regularly consumed chilies.[6] Whereas the 2015 study looked at Chinese adults only, the Vermont project considered people from a variety of ethnic backgrounds, so the more recent research, as the authors put it, "strengthens the generalizability" of the earlier findings.

On the other side of the coin is a body of more nebulous, but nonetheless concerning, research about the possible drawbacks of the overconsumption of chilies. A paper titled "The Two Faces of Capsaicin," published in the journal *Cancer Research* in April 2011, suggested that overuse of capsaicin-based skin creams for pain relief may be linked to an increased risk of carcinogenesis, resulting in skin cancers.[7] Creams, gels, and capsaicin patches have been used in recent years to treat a wide variety of pains, ranging from temporary postoperative pain to the chronic discomforts of osteoarthritis, rheumatoid arthritis, and neuralgia. The medical logic of these treatments is based on the desensitization that builds up after repeated exposure to capsaicin, so that applying a capsaicin cream eventually reduces susceptibility to pain, an effect that is unique among naturally occurring, irritant plant compounds. Whereas the authors of this paper, Ann Bode and Zigang Dong, suggested that the excessive use of topical capsaicin in creams may have adverse effects, their summary states that the normal consumption of chili peppers in food is "not equivalent" to capsaicin's application on the skin. In other words, the possible carcinogenic effects of dermal creams do not translate into a similar risk from eating chilies.

Given the searing heat that consuming chilies generates not just in the mouth but throughout the digestive system, it seems obvious that anybody suffering from a gastric disorder—a tendency to inflammations in the throat or stomach—or a gastric ulcer should avoid very spicy food. But as to whether spicy food can cause these conditions in the first place, the medical jury is very much still deliberating.

What is certainly true for many unfortunate people—and this really is one of those only-one-way-to-find-out dilemmas—is that hot food can trigger digestive spasms, contractions of the intestine that indicate to the body that it has consumed a severe toxin that it must get rid of as soon as possible. (Hello, diarrhea and vomiting.) If you have this sort of reaction at a certain level of chili intensity, you will not necessarily experience the same thing at lower doses; you only need to find your level—the problem then being that, if you haven't cooked the dish yourself, you don't know until you start eating it whether it's going to tip you into the discomfort zone.

Some animal trial studies have tenuously suggested that too much capsaicin can be a precursor to stomach or liver cancer. Two Korean studies from 1985 and 1991 appeared to suggest as much, but in 1998, a Japanese team feeding mice substantial quantities of capsaicin and a related compound for eighteen months found no evidence of carcinogenic activity in any of the subjects.[8] The alternative conclusion, that capsaicin may even be a protective factor against the development of cancerous cells, has not been decisively validated, either. On the question of whether chilies corrode the stomach lining, one set of endoscopy tests conducted in 1987 showed severe irritation and even gastric bleeding. Another set conducted the following year, involving two of the same scientists from the first test, found no evidence of harm whatsoever, even when chili—in the form of ground, dried jalapeños—was introduced directly into the stomach rather than first passing through the esophageal tract.

Perhaps the final say in the matter should be given to the incontrovertible fact of human dietary evolution. If chili peppers were ultimately bad news for us, we probably would not have been eating them for millennia. They certainly would not have been carried around the world and been adopted in a broad range of food cultures in both hemispheres, to the extent that they have.

My guess is this: If you're still reading, you're probably not unduly worried that chilies are bad for you. Neither am I.

2

Apaches, Vipers, and Dragons—Types of Chili

There are now around fifty thousand recognized varieties of chili pepper being grown around the world. Many of these are cultivated only in tiny concentrations in isolated outposts, while others have become part of the repertoire of spicy food in a great diversity of world cuisines. The listing that follows must therefore be highly selective and focus on the most prominent varieties of each of the five principal species, situating them in their respective regions and indicating a little of what they are used for. The estimated Scoville heat unit (SHU) readings for each chili are approximate, reflecting the nature of the measurement system itself, but will give some idea of how much fire to expect in each case. With today's superhots, this system has steadily become impractical, but the readings supplied by liquid chromatography are still translated back into an SHU figure for international use. Ultimately, the best judge of heat is your own bold and willing palate.

Capsicum Annuum

Aji Cereza

Aji is the generic name given to chili peppers throughout South America and the Caribbean, and this variety
takes the name of the Spanish word for cherry, indicating its size, shape, and color. It grows wild in the extensive Peruvian rain forest. The fruit is a round cherry-red
pod, about an inch wide. 70,000–80,000 SHU.

Aji Pinguita de Mono

This *aji* from the Peruvian jungle also grows wild, with
particular concentrations around the central valley of
Chanchamayo. It has a stubby, short fruit ripening to
crimson, barely an inch long, which has earned it the
dignified Spanish varietal name of "little monkey dick."
Although its average heat is about the same on the Scoville scale, this chili tends to be measured more frequently
at the hotter, upper end than the Cereza. 70,000–80,000
SHU.

Aleppo (Halaby)

The spice known as Aleppo pepper in Western kitchens
is derived from a chili also known as the Halaby pepper.
It is grown in Syria and Turkey and is much used in
Middle Eastern and Eastern Mediterranean cuisines.
The reddish pods are partly dried, then deseeded and
ground, the result being an oily, smoky spice that is like
a more characterful cayenne. Usually about 10,000 SHU.

Ammazzo (Joe's Round)

With a name that translates literally as "I kill," Ammazzo is an Italian variety that grows in clumps of twelve to fifteen fruits, each around half an inch wide and maturing from dark green to bright red. Thanks to its jewel-like appearance, it has been grown ornamentally as much as it has been for the kitchen garden, and its Italian name is often mistranslated as "posy" or "nosegay," which is what its clusters of fruits look like. The Ammazzo is also known as Joe's Round. 5,000–6,000 SHU.

Anaheim

Named for the city in Orange County, California, the Anaheim is typically sold as a long, curving, green pepper—about six to eight inches—that is big enough for splitting and stuffing or for grilling over flame. They do ripen to red if allowed to, but the green version is what has become familiar to most consumers. It's a mild variety, especially when still green, with a fairly tough, waxy skin and a mild, sweet taste. 1,000–2,500 SHU.

Ancho

The ancho is a dried poblano pepper (see below). It dries to a deep brown, wrinkled, heart shape, usually around four inches long and nearly as wide, and it has a sweet, mild, smoky flavor. Mexican chefs will reconstitute the dried pepper in warm water for a half hour or so for use in tamales and as one of the varieties in mole sauces. 1,000–2,000 SHU.

Apache F1

Apache is a hybrid chili that produces attractive clusters of short, vivid red pods, about two to three inches long and less than an inch across. Its compactness makes it a favored variety for smaller gardens, and it fruits reliably in cooler climates. For such a vigorous variety, it's hotter than you might expect. (An F1 plant, by the way, is a cross-pollinated, first-generation hybrid of two varieties specifically selected for their particular qualities.) 80,000–100,000 SHU.

Bacio di Satana

An Italian variety whose name means "devil's kiss," Bacio is one of the so-called "cherry chilies," a round, vibrant red type about an inch wide, with a casing thick enough for those with the patience to stuff it. Cram it with mozzarella and pounded anchovies, if you will, prior to grilling. 40,000–50,000 SHU.

NuMex Big Jim

A pepper first bred at the Chile Pepper Institute at New Mexico State University in 1975, Big Jim is the world's largest chili, growing up to a foot long at its most magnificent. The fruit is thick and meaty, and its ample dimensions suit it perfectly for stuffing and roasting. It makes a tastier alternative to an ordinary bell pepper, although the heat output is modest enough. 500–1,000 SHU.

Birdeye (Piri Piri)

So called because it allegedly resembles a bird's eye when viewed end-on, the birdeye, or bird's eye, chili has become one of the truly international varieties. It's inextricably associated with Thai cooking and is often sold as "Thai chili," but it is also grown widely in Africa, especially Ethiopia, where it is known as piri piri. It produces small, thin, tapered fruits that can be used either green or fully ripened to red and have a sweet, fruity flavor with an appreciable punch. 50,000–100,000 SHU.

Boldog

One of the Hungarian paprika varieties, Boldog produces long fruits, up to five inches from top to tail, with thin outer walls that make it highly susceptible to drying. The fruits ripen to dark crimson and have a sweet, noticeably rich flavor that adds substance to paprika. 800–1,000 SHU.

Bulgarian Carrot

The name is both confusing and intuitive. It's actually a Hungarian variety, but it does very much resemble a small carrot, with orange-yellow fruits that grow up to about three or four inches long. The crunchy texture makes it good for pickling, but it also shows up well in spicy chutneys. There is much disagreement about its spice potential, which has been recorded at up to 30,000 SHU. On average, though: 5,000–10,000 SHU.

Capónes

Capónes are dried jalapeños that have been painstakingly deseeded (literally "castrated" like a capon, as the name implies), before smoking and drying. 2,000—10,000 SHU.

Casabella

A dwarf variety that starts yellow and ripens to fiery red, Casabella produces fruits that are between an inch to an inch and a half long. It is widely used for pounding into chili pastes and salsas. 2,000–4,000 SHU.

Cascabel

Cascabel is the dried form of a Mexican variety named Bola ("ball" or "rattle") for the way the seeds rattle inside the dried pod like a maraca. They are an inch or two across, and they have a dark brown, prunelike look when desiccated. They are put to any number of uses in the Mexican kitchen—soups, salsas, stews, and sauces. 3,000–4,000 SHU.

Cayenne

Although apparently named for the city and river in French Guiana, the cayenne probably originated in Brazil. From there, it was transported around the known world by Portuguese adventurers and traders, and it has become one of the world's most widely recognized varieties of chili. It has the classic chili shape of a long, thin pod with undulating skin, tapering to a point, and it comes in dozens of specific cultivars, many grown throughout India and China. In the European context, it was most often encountered in dried and ground form as cayenne pepper, which added a light smoldering of heat to dishes before chili powder was conceived in the nineteenth century. The whole peppers themselves are much hotter than commercial cayenne pepper may suggest. 30,000–50,000 SHU.

Charleston Hot

Charleston is a cayenne variant that was originally bred in South Carolina in 1974 by the U.S. Department of Agriculture, which sought a variety that would be resistant to the root-knot nematode, a particularly pestiferous creature responsible for around 5 percent of global chili crop loss. Typically around four inches long, the Charleston Hot dries well for making chili flakes that add searing heat to dishes. 70,000–100,000 SHU.

Cheongyang

The name is a conflation of two counties in South Korea, Cheongsong and Yeongyang. Used in the spice blend for kimchi and other Korean pickles, it is a long, thin chili that ripens from green to red, and is of medium intensity. 8000–10,000 SHU.

Cherry Bomb F1

A chili pepper with the same name as a firework sounds like a promisingly explosive proposition, but this round, red-ripening variety is actually relatively mild. It grows to around two or three inches in diameter, making it rather bigger than the average cherry, and it is good for both stuffing and pickling. 2,500–5,000 SHU.

Chilhuacle Amarillo
The amarillo variety of the Mexican chilhuacle family is becoming something of a rarity, but is one of the classic three variants of chilhuacle used in mole recipes. It bestows its concentrated tangerine color, as well as a sweet-sour citrus fruit flavor, on mole amarillo sauces. Native to the Oaxaca region, it grows up to four or five inches long and has a puckered skin that needs peeling. 1200–2000 SHU.

Chilhuacle Negro
The brown chilhuacle looks like a small bell pepper in eggplant purple, about three inches long and wide. It is used in the black mole sauces of Oaxaca and Chiapas, and is also dried and ground for other uses. 1,200–2,000 SHU.

Chilhuacle Rojo
Also from Oaxaca, the red chilhuacle is a tapered variety, about two inches across at the top and three inches long. It makes up the trinity of peppers used in mole dishes. 1,200–2,000 SHU.

Chiltepin

Sometimes known as the progenitor of all pepper varieties, the tiny chiltepin still grows wild throughout Mexico and parts of the southern and southwestern United States— principally Arizona, Texas, and Florida—although over-picking has currently left it endangered in its natural habitats. Named from the Nahuatl word *tepin*, meaning "flea," it is a minute berry, usually bright red, although yellow and light brown types have been found in the wild. It has the kind of ferocious heat that mounts a violent attack on the palate but retreats with decent rapidity. Dried and crushed, it is used in soups and stews. It is also sometimes known as the "bird pepper" (not to be confused with the birdeye) for its natural propagation by birds. 50,000–100,000 SHU.

Chimayo

A New Mexico variety named for a town in that state, twenty-five miles north of Santa Fe, the Chimayo is a large red chili that can grow up to seven inches long, usually slightly curved. It is very often sold as molido, the dried powder. 4,000–6,000 SHU.

Chipotle

Chipotle chilies are not, strictly speaking, a variety but a method of processing peppers by drying and smoking them. They are very widely made from jalapeños that have been left to overripen and dry a little on the plant. Traditionally, they are dried in the smoke from a firepit directed over chilies laid out on metal racks above, with as little air getting into the smoker as possible. They end up looking like little prunes, and they confer a piercing smokiness but only modest heat levels, on dishes such as chili con carne. Anything from 2,000–8,000 SHU, depending on the variety used.

Choricero

The Spanish variety most widely used in chorizo sausage is strung in *ristras* and then air-dried. It begins life as a large, fleshy, red pepper that turns to purple-brown with dehydration. Choriceros are then reconstituted with water and pressed into a paste. They are also used in soups and paella. Usually fairly mild. 200–1,000 SHU.

Costeño Amarillo

A southeastern Mexican variety found in Oaxaca and Veracruz, this chili ripens from green to a vivid amber-yellow. The fruits are around three inches long and slender, with thin walls and a pointed tip. They have a lemony citrus flavor when ripe. 1,200–2,000 SHU.

Cyklon

Cyklon is one of the few Polish varieties, a scarlet pepper with a teardrop shape, usually curved toward the tip. It dries well for a fiery paprika and is also good for chunky salsas. 5,000–10,000 SHU.

Dagger Pod

So called because it was once thought to resemble the sheath in which a Gurkha soldier kept his *kukri* (or dagger), this is a thin chili, four or five inches long and less than an inch across, with a crinkled skin that ripens to deep red. Often dried for a hot chili powder. 30,000– 50,000 SHU.

De Arbol

Chili de arbol, the so-called "tree chili," is native to Mexico and grows on a plant that does indeed look like a small tree. Its fruits, which are characteristically long and thin, have been named "bird's beak" and "rat's tail." They can be up to four inches long, a rich, deep bloodred, and are perfect for infusing in oil or vinegar. When dried, they retain their color and are often used for decorative purposes. They have been one of the standbys of Mexican cooking for many centuries. 15,000–30,000 SHU.

Deggi Mirch

In Indian groceries, the term *deggi mirch* most often refers to a mild chili powder a little like paprika, used as a seasoning in gentler dishes, in dal, and in breads such as *paratha*. If it's the real thing, it should be made from the dried and ground chili pepper of the same name, which is a two-inch-long red fruit grown in the northern state of Kashmir, although it is often made from other varieties. 1,500–2,000 SHU.

Espelette

Native to the French zone of the northern Basque Country, the thin, mild, red pods of the espelette pepper have been an *appellation contrôlée* product in the European protected designations system since 2000. They are widely used in southern French and Basque cooking in such traditional dishes as piperade, and they are the centerpiece of an annual pepper festival at harvesttime. 3,000–4,000 SHU.

Facing Heaven

Facing heaven is not the only chili variety to grow with its pods pointing upward rather than hanging down, but for this botanical trait, the pepper was given one of the poetic nomenclatures familiar throughout Chinese taxonomy. It's native to the spice-loving Sichuan province, where its name is *zhitianjiao*. The small, bullet-shaped, thin-skinned pods grow to three inches long, and smaller specimens are often added whole to stir-fries. 30,000–50,000 SHU.

Filius Blue

This strange chili variety fruits in a lustrous purple-blue shade to match its purple-tinged leaves, which it retains tenaciously through the ripening season before finally turning standard red. Its small ovoid pods add sizzling heat to a dish. 40,000–50,000 SHU.

Firecracker

An Indian hybrid variety, the firecracker goes through an astonishing Technicolor spectrum as it ripens, from cream to violet to yellow to orange to flame red, making a single bush with fruits at different stages of the cycle look like nature's own Christmas tree. The fruits are conical, about an inch and a half long, and are small enough to be added whole to simmered dishes or stir-fries. For a small pepper, it cooks up a storm, hence the name. 30,000–40,000 SHU.

Fish

So named not for its shape but for its culinary uses, the fish pepper was one of those varieties that African captives took back to the Americas in the late phase of the slave trade in the nineteenth century. As with Spanish Padrón peppers, there is a great variance in heat levels from one chili to the next on the bush, but at its most pungent, the fish pepper has traditionally been used to season fish and shellfish dishes. Around three inches long, they are often used in the green stage, when they have gentle, creamy white stripes running down the green pod. Their pronounced variance produces a rather elastic heat range of 5,000–30,000 SHU.

Fresno

Despite its California name, the Fresno is a New Mexico variety often mixed up with the jalapeño, which is unfortunate, since the Fresno is considerably hotter.

The conical red fruits grow to around two or three inches long, and they have a rounded fruity flavor. 3,000–8,000 SHU.

Garden Salsa F1
This hybrid variety was specifically bred for use in salsa. Although the peppers ripen to red, they are very often used when still green and require the thick skins to be peeled after roasting. They grow up to seven or eight inches long, with a curved tip. 2,000–5,000 SHU.

Georgia Flame
The long, waxy Georgia Flame hails not from the Peach State, but from the country of Georgia on the Black Sea. It is a thick-skinned variety with a crunchy texture that grows up to six inches long and is good for stuffing and roasting. 1,500–2,000 SHU.

Goat Horn
A long, thin, red chili that twists and curls around, like the caprine appendage for which it is named, it was originally bred in Taiwan and is much used in stir-fried Chinese dishes. It is typically five or six inches in length, very juicy, and relatively mild. 1,000–2,000 SHU.

Guindilla
Originating in the Basque region of Spain, the guindilla is a long, thin variety, up to four inches from top to tip, with enough assertive flavor to make it worth nibbling

on its own. Pickled in white wine vinegar, guindillas are often eaten green as tapas or as an accompaniment to hard cheeses such as manchego, but they ripen to a deep red. It has a gentle rather than a searing heat. 1,000–2,000 SHU.

Hungarian Yellow Wax (Hot)

The Hungarian Yellow Wax is also known as the banana pepper, not for its shape (it isn't always curved), but for the widespread practice of harvesting it while it is still yellow, for use in salsas and pickles. Up to six inches long and an inch and a half wide, its crunchy flesh also makes it appealing when it is sliced into salads. 2,000–4,000 SHU. Its cousin, the Hungarian Yellow Wax Hot, a separate variety, has the same range of attributes but is much fierier in temperament. 5,000–15,000 SHU.

Inferno F1

A hybrid of the Hungarian Wax family (see above), the Inferno isn't quite the hellish proposition it sounds. The large, smooth-skinned fruits ripen to look as red as the flames of hell, but Satan's myrmidons can probably take its mild heat. 2,000–4,000 SHU.

Jalapeño

Very possibly the world's most famous chili variety now comes in cultivars of varying sizes and heat levels. Although jalapeños once had the reputation for being red-hot, today's chili scene regards them as mere beginner's fare. The classic jalapeño is between two and four inches long, generally sold green but ripening to red if given the chance, and prime specimens have a tracery of fine lines along the smooth skin. These days they turn up in everything from pizza toppings to nachos, tacos, and chili con carne, or are prepared as poppers (stuffed with cheese and coated in bread crumbs). The dried and smoked red ones are known as chipotle chilies (see chipotle entry). The Scoville range is fairly wide but is clustered mainly at the lower end. 2,000–10,000 SHU.

Jaloro

The jaloro is a yellow jalapeño, first bred in Texas in 1992 as a disease-resistant alternative to the standard jalapeño, and has about the same heat intensity. 3,000–8,000 SHU.

Joe's Long

It isn't called "long" for nothing. It typically grows to nearly twelve inches but is very thin-skinned and therefore suitable for drying. Joe's Long is a relative of the cayenne but, though pretty hot stuff, it's not quite as scorching. 15,000–20,000 SHU.

Jwala

Often known as the Indian finger pepper, its Sanskrit name means "intense flame." The jwala matures from green to red and is used in a host of different forms, including pickled, dried and fresh. The thin fruits are around four inches long, with a tapered tip and thin walls. 20,000–30,000 SHU.

Mirasol

Like China's facing heaven chili (see entry), the mirasol's long crimson pods "look to the sun," the Spanish meaning of *mirasol*. It can be up to six inches long and has a tough skin that requires soaking or roasting prior to use. The dried version, known as a guajillo, is much used in traditional mole sauces in Mexico and is very popular throughout Peru. 2,500–5,000 SHU.

Mulato

Like the ancho (see entry), the mulato is another dried poblano, though it is considerably darker in color as a result of being left to ripen longer on the plant, and generally quite a bit hotter. It is used with anchos and pasillas in mole sauces and to garnish enchiladas. 2,500–3,000 SHU.

New Mexico No. 9

Of all the New Mexico State University cultivars, the No. 9 has earned its place in history as the first scientifically formulated variety, first bred in 1913. It was developed to be reliable as a crop, marketably mild at a time when Americans were still rather nervous about cooking with chilies, and suitably shaped for canning. It's a long, red, Anaheim-type chili that was grown as the standard American chili until around the mid-twentieth century. 1,000–3,000 SHU.

New Mexico Sandia
What helped displace No. 9 from the commercial center stage was the Sandia, bred at New Mexico State University in 1956, a cross between the No. 9 and another Anaheim subtype. The plant produces a long, broad-shouldered fruit with a flat pod, a little like a runner bean, that is generally sold green, prior to full ripening. 5,000–7,000 SHU.

NuMex Twilight
A New Mexico hybrid developed at the Chile Pepper Institute in 1994, Twilight is another variety that goes through the full color spectrum, resulting in a spectacular display when the different fruits of a single bush are at their various stages. The ripening sequence is: white to purple to yellow to orange to red. Derived from a Thai pepper, it's a hot one, too. 30,000–50,000 SHU.

Orozco
The eastern European orozco could hardly be better suited as an ornamental chili, with its purple leaves, purple-black stems, and carrot-shaped, four-inch-long fruits that ripen from purple to brilliant orange. 5,000–20,000 SHU.

Pasado

The chili of "the past" is so named because it is a very ancient variety, known over the centuries to the native Pueblo peoples of what is now New Mexico. It starts life as a green chili that is roasted, peeled, seeded, and dried, its green color returning a little after its reconstitution in warm water. It has traditionally been added to black bean soups and enchilada sauces. Pasados are often sold with some of the seeds still clinging to them, but they taste a lot better than they look. 2,000–3,000 SHU.

Pasilla

Another one of the essential elements in Mexican mole, along with anchos and mulatos, the pasilla is a variety of dried chili known as chilaca when fresh. Dehydrated to a wrinkled brownish black, it can be up to eight inches long, and its musky, smoky flavor adds a strong aromatic note to dishes. It is often sold in powdered form. Pasilla de Oaxaca is a smoked specialty of that region used in mole negro. 1,000–4,000 SHU.

Peperoncino

A southern Italian variety used in pasta sauces and on pizzas, peperoncini are very mild and sweet, often scarcely spicier than a bell pepper. They are generally sold in the unripe green state and often are pickled or preserved in oil. There are also Greek varieties that are less bitter than their Italian cousins. 100–500 SHU.

Pequin

Like the chiltepin (see entry), the tiny pequin still grows wild in the Mexican highlands, and it makes up for in heat what it lacks in dimensions. It is small enough to be added whole to stews, and it is often pickled or added to oils and vinegars. One of Mexico's bestselling bottled hot sauces, Cholula, uses pequin peppers as well as arbols. 30,000–60,000 SHU.

Peter Pepper

A principally ornamental chili that grows to around four to six inches in length, the Peter pepper is so called for its precise resemblance to a flaccid penis. One can only imagine what our Victorian forebears might have made of it. It is occasionally eaten in its Texas and Louisiana heartlands, and is—perhaps appropriately—pretty hot stuff. 10,000–25,000 SHU.

Pimiento

A large, heart-shaped cherry variety, the pimiento is prized for its vibrant color and sweet taste. It is doomed to be confused with the Spanish word for a generic bell pepper, but it is a distinct variety with fruits that look like small bell peppers, on average four inches long and three inches wide. The spice level is very mild, similar to Italian peperoncini (see entry). 100–500 SHU.

Pimiento de Padrón

A much-loved feature of worldwide tapas menus, pimientos de Padrón come from the district of the same name in Galicia, in the northwest corner of Spain. They are generally flash-fried in olive oil, salted, and then nibbled off the stem while still warm. The fascination of Padrón peppers is that only the occasional one has any chili heat. It often seems as though the hot ones, which used to be one in four of any given batch, are getting rarer—one in ten perhaps—the result of inaccurate watering of the plant. 500–2,500 SHU at the hotter end, if you're lucky.

Poblano

The original fresh version of various dried chilies including anchos and mulatos (see entries). Originating in the eponymous state of Pueblo, Mexico, the poblano is a weighty variety, typically five inches long and three inches across. It tends to be sold in the less ripe—and less fiery—green state, although it does turn red and get hotter when ripe. The poblano's size and tenderness makes it perfect for chiles rellenos, and it is usually one of the elements in the national dish, chiles en nogada, made with ingredients in the three colors—red, white, and green—of the Mexican flag. 1,000–2,000 SHU.

Prairie Fire

The conical fruits of this Mexican variety, also known as Christmas peppers, look a little like old-fashioned tree lights, more so when they ripen at different rates on the bush, and a mass of green, yellow, orange, and red pods is displayed. They have a pronounced fruitiness, and a powerful capsaicin hit. 70,000–80,000 SHU.

Riot

Another upward-growing variety, which makes its orange and red color spectrum look like the leaping flames of the civil disturbance suggested by its name. Usually around three inches long, it was originally bred at Oregon State University. 6,000–8,000 SHU.

Santa Fe Grande

A very prolific variety grown in New Mexico and throughout the Southwestern United States, Santa Fe Grande produces conical fruits with a blunt end that have a sweet flavor and the gentlest kick. 500–1,000 SHU.

Santaka

The Japanese variety Santaka is commonly used in that country in stir-fried dishes and in chili condiments. It is a thickish, tapered, conical pod, about two inches long, with a delicate skin ripening to a deep cranberry-red shade, and it is distinctly fiery. 40,000–50,000 SHU.

Sebes

Originating in the Czech Republic, this is another one of the waxy, bananalike varieties, about an inch wide with a flat five-inch-long pod that ripens to a bright yellowy orange. 2,000–4,000 SHU.

Serrano

Hailing from the mountainous regions of Puebla and Hidalgo, the serrano chili is widely used in Mexican cooking, its thin skin making it a versatile resource. It's often compared to the jalapeño, but the serrano is hotter, even in its more commonly used green state. Some varieties of serrano mature to purple. 10,000–25,000 SHU.

Shishito

The Japanese shishito is a long, thin variety, about four inches long, with a very wrinkled skin, usually sold green. Fancy has it that the tip end looks like a lion's head (the Japanese for lion being *shishi*). Shishitos are fried in oil or stewed in soy sauce and dashi stock. Like Padrón peppers, only the odd one—about one in ten—has any heat, and fairly modest heat at that. 100–1,000 SHU.

Super Chili F1

Derived from Thai varieties in the 1980s, the super chili is a vigorously fruiting pepper that produces a wealth of three-inch-long pods that ripen along the spectrum from green to orange to red, increasing in potency as the colors change. The name denotes the chili's ambition in the heat stakes, although today's superhots have since left it far behind. 20,000–50,000 SHU.

Szentesi Semihot
A bulbous variety that grows to four or five inches long and two inches wide, the Szentesi was developed in Hungary. It isn't the most obvious candidate for the paprika industry, since its rather thick-skinned nature makes it hard to dry. It's better stuffed and baked. 1,500–2,500 SHU. (If "semihot" sounds a little milk-and-water, rest assured that there is now a hot variant.)

Takanotsume
A Japanese chili known as the "hawk pepper" for its talonlike shape, this is another upward-pointing variety, growing in three-inch-long red claws and used fresh or dried in stir-fries. 20,000–30,000 SHU.

Tears of Fire
A very hot relative of the jalapeño with teardrop-shaped, thick-walled pods. The name is something of a clue here: It ripens from green through a brown stage until it reaches its final, shrill cherry-red, when it's ready to make you weep ardently. 30,000–40,000 SHU.

Thai Dragon F1
One of the staples of the Thai kitchen, the dragon produces thin, bright red fruits about three inches long, tapering to a blunt point and growing upright. Also known as the Thai volcano, it contributes rollicking heat to soups, stir-fries, red curries, and salads. 50,000–100,000 SHU.

Tokyo Hot F1
Despite the name, this is a Mexican hybrid growing in very slender, red pods with curved ends. The Tokyo hot has cayenne in its parentage, and it is a versatile pepper for Thai and Mexican food as well as Japanese. 20,000–30,000 SHU.

Capsicum Frutescens

African Birdeye
Not to be confused (though it inevitably is) with the Thai birdeye chili, which is C. *annuum*, this African pepper is a relative of the tabasco (see entry). It grows in stubby, red pods facing upward, and it is extremely hot. Following the importation of chili seeds to Africa in the sixteenth century, it became a flourishing wild variety, and it has been used for centuries in stews, soups, and hot sauces. Also known as piri piri, which creates another layer of confusion, and African Devil. 150,000–175,000 SHU.

Bangalore Torpedo
An Indian pepper that's similar to a classic cayenne, the torpedo is a long, twisted pepper that matures to around five inches long, changing from vivid green to scarlet as it ripens. Used in stir-fried dishes and chopped into salads, it adds medium warmth to most regional styles of Indian cooking, too. 30,000–50,000 SHU.

Bhut jolokia

Also known as naga jolokia, named after the Naga war-
riors of Indian history, or—more hauntingly—as the
ghost pepper, bhut jolokia enjoyed a brief spell in the
late 2000s as the hottest chili in the world. A hybrid
variety initially cultivated in Assam, Northeast India,
from both C. *frutescens* and C. *chinense* parentage, it
has a lumpy-contoured, flattish pod, about three inches
long and an inch wide, ripening to orange, red, and
sometimes a deeper chocolate-brown. The heat is un-
believably intense, and this pepper has been used very
sparingly in Indian cooking, but also for the kinds of
chutneys and relishes that will lift the top of your head
off. 850,000–1,000,000 SHU.

Japones

It originated in Mexico, where it bears a passing resemblance to the chili de arbol (see entry), but the
japones has become an East Asian specialty, cropping
up widely in the cooking of Thailand, Japan, and China,
especially that of Sichuan and Hunan. It has a thin
pod with a curved end, and grows up to three inches
in length. The japones is often sold dried and whole,
though it is also commonly ground for powder as well.
This chili has a wide spice range at the hotter end of
the spectrum. 25,000–40,000 SHU.

Kambuzi

Native to the small landlocked central African country of Malawi, kambuzi is a cherry chili similar to the habanero. It resembles a pointy-tipped cherry tomato in various shades ranging from orange to red. The name means "little goat," a reference to goats' predilection for the plant's leaves. Kambuzis have a broad spice range and can get very hot indeed. 50,000–175,000 SHU.

Malagueta

The malagueta is easily confused with melegueta pepper, which is not a chili variety at all but an African spice commonly known as grains of paradise. It is also one of the peppers known in Africa as piri piri, which is also the name of another species (see entry). The true malagueta is an indigenous Brazilian chili that was transported by the Portuguese to their colonies in Africa, notably the São Tomé and Príncipe islands and Mozambique. It is still very popular in the eastern Brazilian state of Bahia. It grows in thin pods about two inches long, ripening to vibrant red, and is incandescently hot. 60,000–100,000 SHU.

Siling Labuyo

A wild variety native to the Philippines and widely used in the islands' cuisine, its name is Tagalog for nothing more picturesque than "wild chili." It produces small, tapering, budlike fruits, growing upward and usually no more than an inch long, that come in a variety of ripe colors, including Halloween orange, bloodred, and even inky black. These peppers are pretty hot stuff for their diminutive size. 80,000–100,000 SHU.

Tabasco
This Mexican chili's name is forever synonymous with McIlhenny's Tabasco pepper sauce, a brand first produced in 1868 and world-famous to this day. The upward-pointing fruits are usually no more than an inch long, bright red, and appealingly juicy inside when fresh. 30,000–50,000 SHU.

Capsicum Chinense

Adjuma
A Brazilian variety that is often confused in the markets with Suriname Yellow (see entry), adjuma produces bulbous fruits that look like small bell peppers and ripen to yellow or red. Its heat level is comparable to that of the very hottest habaneros. 100,000–500,000 SHU.

Aji Dulce
A local Venezuelan variant of the habanero family, aji dulce (the "sweet chili") has spread into the Caribbean, too. It's on the milder end of the spice range, with misshapen, blocky fruits, and it is used in sofrito and salsa. 500–1000 SHU.

Aji Limo

Much hotter than its Venezuelan cousin aji dulce, the limo is a Peruvian variety with a bulbous, two-inch-long pod growing to a pointed end, ripening to a range of colors from carrot orange to flame red. It's popular as a component of ceviche fish marinades, and it has an attractive citrus flavor when cooked. 50,000–60,000 SHU.

Carolina Reaper

At the time of this writing, and since 2013, the official hottest chili pepper in the world is still this one, bred by Ed Currie at the PuckerButt Pepper Company in South Carolina. It has a purselike, wrinkled pod in vivid red, not much more than an inch and a half across, with a little appendage at the bottom that looks, very appropriately, like a hornet's stinger. The average strength of the batch tested by a team at Winthrop University was 1,569,300 SHU, but the hottest individual pepper measured an incendiary 2.2 million, suggesting there is potential for a pepper variety that will average out at greater than two million, should the world feel it needs such a thing. On this note, see Dragon's Breath on the following page.

Datil

The story has it that datil came to the Americas with indentured laborers from the Mediterranean island of

Menorca in the 1770s. Its production is now concentrated around Saint Augustine, Florida, and it remains popular with people of Menorcan heritage. It produces a very misshapen-looking, orangey-red fruit with scorching heat levels but a pleasantly sweet, habanero-like flavor. 150,000–300,000 SHU.

Dragon's Breath

In 2017, a plant breeder named Mike Smith in Saint Asaph, a city in Denbighshire, in North Wales, announced that, in the course of attempting to breed a new, attractive ornamental chili in concert with a research program at Nottingham Trent University, he had produced what appeared to be a new record-breaking pepper. He named it in honor of the Welsh dragon and claimed that it had an SHU reading of approximately 2,480,000, which would make the pepper a new world's hottest if verified. Rumors that an even hotter chili (the ominously named Pepper X) would soon emerge from South Carolina breeder Ed Currie's PuckerButt operation, before the Dragon's Breath could be accredited, indicate the arms race that the competitive cultivation of chilies has now become.

Fatalii

A probable descendant of the habanero, native to central and southern Africa, fatalii is instantly recognizable for its banana-yellow color when ripe, although there are red and brown variants, too. It grows in wrinkled pods about three inches long and an inch wide. It has a bright citrus flavor when cooked and is often used in the production of African hot sauces, along with citrus fruits themselves, mango, and pineapple. It is extremely hot. 100,000–325,000 SHU.

Habanero
The ancestor of all the *Capsicum chinense* cultivars, the habanero (named for the city of Havana, Cuba, but grown all over Central America) is one of the most widely recognized hot peppers in international cuisine. Evidence of domesticated habaneros in Peru dates their cultivation back to at least 6500 B.C.E. The habanero loves very hot tropical climates, where its lantern-shaped fruits mature to a characteristic orangey-red, with thin, waxy skins. Milder versions of the habanero have been bred in Texas, but the original should be around 200,000–300,000 SHU.

Hainan Yellow Lantern
The *huang deng long jiao*, to give it its Mandarin name, is also known as the yellow emperor, and has a small, gently puckered fruit growing to about two inches long and a little less across, with an arresting golden yellow luster when ripe. It is native to the southern corners of Hainan, an island province off the coast of southern China. It is mainly processed into chili sauce. 250,000–300,000 SHU.

Infinity
The infinity pepper was, for a blink of an eye in 2011, the hottest chili in the world, before the naga viper (see entry) steamed past it. Bred by Nick Woods at Fire Foods in Lincolnshire, England, the infinity has heart-shaped pods that ripen to an orangey red with a wrinkled, rough-textured skin. It has an initial fruity taste before the blinding scorch takes over. 1,000,000–1,250,000 SHU.

Jamaican Hot Chocolate
Legend has it that the hot chocolate first came to light at the street market in Port Antonio, Jamaica, where its small, wrinkled pods attracted notice for their prune-brown color. It's rarely more than about an inch or two long, and it has a potent, smoky flavor. Excellent in Caribbean hot sauces. 100,000–200,000 SHU.

Naga Morich
Also known in India as the serpent and (in the United Kingdom) as Dorset naga, the morich originated in Assam, Northeast India, and is also grown in Bangladesh. It is similar to bhut jolokia (see entry) but with a smaller pod that has an uneven, knobbly surface, and it is even hotter. 1,000,000–1,500,000 SHU.

Naga Viper
Bred by Gerald Fowler at the Chili Pepper Company in Cumbria, northwestern England, the viper was the world's

hottest for a tantalizingly brief spell from 2011 to 2012. It's a shriveled-looking, shiny red pepper, and it has a tripartite parentage in bhut jolokia, naga morich, and moruga scorpion (see entries). 1,382,000 SHU.

Paper Lantern

A longer variant of the habanero that matures to a raspberry-red, pointy-ended pod of about three inches, the paper lantern is not as fragile as its name would suggest. It fruits vigorously even in cooler climates and makes an explosively hot base for a chili relish. 250,000–350,000 SHU.

Pepper X

Whether Dragon's Breath was hotter than Carolina Reaper will soon be irrelevant, as PuckerButt's Ed Currie bred a pepper in 2017, given this mysterious temporary code name, that is averaging over 3 million SHU. That's about twice the intensity of the Reaper. It's a gnarled, greenish yellow chili that has so far been used as the key ingredient of a hot sauce called the Last Dab (slogan: "It's a tough one"), revealed on Currie's YouTube channel, Hot Ones, in September 2017. Demand for the sauce shot into the stratosphere on news of its release. Hot peppers are not going away any time soon. 3,000,000 SHU.

Red Savina

Developed in Walnut, California, in the 2000s, the savina enjoyed the accredited title of world's hottest chili until it was overtaken in 2007 by the bhut jolokia (see entry). It has a round fruit that ripens to deep Crayola red and the kind of heat level that requires protective clothing for handling it. 350,000–550,000 SHU.

Scotch Bonnet

Along with the habanero, to which it is related, Scotch bonnet is probably the most famous of the *chinense* varietals. It was named for its speculative resemblance to the Scottish tam-o'-shanter, a flat cap with a pom-pom. It has become a firm favorite of the Caribbean islands, where some producers have bred sweeter variants of it, but it is also common in Central America and Africa. Ripening to orange or red, it's added to many different dishes and to bottled hot sauces, but it is most characteristically known as the fire-raiser in jerk chicken and pork recipes. 100,000–400,000 SHU.

Suriname Red (or Yellow)

Originating in Suriname (formerly Dutch Guiana) in northern South America, these interlinked varieties produce a stubby, curved pepper with puckered skin and elevated levels of heat. The yellow version, also known as Madame Jeanette (allegedly after a celebrated

Brazilian bordello proprietor), is the more popular, and it is more closely related to the Scotch bonnet and original habanero. The yellow is said to have a pineapple taste when ripe, while the red has a more savory edge. 100,000–350,000 SHU.

Trinidad Moruga Scorpion

Closely related to the Butch T scorpion (see entry), the moruga hails from the district of the same name in the Trinity Hills in central south Trinidad, where it was bred by Wahid Ogeer. It also had its moment of glory as world's fieriest from 2012 to 2013. It produces a squat, rounded pod that ripens to scarlet, with a sweet flavor and—of course—a raging conflagration of capsaicin. 1,200,000–2,000,000 SHU.

Trinidad Scorpion Butch T

The Trinidad scorpion is another variety that has recently enjoyed a moment in the limelight as the world's hottest pepper. It is derived from the much less feral Trinidad scorpion, but with the aid of seeds supplied by a Mississippi grower, Butch Taylor. Like the Carolina Reaper (see entry), it has what looks like a thick stinger protruding from the bottom end of a bulbously flared body, and it ripens to a shrill scarlet. The scorpion has been readily adopted in its ancestral home of Trinidad and Tobago for use in bottled hot sauces. The secret to the scorpion's fire is that the soil in which it was originally grown was fertilized with liquid runoff from a worm farm, the sort of detail that you may not want to dwell on as you're sprinkling the hot sauce over your oysters. The theory is that chitin from the dead insects eaten by the worms triggers the plant's natural defense systems, encouraging it to make itself furious with deterrent heat. Up to 1,463,700 SHU.

Capsicum Baccatum

Aji Amarillo
The yellow *aji* is the most common variety in Peru, and it is grown all over the Andean region. It grows to around four inches long, with a tapered end, and it has a deep orange-yellow color when ripe. Used in many indigenous dishes and in salsas, it is also sold dried and powdered. 40,000–50,000 SHU.

Aji Limon
Another Peruvian *aji* variety, but distinct from the aji limo (see entry), the limon, or lemon drop, is a two-inch-long pepper with a crinkly skin that ripens to a light lemon yellow. Its users insist that its name derives not from its color but from its strong citric flavor, though some find it excessively perfumed in a soapy way. It comes into its own for infusing in vodka to make an aromatic *limonnaya*. 15,000–30,000 SHU.

Brazilian Starfish

The flat, red pods really do suggest the stellate form of the marine starfish, although they mature only to about two inches across. It has a sweet, fruity flavor, too, and a pretty big punch of heat. Creative slicing to emphasize the shape is a must. 10,000–30,000 SHU.

Christmas Bell

A chili pepper must be trying to get this weirdly shaped, but this one has a bell-shaped form with a flared bottom end and something reminiscent of a clapper peeping out below. In Brazil, where this pepper came from, they call it Ubatuba Cambuci, after the two locations where it is mainly found. It's also been called the bishop's hat. It ripens to a very festive Santa Claus red and is at the milder end of the heat scale. 5,000–15,000 SHU.

Criolla Sella

Originating in the Bolivian highlands, the criolla sella is definitely a looker. It produces golden-yellow fruits in two-inch-long pods, and it is thin-skinned enough for drying, but it makes a colorful addition to chunky salsa, where the citrusy, smoky flavor comes into its own. 20,000–30,000 SHU.

Peppadew

One of the truly global chili varieties appears to have originated by happenstance in a garden in the Limpopo province of South Africa in 1993. The fruits look like ripe cherry tomatoes, and they are generally sold in a sweet pickling brine. 1,000–1,200 SHU.

Capsicum Pubescens

The C. *pubescens* species is the rarest of the five chili types, and it may never have existed in the wild state at all. Its principal Central and South American variety is variously known as rocoto, locoto, or manzano, the last from the Spanish word for "apple," which it very closely resembles in miniature. The mostly deep red, shiny fruits are only about an inch across, containing seeds that are the dark brown of apple pips rather than the normal white, and they can ripen in relatively cool climates. The *pubescens* species name derives from the hairiness of the leaves and stems. Regional variants of the rocoto include a yellow version called canario, the pear-shaped perón, and the elongated rocoto longo, which was bred in the Canary Islands. The heat intensity varies very widely according to the provenance and subtype. 50,000–250,000 SHU.

Part
TWO

HISTORY

3

Spice of America—
The Chili in Its Homelands

Of the twenty to thirty wild species of chili pepper found across Central and South America, just five have been subjected to domesticated cultivation. All of these domestications happened in pre-Columbian antiquity, and all chili varieties found throughout the world today belong to one or another of those five types.

The two most widely encountered species—*Capsicum annuum* and *C. frutescens*—as well as *C. pubescens*, appear to have been first domesticated in the northern sector of Central America, most probably in what is now Mexico. There is archaeological evidence of domesticated chili in use in the Tehuacán Valley of southeast Mexico dating back around 6,000 years ago.[1] These findings are of *C. annuum* residues. Intriguingly, the earliest records of the other two species—*C. baccatum* and *C. chinense*—give evidence of their domestication in two sites, Loma Alta and Real Alto, in southwestern

Ecuador at roughly the same time. These are culturally quite distinct developments, and yet they were very likely motivated by the same impulse: to provide a ready supply of a plant that had preservative and antimicrobial properties and that contributed to overall human health and well-being.

Exactly how chilies were consumed at these earliest times remains a matter of speculation, but some educated guesses can be made from the residual fossil evidence. The residues have been found on a number of different types of vessel: cooking pots, grindstones, and spouted jars or jugs. It seems certain that chilies were ground up or chopped very finely and added to the other ingredients in a cooked dish, but at some stage they began to be made into a paste or salsa on their own, for use as a condiment. We cannot know precisely when this later development began, but by the time of the Middle to Late Preclassic period in Mexico (400 B.C.E.–300 C.E.), according to the findings of a team working in Chiapa de Corzo in Tehuacán, chilies were apparently being prepared in this way and stored in spouted jars. Originally, archaeologists assumed this widespread vessel was used purely as a form of decanter, for pouring out liquids into smaller containers, but the presence of chili residues suggests that it might have been a serving vessel in its own right. It may well have been the precursor of chili sauce bottles, its contents stored separately because of their incendiary effect on other foods, with small amounts sprinkled as seasoning for other foods at a communal meal. If these vessels had been used only for storing whole chilies, there would be a strong likelihood of finding whole seeds in the archaeological remains, but there are none at all, which suggests that the seeds had been crushed or, less likely, removed before the jar was filled with the chili relish.

What would substantiate the chili sauce theory would be the discovery of grindstones or tools from the same era showing evidence of chili deposits. The principal means of grinding at this time was the *mano* and *metate* method in which the material to be crushed was laid on a large, round, flat stone with a depression in the middle (the *metate*) and pounded with a smaller, handheld stone about the size of a bar of soap (the *mano*). This technique was eventually superseded by the *molcajete*, the ancestor of the mortar and pestle, but there is no evidence that this tool was used in Mexico until the Postclassic period, about 1000 C.E. at the earliest.

The other possible reason for the presence of chili on the insides of spouted jars is that it may have been applied to the interior surfaces of the vessel to preserve some other food that was stored there and to repel insects. In certain instances, there is evidence of chili residues that appear to have been mixed with wood ash, and such a mixture would have been used more likely for preservation than for consumption.

These findings come from a region of southeastern Mexico that covers the Tehuacán Valley and from the present-day states of Oaxaca and Veracruz. This area was already home in the Middle to Late Preclassic era to two prominent related cultures known as the Mixe and the Zoque, whose languages are related and each of which is thought to descend from the Olmec people, the first large-scale civilization of Mesoamerica. Writing home to the Spanish king Charles V in the sixteenth century, the conquistador Hernán Cortés reported that the Mixe-Zoque peoples were the only native populations whom the Spanish forces had been unable to quell, owing partly to the rough inhospitableness of their terrain, and partly to the fact that the native peoples were so disobligingly warlike in defending it. Armed to the teeth and fiercely territorial, the Mixe-Zoque people resisted any incursion on their culture other than the partial success of the spiritual variety undertaken by Catholic missionaries, and their culture has endured to the present day, even while other small tribal groups were wiped out by conquest and contact with European diseases to which they had no natural immunity.

One factor seems to link the contexts in which the Chiapa de Corzo findings were unearthed. They are all associated with social elites, either from the burial remains in the tombs of high-status individuals or from temple complexes where religious rituals took place. Chili preparations seem to have been consumed at tribal feasts to mark the passing of elders, and the empty pots and vessels that had contained the peppers were then deposited among the grave goods. As well as being a ritual food, chilies were, as we know, also used medicinally for their antibacterial properties, and bowls and jugs that had contained chili may well have been deposited in tombs to protect the deceased on their passage into the next world.

We know that chili has been used since ancient times in the Mesoamerican world to flavor hot drinks made from cacao, this, too, being a luxury preparation as is indicated by the ostentatiously decorated tall ceramic jars, *tecomates,* in which it was served in the Olmec period, at least as far back as 1900 B.C.E. Indeed, the elites of Aztec society still drank cacao in this way when the Hispanic colonists arrived and first observed the custom in the early sixteenth century. That great anthropologist *avant la lettre,* Bernardino de Sahagún, field researcher of the Spanish conquests, describes the retailing and preparation of a hot chocolate drink in his journal of the 1560s. When he comes to enumerate the additional flavorings that go into it, what he calls "chile water" is the first mentioned, followed by the aromatic repertoire of vanilla, fresh or dried flowers, and honey. The tantalizing question, reaching back into antiquity, is which came first: the chili or the chocolate? Was chili one of various means of flavoring bitter hot chocolate, as food historians have traditionally believed, or was the drink originally a chili pepper preparation to which cacao was added to make it a little less ferocious? The latter hypothesis gains a little credence from the failure to find chocolate residues in those chili-laced vessels at Chiapa de Corzo. Then again, perhaps the recipe was accidentally discovered when a chocolate drink was poured into jars that had been swabbed with chili as an insect repellent and preservative.

Even the Olmec were not the first adopters of chili in these parts. Evidence of domesticated chili strains has been discovered from periods predating even the systematic production of ceramic ware, meaning that the chili plant must have been previously cultivated by one of the settled trading communities that sprang up all over the ancient Americas. Archaeobotanist Linda Perry favors the theory that the first domestication of chili peppers happened in what is now Peru and Bolivia. The remains of cultivated chilies that her team un-earthed in southern Ecuador, reported in *Science* magazine in February 2007, were around 6,250 years old, and since there are no wild chilies in this region, she speculates that these remains must be the descen-dants of plants brought there from neighboring zones.[2]

According to this account, the chili was first domes-ticated in the northern zones of South America before being traded northward into Central America as far as Mexico. What seems to contradict this theory is that the two distinct cultivation areas are characterized by the occurrence of different species of *Capsicum*, suggest-ing that domestication was a process that happened at roughly the same time in these two distant areas of the American landmass.

As we follow the progress of the chili around the world, we need to consider it everywhere in its culinary contexts. What was it eaten with? How was it prepared? Was it used as a seasoning or eaten as a vegetable on its own?

In the ancient Americas, the staple grain of the cooking systems that traveled most widely across the continent was maize. The earliest wild antecedent of cultivated maize, which can be traced in central Mexico at least as far back as 7000 B.C.E., was a miniature version, teosinte, that had tiny cobs no more than about three inches long. Its domesticated descendant, the prolifically fruiting form familiar today for its large yellow kernels, was probably developed around 1500 B.C.E. Both the plant itself and the technologies used in preparing it for cooking—a dipped grindstone and pummeler—made their way along the Mexican Gulf Coast. This diffusion coincided with the rise of the Olmec culture, about which tantalizingly little is still known, but we do know the Olmec people subsisted on what became the indispensable Mesoamerican food trinity of maize, beans, and squash. The maize appears to have been either ground and boiled in water for a loose gruel known in Spanish as *atole,* or parceled in leaves for tamales, steamed dumplings in the manner of Chinese *lo mai gai* (lotus-leaf rice wraps). These maize dishes were eaten with a wide variety of meats— including that of birds, raccoons, deer, opossums, peccaries (a species of wild boar), and domesticated dogs—as well as saltwater and freshwater creatures such as turtles, fish, mollusks, and other shellfish. In addition to the squash, beans, tomatoes, and sweet potatoes cultivated in fields outside the villages, and avocados harvested from their soaring trees in the rain forest, chili peppers were grown in little enclaves of cleared forestland, in the vicinity of cacao bushes for making the chocolate drink that the Olmec almost certainly pioneered.

Maize meal, along with the meat of domesticated animals, formed the basis of offerings to the gods in rituals that took place on stone platforms elevated high above ground level. The Feathered Serpent—half-divine and half-mortal, and common to later Mesoamerican cultures including the Aztecs and the Maya—may well have originated among the Olmec, and there were also meteorological spirits, bringers of rain and sun. Whether the Olmec practiced human sacrifice, as the Aztecs certainly did, is less clear. The culture did not encompass a priestly caste as such, and the offerings were mostly carried out by local rulers in each community.

Chili underpinned a great deal of what the Olmec ate. The seeds and other residues found in firepits that were traditional for cooking, in traces inside ceramic vessels, and in garbage dumps indicate that hot peppers were ever present. In time, they came to be used as a flavoring element in the bitter chocolate drink, in bland atole gruels, and, ground up with water and perhaps other herbal ingredients, as the basis for pungent relishes and salsas to accompany the food of the elites. The use of dressings to supplement whatever seasoning the main dish contains is indeed one of the hallmarks of elite food, representing a gilding of the lily that is not nutritionally necessary but that adds aesthetic pleasure to the taste of food.

When a food item becomes one of the staples of a diet in any region of the world, it takes on two almost contradictory meanings. Its commonness makes it a humdrum, quotidian part of the daily fare, and yet, precisely because it is so widely used, it becomes indispensably precious. Imagine life without salt. To the early Mesoamerican peoples, chili had become virtually as essential as salt, especially when the pepper's obscurely understood nutritional value was taken into account. By the time of the Aztec civilization, eating any meal, or even any dish, without chili had the same privative drabness as Lenten fasting had to the Spanish voyagers who eventually appeared on the horizon. Chili was used to season meat and fish, was added to flatbread doughs, and was nibbled in a shriveled, dried form to ward off illness.

Such a valuable plant food had other, nondietary uses. Dried chilies were rubbed on the soles of a baby's feet to ensure health and long life. The pungent smoke was put to many uses, both sacred and profane. It helped to drive off malignant spirits during funeral ceremonies, and it could also be a means of chastising a raucous child, who only had to be held near the fumes of roasting chilies to be reduced to teary-eyed, choking remorse. Two adjacent images in the *Codex Mendoza* of the late 1530s, completed around twenty years after the Spanish conquest, make the latter practice graphically clear: While a mother shows her infant daughter the smoke, as though threatening her into good behavior, her husband is holding their son's face directly over the fumes. The chili also became an item of currency in many areas, and it played a central part in tribute systems. By the time of Columbus's first voyage, the people of each province in Mexico were duty-bound to pay a yearly tribute to the emperor, Montezuma II, of 1,600 bales of chilies.

Alongside the Olmec, the Mayan civilization grew to cover around one-third of the Mesoamerican landmass. Once thought to have emerged around 2000 B.C.E. at the dawn of what is known as the Preclassic era, archaeologists have now pushed back its origins to at least six hundred years earlier. The Mayans enjoyed friendly trading relations with their neighbors and developed much the same diet. The tripartite carbohydrate system of maize, beans, and squash was supplemented by the cultivation of chili peppers. Their remains are present at Joya de Cerén, a site unearthed in western El Salvador in 1976 and known as the Pompeii of the Americas. A volcanic eruption around 590 C.E. covered the village in fourteen successive layers of ash, perfectly preserving a snapshot of an agricultural community at work. The manioc fields were freshly planted only hours before the devastation, while cotton seeds were in the process of being ground, probably for cooking oil. Among the items found in the food stores are tomatoes and chilies, staples of the diet here and elsewhere in the region. The only thing missing is the people, who, in contrast to their unluckier counterparts in Pompeii, had apparently managed to flee in time, despite the overwhelming suddenness of the eruption. Their half-eaten meals testify to the crash of dire emergency.

The Mayan civilization would eventually collapse catastrophically, succeeded by the Aztec in Central America around 1300 C.E. They dominated the Mesoamerican region from the fourteenth to the sixteenth century, when the Spanish arrived. To a much greater extent than their predecessors, the Aztecs left behind a rich legacy of written source material, artifacts, and buildings, supplemented by the eyewitness accounts of incoming Europeans, who were alternately fascinated and repelled by Aztec custom. In matters of diet, the Aztec sought a very classical-sounding balance between indulgence and abstemiousness, practicing regular fasts in which they would abstain not from meat and sweets in the European fashion of Lent, but more radically from the fundamental elements of seasoning—salt and chilies—without which food would taste joyless and unsatisfying. Chili was as important a factor in the diet as it had been for the Aztecs' cultural predecessors in the region, but it had been elaborated by now into a formidably complex taxonomic system of almost Linnaean exhaustiveness.

Once again, we have the Spanish Franciscan friar, Bernardino de Sahagún, to thank for the most diligent ethnographic account of the way of life in the Aztec villages. In the tenth book of his encyclopedia of the indigenous way of life, known as the Florentine Codex, written over several decades for a Spanish monarchy agog for stories of the New World, he paints a picture of the Aztec people and their customs, including what has become one of the more famous word portraits of a food merchant and his wares in gastronomic history:

> The good chili seller sells mild red chilies, broad
> chilies, hot green chilies, yellow chilies, cuitlachilli,
> tenpilchilli, chichioachilli. He sells water chilies,
> conchilli; he sells smoked chilies, small chilies,
> tree chilies, thin chilies, beetle-like chilies. He
> sells hot chilies, early-season chilies, hollow-based
> chilies. He sells green chilies, sharp-pointed
> red chilies, late-season chilies, chilies from
> Atzitziuacan, Tochmilco, Huaxtepec, Michoacan,
> Anauac, the Huaxteca, the Chichimeca.
> Separately he sells strings of chilies, chilies cooked
> in an olla [a broad-bellied cooking pot], fish
> chilies, white fish chilies.

There is an incantatory feeling to this listing that suggests something of the traditional merchants' songs of the European markets, but Sahagún does not scruple to give the negative side, too. There are bad chili sellers whose wares include such impertinences as "flabby chilies" and—the ultimate ignominy—"chilies without heat":

> *The bad chili seller sells stinking chilies, sour*
> *chilies, foul chilies, rotten chilies; waste from*
> *chilies, runty chilies, chaff from chilies. He*
> *sells chilies from the wet country, chilies without*
> *heat, chilies without taste; malformed chilies,*
> *flabby chilies, unripe chilies, embryonic chilies.*[3]

Further south, in the highlands of South America's upper reaches, the Inca Empire was the largest world empire of its day, the most extensive of all in the pre-Hispanic Americas. The Incas' origins are lost to recorded history, but they appear to date back as far as the thirteenth century, when they emerged as a pastoral tribe in the Cusco region of what is now Peru. Theirs was a true empire in the sense that its ethnic composition was very diverse: people of unmixed Incan ethnicity themselves represented no more than about 0.25 percent of the approximately ten million people over whom they held sway. The heyday of the civilization extended for a century from the 1430s, when the Incas began a sweeping campaign of territorial expansion, but their culture would be brought to an ignominious demise by Spanish conquest under the Pizarro brothers from the 1520s on. One tribal ruler after another was humiliated and executed until the last Inca stronghold was captured and subdued in 1572. The Inca people were made subjects of the Spanish crown, and their gradual extinction through forced labor in warfare and in the silver mines was ruthlessly compounded by rapidly spreading epidemics of European diseases.

The Inca diet was based on tubers and roots, predominantly the thousands of wild varieties of potato, which is native to Peru. Meats and fish were preserved for the winter months by drying and salting, and the Incas also practiced the earliest known prototype of freeze-drying, laying out harvested potatoes under cloths to freeze through the mountain settlements' cold nights. In the mornings, the people literally stamped out the excess water from them under the cloths, and then the potatoes were exposed to the dehydrating heat of the day. This process, repeated over several days, produces a lightweight and very durable food (known as *chuño* in the Spanish derivation of the native Quechua) that was perfect kit bag sustenance for soldiers on campaign.

Underpinning the Inca diet were chili peppers of the *Capsicum baccatum* and *chinense* varieties. Like the Olmec, Maya, and Aztec peoples, the Incas used chilies as talismans against evil spirits, as medicinal aids in the treatment of diseases, and as a trading commodity. Peppers play a central role in the Inca foundation myth, which told of four brothers and four sisters emerging from caves at the dawn of time to populate the earth. One of the brothers, to whom the plant was considered to be sacred, went by the honorific title of Ayar Uchu (Brother Chili). The empire's extent over four distinct climatic zones from north to south meant that many different types of chili were cultivated throughout it, the peppers' different levels of heat intensity adding variety to the foods they flavored. As with the Aztec people, the Incas practiced periodic salt and chili fasting. Peppers appear in textile and ceramic designs, a tradition in this region that predated the Inca themselves. The Nazca people of southern Peru also decorated their pottery with graphic depictions of foods, such as the six large, gaily striped chili peppers that ornament a small, double-spouted bottle made somewhere between the third and sixth centuries C.E.

The part-Inca historian Garcilaso de la Vega, writing a cultural history of the civilization in 1609, notes the prevalence of *uchu* (chili) in the Incan diet. There was no method of cooking to which it was not considered suitable. When rigorous fasting mandated abstention from chili in all its forms, the ordinance noted both the everyday indispensability of the plant and its sacred character. Garcilaso even delineates for a seventeenth-century readership two of the three varieties of chilies cultivated in the region at the time (the one whose name he cannot recall was the crème de la crème, reserved only for consumption in the imperial household of the Inca ruler's family): There were *rocot uchu* (thick pepper), a variety of *Capsicum baccatum* whose pods are as long and thick as those of runner beans, and *chinchi uchu,* the cherry chili, the type confusingly now known as rocoto, fiercely potent and rarer than the rest, which looked for all the world like a round berry on a stalk, and belonging to the cultivated C. *pubescens* species. In a moment of pathos, Garcilaso relates how the Incas made offerings of chilies to the conquistador Francisco Pizarro and his army in vain appeasement of the worst intentions of colonial rapacity. The chili's real victory would have to wait until it was transported back to Europe, when it took its place among the traditional Eastern spices of the refined cuisines of the Iberian peninsula.

A further suggestive aspect of the foundation myth has Ayar Uchu as the focal point of a ceremony marking the transition to adulthood. His stone shrine stood on the summit of the Huanacauri mountain, which an Inca youth would ascend at the appropriate moment of his life to become a man. In a kind of transubstantiation narrative, the stone idol was said to assume a living form, taking on wings like those of a condor, on which it would soar into the heavens to converse with the sun, before returning and repetrifying to do service to the next generation. When the new young men returned from their initiation, their youthful long hair had been cut short, and they had been adorned with golden ear spools, invested with their first breechcloths, and entrusted with their first weaponry. In this mythic structure, we can see the transcendence of the chili as a taste element that soars above all else, its hotness attested by the shape-shifting deity's familiarity with the equally fiery and life-giving sun, and note its pivotal symbolic role in the transition to adulthood. An appreciation of the fire of chilies is a taste that must be both learned and earned. The sacred colors of the Inca, red and yellow, are the predominant shades of ripe rocoto peppers.

Through these long millennia of pre-Columbian history, the taste of chili peppers was known only to the indigenous peoples of Central and South America. The chili was a linchpin of the diet, already multifarious in its varieties even within each of the domesticated species, a source of fascination and reverence for its copious purposes. It was prophylactic, medicinal, an aid to food preservation and hygiene, and a commodity in intertribal trade. It was a sacred currency, too, an emblem of origin myths in many zones, an offering and an honor, a food of the gods that could be shared by mortal people—or at least, in the case of some chili varieties, by the more privileged among them. Proffered in the right spirit, the chili might just pacify the hostile intent of pallid outsiders from far away.

When the conquistadors arrived in the Americas on their missions of conquest from the farthest foreign monarchies, what they wanted, along with land and riches, was spice. Intriguingly, they ascribed to spices of the East many of the same attributes as the American chili. Asian spices contributed to gastronomic enjoyment but could also be pharmacological agents, preservatives, even aphrodisiacs. They supported a vastly lucrative mercantile profit economy, and they forged indissoluble cultural ties between different peoples and traditions. All chilies lacked for the Spanish was the element of the sacred, and that lack, together with the colonist's unshakable belief in his own innate superiority over what he saw as benighted savages, was what set the mood for the reckless despoliation and plunder that would carry a thoroughly desacralized chili pepper all through the wider world.

4

Three Ships Come Sailing—The Columbian Exchange

The three ships that set out from Palos de la Frontera in August 1492, under the command of Christopher Columbus, were on a mission from the Spanish crown to find a shorter maritime route to India and the riches of the East. The Spanish believed so tenaciously they would come across the Indies, to which they were used to traveling in the opposite direction, that we still use their misnomers today, referring to the Caribbean islands as the West Indies, while for many generations the native peoples encountered in the Americas were universally known to outsiders as Indians.

Columbus's first voyage, which returned to Spain in January 1493, was effectively a whistle-stop tour of the Greater Antilles, calling at what are now the Bahamas and Turks and Caicos Islands, and then the northern coasts of Cuba and Hispaniola (Haiti and the Dominican Republic). This odyssey introduced the voyagers to groups of peaceful islanders, some of whom were so friendly indeed that Columbus felt confident, with the agreement of the local chieftain, about leaving behind thirty-nine of his men to go native. La Navidad, on the north coast of present-day Haiti, was the New World's first, though short-lived, European settlement. In addition to meeting the locals, the conquistadors also encountered their food.

By the time he returned to Spain, on a rather rougher Atlantic crossing than the expedition had endured going out, Columbus was able to introduce his royal sponsors, King Ferdinand and Queen Isabella, to a handpicked group of wide-eyed, deracinated natives, or at least the eight of them who had survived the journey, as well as some of the things these people ate. There was a peculiar-looking domestic fowl given the name of *gallina de la tierra* (the "land chicken," whose international names would eventually become a linguistically incoherent repertoire of references to India, Peru, and, most familiarly, Turkey). There was a large, spiny fruit that yielded a deliciously sweet, juicy, golden flesh—the pineapple. There was sweet potato and probably the first seeds of an unfamiliar grain eventually known as maize. The leaves of the tobacco plant would enjoy a spectacularly successful worldwide career when the principle of inhaling their burning fumes was learned. What was missing, however, was spice.

This was a major blow. The entire point of the expedition had been to open up new and more commercially

profitable routes to the Asian heartlands, where the lucrative cash crops of pepper, cloves, cinnamon, and ginger provisioned the most valuable import trade in the
world. None of these commodities was found in the New
World, although Columbus would be erroneously convinced on subsequent voyages that he had found slightly
more bitter versions of both cinnamon and ginger.
(Sadly, the former was just regular tree bark, and the latter was probably some unidentified vegetal root.) What
there was instead was a condiment that appeared uni-
versal throughout the region. "There is plenty of *aji*,
which is their pepper," he wrote in his log, "and which
is more valuable than black pepper, and all the people
eat nothing else, it being very wholesome."

Aji was what the Taino and other Arawak people in
the western Atlantic islands called chili. Indeed, the
term is still widely used today as one of the South American words for the chili pepper, reflecting the plant's
geographical origins. Whether it was carried to the
islands in distant pre-Columbian antiquity in the boats
of migrating peoples or propagated by the flights of birds
that had consumed it is uncertain, but two things are
significant about Columbus's description of the plant.
One is that he assumed it was a kind of pepper, so-
lidifying another inaccurate nomenclature in European
usage for centuries to come, and the other is that he gave
it a potential monetary value, as if to entice the import
merchants back home with the expectation of riches to
be made, to the same degree as in the Eastern spice

trade. Chilies would certainly become a significant element of the European and later the global diet, but, as we shall see, they were to be anything but another priceless support of the international capital economy.

Nor was the chili only a culinary staple. The first European exposure to an alternative use for it may well have occurred when the Taino people attacked the Spanish fort at La Isabela, after Columbus had embarked on the return journey to Spain. La Navidad had been reduced to ashes within a year of its foundation, probably as a result of the colonists' contemptuous treatment of the native peoples, which eventually fomented a rebellion against it. At the beginning of 1494, Columbus established a second colony farther east along the coast and named it for the Spanish queen. A two-story fortress and an encampment of around two hundred small dwellings under its protection were constructed. In the founder's absence on another fruitless marine quest for the Far East, the administration of La Isabela disintegrated into shambles, and the colony's inhabitants raided the local people's food stores to keep themselves alive. Full-scale war broke out.

During their assaults on the Spanish fort, an alliance of four Taino communities, who had no metal weapons of their own with which to counter the colonists' lethal steel swords, employed a prototype of chemical warfare, hurling gourds full of ashes laced with ground-up chilies at the Spaniards. When these spice bombs burst among the fort's defenders, the ash carried the particles of chili into the air, forming a lethal dust that stung and blinded their eyes and choked their throats. With the enemy in sensory disarray, the besiegers were able to move in, their faces covered with bandanas worn as protective masks, and pick off as many of the Spaniards as they could.

The physician appointed to Columbus's second voyage to the Americas in 1493, Dr. Diego Alvarez Chanca, was to be the most significant evangelist for the chili pepper back home. In his account of the voyage, written to the Spanish court the following year, Chanca enumerated the staple foods eaten by the various native peoples of the West Indian islands. At Santo Domingo (Hispaniola), he came across the *caumaná* tree, which he misidentified as a type of nutmeg; what he wrongly takes to be inferior wild cinnamon; a bit of wrinkled "ginger root" worn around a tribesman's neck; yellow paradise plums fallen from their tree and partially rotting on the ground; palm nuts; maize from which the islanders made a kind of bread; a tuberous root known as *age* (either from the yucca plant, or possibly sweet potato); and, last but by no means least, the indispensable condiment for this tuberous root and for much else besides: "They use, to season it, a vegetable called *agí*, which they also employ to give a sharp taste to the fish and such birds as they can manage to catch, of the infinite variety there are in this island; dishes, all of them, that they prepare in different ways."[1] In other words, here we have an early indication of the ubiquitous and endlessly versatile use of chili, known as *aji* throughout these regions.

Inevitably, the voyagers considered the native foods worth trying, though the idea of eating insects instinctively deterred them, the frothy turbid chocolate drink looked dirty, and the habit of popping out and snaffling down the eyes of fish prior to boiling seemed frankly disgusting. Often the voyagers' curiosity was severely punished by nature. Nothing could have prepared them for the effect of the innocuous-looking fruit of the man-chineel tree (now candidly known as the death-apple), of which Chanca records: "There were wild fruits of various kinds, some of which our men, not very prudently, tasted; and upon only touching them with their tongues, their countenances became inflamed, and such great heat and pain followed, that they seemed to be mad, and were obliged to resort to refrigerants to cure themselves."[2] But neither could anything, as every chili novice since could advise them, have suggested how vicious the first effect of hot peppers would be. Had someone told the voyagers that, within a generation, the folks back home would be gleefully using them to fire up savory sauces for their meat and fish, they would doubtless have considered a collective madness to have overtaken polite society.

Columbus had already noted the importance of chili peppers in the local diet, but he convinced himself—in defiance of the habitual logic of capital markets—that their ubiquity should not stop them from being a potentially lucrative commodity. He observed on his first voyage that "the pepper that the local Indians use as spice is more abundant and more valuable than either black or melagueta pepper." The insistence that anything spicy must be a form of pepper has stayed in the European nomenclature ever since, even though the chili has no biological connection with either black pepper (*Piper nigrum*) or melegueta (*Aframomum melegueta*), the latter the sharp-tasting seeds of a bright red fruit more commonly known as grains of paradise, now confined to specialist delicatessens. The latter comparison would have been especially suggestive. Melegueta was a spice plant native to West Africa, where it was grown on trellises as hops were. It was first transported to Europe by Portuguese traders in the mid-fifteenth century, quickly becoming an item in maritime trade, and also was carried by caravan across the Sahara and along the commercial routes where West African gold and slaves were traded. By the time of Columbus's voyages, melegueta was even more valuable in European markets than Indian black pepper, which was itself known as "black gold." Even if the distribution systems of commodities such as these were anything but heavenly, the idea of paradise—a symbolic terrain of otherworldly mystery as ancient as time—lies at the heart of the exotic cachet that clung to the spice trade. As spice historian Jack Turner puts it, "for centuries spices and paradise were inseparable, joined together in a relationship whose durability was guaranteed by the fact that it could not be disproved."[3] The circuitous spice routes out of the East were already of such piecemeal construction, with each trader along the way knowing no other agent than his immediate predecessor, that the geographical origins of spices remained mysterious to the traders themselves and entirely opaque to their consumers in the markets of Europe. That the Caribbean chili might prove to be an even more valuable import crop than grains of paradise was an all-too-tantalizing prospect. (To add to the confusion, one of the principal Brazilian varieties of *Capsicum frutescens* is known today as malagueta, a chili variety that has no biological relation to grains of paradise.)

On his second voyage to the Caribbean islands, the one that Dr. Chanca accompanied, Columbus wrote again in his journal about the chili: "In those islands there are also bushes like rosebushes that make a fruit as long as cinnamon, full of small grains as biting as pepper; those Caribs and the Indians eat that fruit as we eat apples." Here at the outset of the European encounter with chilies is the mistaken notion that the seeds are the hottest part of the chili, but the comparison to pepper suggests that Columbus was no longer viewing this plant as a type of pepper itself. The fact that the fruit was eaten whole is also fascinating. Melegueta pepper production involved extracting seeds from the fruit in which they were housed, but chilies were eaten entire, a very peculiar practice to the curious European observer.

Meanwhile, in a journal of September 1493, eventually incorporated into a compendious ethnographic work titled *De Orbo Novo* (*On the New World*), an Italian historian at the Spanish court and tutor to the royal princelings, Pietro Martire d'Anghiera, recorded an impressively accurate classification of the indigenous spice ingredient of the Caribbean, based on diligent interviews with men who had been present on Columbus's first voyage: "Something may be said about the pepper gathered in the islands and on the continent—except that it is not pepper, though it has the same strength and the flavor, and is just as much esteemed. The natives call it *axi*, it grows taller than a poppy. When it is used, there is no need of Caucasian pepper."[4]

When this not-pepper version of pepper began to find favor among potential client European populations, as was often the case with new foods, its virtues were advertised as primarily medical. Thus we find a Spanish physician in the 1570s claiming of the chili (in a contemporary English translation), "it dooeth comfort muche, it dooeth dissolve windes, it is good for the breaste, and for theim that bee colde of complexion: it doeth heale and comforte, strengthenyng the principall members."

It was not only the Spanish who would ply the transatlantic routes of colonization and conquest. Their Iberian neighbor, Portugal, was among the world's most advanced seafaring nations, with a reach and influence out of proportion to the modest size of the mother country. In 1494, the two kingdoms signed the Treaty of Tordesillas, in which they agreed to divide up the spoils of the so-called New World between them. They drew a notional line of longitude, known as the Tordesillas Meridian, through the map of South America, disposing everything to its eastern flank in Portugal's favor and the substantially vaster tracts on the west in Spain's. In practice, the treaty was often honored more in the breach than in the observance, and the meridian line shifted to left and right according to who was drawing up the latest map, but both signatories to the treaty recognized the immense advantages of avoiding an international conflict in the exploitation of the resources beyond Europe's shores. In 1500, the Portuguese navigator Pedro Alvares Cabral made an expeditionary landfall on the coast of what is now Brazil and claimed the territory on behalf of King Manuel. The extent of Portugal's global empire meant that the new territory was fated to be linked with its colonial possessions in West Africa, and any slack in working the new plantations with indigenous peoples could be taken up by forcibly transported black African labor, so laying the grounds for the centuries-long crime against humanity we know as the slave trade.

Sugarcane was the most intensively grown crop, cultivated on an industrial scale to satisfy the taste for sweetness that was spreading like wildfire among refined palates back home. In the case of chili peppers, which the Portuguese encountered in the diets of native Brazilian peoples as frequently as the Spanish had encountered them farther north, there was the same initial blank incomprehension. The Portuguese took chilies back to their homeland, as Columbus had done, very possibly having acquired their earliest import samples from the Spanish themselves. But the evidence indicates that, in both Spain and Portugal, chilies were initially grown at home as botanical curiosities, not for any gastronomic role they might fulfill. Yet the explorers themselves, and the settlers who came after them, eventually took to the chili with true gusto once they were stationed in the plant's native lands. As historian Lizzie Collingham writes, "The Spaniards used chilies in much the same way as black pepper. They flavored pork dishes with them and invented spicier versions of staple Iberian recipes. It was claimed that the sweet pork from the Toluca Valley, west of Mexico, when combined with chilies, made a chorizo sausage to rival any found in Old Spain."[5]

Any hesitation about chilies' culinary value did not last long, however. By 1535, the Spanish traveler and historian Gonzalo Fernández de Oviedo y Valdés, in his great *General and Natural History of the Indies*, could already note that chilies were in frequent use as a kitchen ingredient in both Spain and Italy, that consuming them was particularly good for health in the cold winter months, and moreover that they were superior to traditional Indian black pepper for seasoning fish and meat.

The chili would eventually find its way into Portuguese cooking, too—in the form of hot piri piri marinade, without which the cuisine of Portugal today is unimaginable—but by a considerably more circuitous route. Spanish ships returning to and leaving from the Iberian Peninsula often made their first or last ports of call at Lisbon, thus securing the chili's symbiotic adoption into the parallel culinary cultures of Spain and Portugal. Chilies may well have undergone a transitional movement into Europe, alongside the importation of maize, courtesy of the Portuguese. Pepper historian Jean Andrews argues that they were probably planted early on the mid-Atlantic islands of the Azores and Madeira (still Portuguese territories today, albeit autonomously governed ones), on the Cape Verde islands off West Africa, in what is now Guinea on the internationally colonized Gold Coast, and in Angola farther south, and that this piecemeal propagation took place when Portuguese traders acquired the seeds from an unknown Spanish source late in the fifteenth century. That source could have been in Spain itself or in the lightly patrolled territories of the Spanish Main off the Americas, where the terms of Tordesillas theoretically prohibited the Portuguese from going, but where there was more often than not nobody in Spanish uniform around to stop them. A key factor in the dispersal of the plant was the high status that specialized horticulture enjoyed in Portugal relative to Spain, where the elite tended to view botanical dabbling as a rather lowly pursuit.

Beginning at the turn of the sixteenth century, via the world-encircling tentacles of the Portuguese maritime trade, the transfer of the chili to the culinary cultures of Africa and Asia would prove both rapid and profoundly transformative. While chilies inveigled their way into European cuisines at the margins of the everyday diet, adding subtle touches of spicy warmth as a further dimension of existing complexes of seasonings, chilies became all but constitutively indispensable in African and—especially—Asian cooking, a status underpinned by the versatile plant's adaptability to a diverse spectrum of growing conditions. Different varieties of chili have been developed in different parts of the world, and their transportability meant they never became as preposterously valuable in economic terms as pepper and ginger once were, but would be embraced by at least a quarter of humanity.

5

Blazing a Trail—Chili's Journey Through Asia and Africa

The period of the Columbian Exchange in the early sixteenth century has accurately been pinpointed as the origin of globalization. While new ingredients—tomatoes, potatoes, sweet potatoes, maize, beans, peanuts, pineapples, chocolate, and chili peppers—poured forth from the Americas, the staple livestock of European culinary cultures—domesticated cattle, sheep, pigs, and goats—flowed in the reverse direction to the New World. This mutually profitable intermingling of traditions was greatly extended by the involvement of Iberian, and later other European, trading nations in commercial interchanges along their established colonial and mercantile routes, southward into Africa and eastward to the Middle East and central Asia. The transport of chilies to these territories outside the old European heartlands, where gastronomic taste remained strictly stratified and only the elites in society tended to come into contact with new foods in the earliest periods of their importation, was responsible for the rapid global diffusion of the chili.

The adoption of chilies in African cooking was particularly fast—substantial quantities were already being imported by the early 1500s—and was inevitably embroiled in the slave trade. Portuguese slave traders often paid for their human cargoes partly with chilies, which had evidently become everyday items in the regional economy at an early stage. A notably insidious piece of political calculation accounts for the dispersal of chilies across the vast expanses of African territory. Slave traders were aware from experience that African captives were more likely to rebel if they were taken in homogeneous bundles from one community at a time. To counter this risk, the traders gathered people from different areas of the continent that came under their colonial jurisdiction, so each individual cargo comprised captives who had no shared language or culture and therefore much less ability to work together to mount an uprising. As a result of this policy, which linked the isolated Cape Verde islands off West Africa to the territory of present-day Mozambique in the southeast of the continent, the traders had, by the end of the sixteenth century, spread the chili peppers they had brought with them over a huge geographical distance. Chilies also moved along overland trading routes within the African interior, but nothing was quite as effective in dispersing them as the slave trade was. Indeed, as slavery continued through the centuries, Africans would in due course bring their own newly developed spicy dishes to the plantations of the Caribbean and South America. Once this reverse exchange was well established in the seventeenth century, virtually nobody remembered that the chili pepper, far from migrating out of Africa, was in fact coming home.

What facilitated the adoption of chilies, in West Africa at least, was the presence of pungent precursors in the local diet. "African cuisine was already spicy," writes food journalist Angela Garbes, "using native 'grains of paradise' [melegueta pepper], so it's no surprise that people took to the chili pepper with enthusiasm."[1] By the time the British were the unchallenged overlords of the transatlantic slave trade in the later seventeenth and eighteenth centuries, chili peppers had become such an integral part of the pan-African diet that the traders made sure their ships were provisioned, among other requisites, with chilies as an indispensable staple.

In addition to the slave trade, which was responsible for distributing the *Capsicum annuum* and C. *frutescens* species into Africa, and possibly C. *chinense,* too, some diffusion of the plant came from less brutally commercial exploration of the continent. When Spanish and Portuguese expeditions ventured into the interior of West Africa and down to the Congo Basin as the sixteenth century progressed, they brought chilies, in the form of either whole fruits or seeds, as trading counters, as components of educative missionary work, or as routine elements of colonial settlement. A peripheral route of dispersal came about in the following century when British, Dutch, and French colonists brought chilies into Africa from plants grown experimentally or decoratively in botanical gardens. These colonists were not misguided in thinking that a plant originating in the torrid climates of the Central and South Americas might well thrive in the broiling African heat.

Of the two principal species to have become widely established in Africa, C. *annuum* varieties tend to be grown as vegetables, while C. *frutescens* are cultivated for processing into spicy seasonings and condiments. Variations of African hot pepper sauce remain a standby ingredient and relish in many parts of the continent to this day. Ordinary habanero peppers are popular, but for the full blast, many recipes call for Scotch bonnet, birdeye, or savina peppers, the last a particularly fiery red subtype of habanero. African chilies are typically pounded in oil with tomatoes, onion, garlic, salt, pepper, herbs (marjoram, basil, bay, parsley), and other spices (ginger, ground coriander seed, paprika). This mixture is, historically speaking, an African variant of Portuguese piri piri sauce, and in some African regions, the birdeye pepper variety is known as piri piri, or peri peri ("pepper pepper" in languages throughout the Bantu linguistic complex of southern and eastern Africa, including Swahili).[2]

The opening chapter in the story of the globalization of trade is marked by rapid development in many directions at once. Spanish and Portuguese trading ships established new maritime routes across the Atlantic and Pacific Oceans in the sixteenth and seventeenth centuries, bringing colonial settlers, missionary clergy, and freebooters of all stripes to new towns and plantations throughout the coastal zones of the Americas, the Caribbean, and the Atlantic and Pacific islands. In 1497, when the Portuguese navigator Vasco da Gama sailed in quest of spices around the Cape of Good Hope at the southern tip of Africa and back northward through the Indian Ocean, he opened up access to the Persian Gulf region via the Strait of Hormuz. The state of Goa on the west coast of India became a Portuguese outpost in 1510, and the eastward expansion continued to Malacca on the Malay coast, which was a lucrative conduit for Europe's supplies of nutmeg and cloves from the Spice Islands of the Moluccas and eastern Indonesia, and then to a southern Chinese base at Macao. In the other direction, Spanish conquistadors declared Manila in the Philippines to be the headquarters of its eastern empire in 1571, establishing a hazardous but busy trading and passenger route across the Pacific between the Americas—Mexico, Panama, and the territory of the defeated Inca empire in Peru—and East Asia.

The technique of crushing chilies and other spices on a grindstone that the Spanish encountered among Aztec peoples in Mexico was adapted by the settlers and their criollo descendants in the region. Mole sauces in which meat was stewed were based on ingredients that had been ground up on the metate. In Puebla, a version that incorporated chilies and chocolate, *mole poblano,* became the canonical version in criollo cooking. Another sauce traditionally served with braised poultry, a tomato-based hot chili preparation with garlic and coriander, was called mestizo: the name designates mixed race, because it incorporates ingredients from European and Islamic cuisines with indigenous tomatoes and peppers, and because the chicken that was served with it was also an imported culinary tradition in the Americas. Versions of these recipes made it to the Spanish settlements in the Philippines, although the optimal use of chili was not immediately understood, as food historian Rachel Laudan explains: "In most places (except perhaps North Africa) the dried chilies were not rehydrated and sheared to produce a pureed sauce. As a result the color, texture and fruity tastes they could contribute to dishes were not appreciated."[3]

At least three varieties of chili pepper were growing in the Portuguese enclave of Goa by 1520, transported there from Brazil via Lisbon. The influence of Portugal on local culinary tradition was dramatic and deep-rooted. Indian flatbreads began to rise, owing to the addition of European yeasting techniques, while Portuguese recipes from back home were adapted to local conditions, with sesame oil standing in for olive oil, pickled green mango for green olives, and coconut milk for almond milk. A classic Portuguese meat dish, *carne de vinha d'alhos,* pork in wine vinegar with garlic, gained a strongly spicy element from chilies, often ground up in the vinegar beforehand, and became Goan vindaloo. In its origin, this dish is characteristic sailors' fare, constructed from barrel-preserved meat and from garlic reconstituted by marination in red wine or wine vinegar. In Goa, palm vinegar became the accepted substitute, and a host of local spices was added to enliven the dish, with ground dried red chilies the invariable base. So rapid was the adoption of this dish that vindaloo, a chili-laden staple of Indian restaurant menus the world over today, is hard to imagine as being anything other than indigenous to western India, but Europeans had brought the peppers that are indispensable to vindaloo's assertive fieriness from even farther away in the Americas in the first place. A pot of vindaloo large enough to feed a family typically contains at least ten and up to twenty chilies, simply split lengthwise and allowed to release their oils into the dish. Even in India, this quantity of chili is considered a challenge to the palate, and modern cookbooks suggest courteously advising your guests how hot the dish is going to be before they begin eating.

Originally known in Goa as "Pernambuco pepper," named after the Portuguese outpost in Brazil, the chili pepper was adopted in regional cuisines across the Indian subcontinent quickly enough that it became a suitable replacement for indigenous black pepper, almost as though Indian cooking had always been awaiting something stronger than peppercorns. The incorporation of chilies is reflected in the linguistic proximity of terms for black pepper and chili, just as the European languages cheerfully mixed them up: in Hindi, they are respectively *kalimirch* and *harimirch*, in Tamil *milagu* and *milagai*, the latter term a contraction of a phrase meaning "pepper fruit." Indians saw chili as strong pepper in the form of a fruit. Furthermore, whereas the black peppercorn vine was limited to a growing region around the southwestern coastal zone of Kerala, the chili plant turned out to be happy to grow just about anywhere. Of course, black pepper does still play a supporting role in the cooking of the Indian regions, but its significance as the chief provider of spicy heat was overtaken in the sixteenth century, to the extent that local people soon came to regard the chili as an indigenous ingredient.

The chili's transformation of Indian cuisines happened not primarily for gastronomic but for economic reasons. Precisely because it was easier and cheaper to grow, the chili began to overtake black pepper and its relative, long pepper, in Indian agriculture during the sixteenth century, rapidly gaining for itself a reputation as an asset to the diet of the poor. It supplied a whole new dimension of sizzling pungency and complexity to food, but it was also appreciated for its obviously nutritive properties relative to the peppercorn. By the time European botanists began to explore the wild and cultivated flora of India in the 1540s, chilies were already so widely adopted that it was repeatedly assumed that they were a native plant.

In 1511, the year after they commandeered Goa, the Portuguese sent a diplomatic emissary to the Southeast Asian kingdom of Ayutthaya, modern-day Thailand. Within a few short years, a full-scale, two-way trade had been established between the territories, and chilies, which the Portuguese might well have offered to the Thai people in that earliest visit, had put down roots as swiftly as they did in India. Once again, chilies became the food of the poorest people and supplemented a whole diverse array of regional dishes that sprang up throughout the kingdom. Whereas Indian cooks blended chili into the spice mix of slow-cooked dishes, the typical Thai practice was to use chili as a condiment or as the basis of a side dish. The whole family of chili relishes known as *nam phrik*—variations on mixtures of *nam pla* (fermented fish sauce) or dried shrimp paste with garlic, shallots, lime juice, and often sugar with chopped fresh or dried chilies mixed in—has been the central support of Thai cuisine ever since. Served in small, shallow dishes, *nam phrik* is used as a dip for the principal food items it accompanies, whether fish, meat, or vegetables. Salted duck egg and fresh green vegetables are usually paired with a fruity version called *nam phrik long ruea,* made with sour green madan fruit and lime. *Nam phrik phao,* made with tamarind paste and palm sugar, is generally added to tom yum soup but can also be eaten as a kind of spicy marmalade spread on toasted bread. A truly unique experience is the flavor of *nam phrik maeng da,* which incorporates the dried and pounded flight muscles of *Lethocerus indicus,* a gigantic bug caught nocturnally in floating light traps on freshwater ponds. Chili historian Heather Arndt Anderson notes that the sauce's flavor resembles a "delectable combination of lobster, rose petals, orange peel, black licorice and Gorgonzola cheese."[4] It also, of course, contains chili.

Bottled Thai chili sauce is one of the perennial standbys of the region's cooking, splashed liberally into stir-fried noodle dishes and used as a side dip. The internationally known sauce in this style is sriracha, named for a town on the east coast of the Gulf of Thailand. A local shop owner probably first formulated it there in the 1930s to sell to migrant Burmese sawmill workers, who were in the habit of concocting their own relish from pounding chilies with vinegar, salt, and sugar. Various proprietary brands quickly sprang up, and the rest has been commercial history. Despite its geographic name, sriracha is produced in many different countries now, the non-Thai versions tending to have a sweeter flavor and thicker, more ketchuplike consistency than the Thai ones, which emphasize the vinegar behind the chili and are characteristically thinner, like a true *nam phrik* dipping sauce.

The Portuguese and Japanese first made contact in 1543, and in little more than a decade, an annual trading itinerary was set up out of the port of Goa to Macao and Nagasaki. Goa was the site of the largest Jesuit mission in Asia, and the Catholics introduced potatoes, refined sugar, and chilies, as well as the technique of deep-frying in batter that would become Japanese tempura. The Jesuits' ingredients and methods were cautiously incorporated into the local cuisine, which was otherwise based on strictly interpreted Buddhist principles. By the early seventeenth century, spice merchants in the markets of Edo (the city that became Tokyo) had devised a proprietary blend called *shichimi togarashi* (seven-flavor chili pepper), the principal ingredient of which—in addition to some combination of sesame seeds, dried citrus peel, hemp seeds, ginger, seaweed, and sansho, the peppery fruit of the prickly ash—was ground, dried red chili. Togarashi is a staple condiment to this day, used for pepping up rice cakes and crackers and for sprinkling on noodle dishes and soups. Otherwise, there isn't a great deal of chili in Japanese cooking, much of its heat being generated by the horseradish-like brassica wasabi and by raw ginger.

In Macao, the Portuguese culinary influence was noticeably stronger than it would be in Japan. Bacalhau (dried salt cod) easily entered a culinary idiom that already knew dried shrimp. Duck cabidela had made a very long journey from Portugal's Brazilian entrepôts, where the dish was more usually made with chicken. Cabidela consists of poultry cooked in its own blood with vinegar and rice. Rabbit casseroled in wine with aromatic Asian spices such as star anise and cinnamon is an exemplary crossover dish, and the Portuguese *pastel de nata,* a sweet egg tart made with the yolks only (and in China without the milk), is a feature of both Macanese cuisine and Chinese dim sum menus the world over. Chili also found its way into stir-fries of large prawns and crab, and its use would spread like wildfire through the regions of China, as we shall see in the next chapter.

The last port of call on the eastbound tour of the Portuguese in Asia was the Korean Peninsula. Once again, the chili pepper was quick to find a home here in the mid-sixteenth century, inveigling itself into what was essentially an ancient agrarian culinary culture. Seasoning in Korean food had traditionally been assertive anyway, including *jang,* a blended paste made from glutinous rice, powdered fermented soybeans, malted barley, and salt, spiked with black pepper and chopi (berries of Korean pepper, *Zanthoxylum piperitum,* the local variant of Japanese sansho). Following the Portuguese exchange, chili was incorporated into *jang* preparations in the form of *gochugaru,* powdered or flaked sun-dried chili peppers that transform the all-purpose paste into *gochujang,* an essential element of Korean cuisine ever since. *Gochujang* is used in slow-cooked dishes, as a marinade for meat, and as a table condiment like Thailand's *nam phrik.* It has an intriguingly complex range of flavors, encompassing sweet, smoky, and sour elements, the last resulting from its open-air fermentation in traditional ceramic jars. It also covers a broad range of hotness, for which the Koreans have devised their own measurement system, GHU (Gochujang Hot Taste Unit), based on gas and liquid chromatography rather than the more subjective basis of the Scoville scale. Preparation of homemade *gochujang* was still popular throughout Korean kitchens as recently as the 1970s, when it began to be mass-produced commercially and sold in supermarkets. There are more complex blended sauces based on *gochujang,* such as *ssamjang,* which adds soybean paste, onion, and other seasonings to the basic template.

The chili made its way into Korean agricultural treatises in the late seventeenth century, when it appears in the *Sallim gyeongje* (Book of Farm Management) of Hong Man-seon, a digest of practical advice ranging from house-building to looking after your musical instruments. Interestingly, Hong suggests using chili in the ancient Korean side dish kimchi, the staple mix of fermented cabbage and radish that goes back to at least the first century B.C.E. This proposition was avant-gardism of the most venturesome kind: *Gochugaru* chili powder did not become a fully established ingredient of kimchi until the early nineteenth century. Studious cultivation of the chili has remained a widespread enterprise down to the present day. The most favored chili for today's chefs is a variety of *Capsicum annuum,* the Cheongyang chili, whose name is a hybrid of two southern counties, Cheongsong and Yeongyang. The pepper is also a botanical hybrid of the birdeye and the

Jeju island chili. At its most concentrated, the Cheon-gyang is the hottest variety grown in Korea.

In addition to the exploratory voyages of the Iberian traders, the Venetian Republic led the other major route of commercial exchange from the eighth century on, long before Europeans made landfall in the Americas. This route traversed the great empires of the Middle East, the Arabic and Persian heartlands, the Muslim caliphates, and—starting at the end of the thirteenth century—the Ottoman Empire. The Dutch and, once again, the Portuguese came to be principal players in this arena. Introductions of new ingredients and culinary techniques had helped transform Middle and Near Eastern cooking during the Arab trade with the Spice Islands in the Middle Ages. These food traditions already had a strong aromatic base, derived from imported spices that came via the eastern maritime and overland routes to the great trading hub of Venice. Nutmeg, cloves, cinnamon, and ginger are all conspicuous seasoning elements in Middle Eastern cuisines, and they made their way around the Mediterranean basin to Southeast Europe and North Africa. Trade between the Arabian Peninsula and Africa was a long-established enterprise. Coffee spread from Ethiopia throughout the Middle East in the fifteenth century, and the same channels brought melegueta pepper to the region. By one or another of these routes, Portuguese and perhaps also Spanish chilies eventually made their way there, too.

The Arabian peoples were used to adopting gastronomic traditions from both hemispheres, since their region had been a way station for two-way traffic between the Greek and Roman civilizations and India and China since classical times, and the chili was welcomed as readily here as it was farther east along the Portuguese colonial pathway. An emblem of its influence is the merguez, a North African and Arabian mutton or lamb sausage. In the thirteenth-century cookbook *Al Andalus,* a compendium of Moorish Andalusian and Maghrebi cuisine, *mirkâs* is seasoned with *murrī* (fermented barley sauce), cinnamon, lavender, coriander, and black pepper. By the sixteenth century, the recipe was all but unthinkable without dried chilies. Hot peppers made their way into harissa, the fiery red paste of the Maghrebi kitchen, and into *ras el hanout,* a mix of various dry spices. The chili made its way more surreptitiously into Persian cuisine, which was characterized less by sharp fiery seasonings and more by mellow fruit flavors.

Meanwhile, two hundred years after its introduction to India in the sixteenth century, the chili penetrated via Indian pilgrims and traders, into the landlocked kingdom of Bhutan, wedged in the Himalayas between Tibet to the north and Assam to the south. Chilies were adopted here for precisely the opposite of the reason they were widely used in tropical zones: Instead of keeping people cool in broiling heat, peppers were eaten to stay warm in the vicious winters experienced on the rooftop of the world. Chilies also found an interesting place in folk belief that was strikingly similar to their purgative function in Mesoamerican cosmologies: Burning chilies in the house was thought to keep invisible demons away, a practice still widely undertaken today. Soon every small farmer with a bit of land would grow chilies among their other vegetables, a practice that persisted until the late twentieth century, when commercial markets began to fill in for the drop in private production caused by people migrating to the urban centers. In the villages, chilies are hung out to dry in what Mexicans would call *ristras,* draped from little balconies on the fronts of houses and on rooftops. The result has been what is probably world cuisine's most single-minded dedication to chili. Not only are chilies used as seasonings and condiments; they are eaten in Bhutan in side dishes and salads as vegetables in their own right. They are even eaten for breakfast.

The national dish is *ema datshi* (chili cheese), a mixture of fresh or dried *sha ema* chilies with defatted curd cheese made from yak milk. This dish may be eaten on its own, with red rice, or alongside other vegetable dishes such as mushroom chili curry. Side orders of salted, whole chilies are quite commonly eaten with other dishes, resulting in a full-blown incendiary assault

on the taste buds. The Bhutanese people have become
so used to this diet that they consider any meal without
much chili to be drearily bland. At celebrations, the
customary libation is the local distilled rice spirit, *ara*,
in which whole chilies are often macerated, as much
for good fortune as for their sizzling heat. As in India,
China, and Japan, the regional cooking of Bhutan has a
precedent for a pungent ingredient, in this case an
aromatic herb called *namda* (*Pogostemon amaranthoi-
des*), which contributes a hot, bitter taste to a dish when
it is boiled in it. Chili, as in many other locales, quickly
became the preferred way of focusing the pronounced
piquancy that the Bhutanese already valued. Today,
a great range of chili varieties is grown in Bhutan,
and the average family consumes a staggering one kilo
(2.2 pounds) of chili every week. The taste for chili is
encouraged early. Children as young as four or five have
their tender young palates introduced to it, the more so
in the most recent generation as an insurance against
the Westernizing tastes of teenagers for blander, fattier
food. Even *ema datshi* begins to look boring when burgers and pizza come on to the radar.

A faint ripple of medical concern has begun to spread
among the Bhutanese. Is the consumption of so much
chili responsible for a recent increase in cases of peptic
ulcers? People are succumbing to the kind of suggestibility with regard to food-based health scares that has
long possessed the affluent world. A man in a shack café

in Thimphu, the kingdom's capital, told a reporter for Al Jazeera, "These chilies, they are not good for your brain. That's why we Bhutanese people haven't made much progress! If you have a 2 GB memory, you'll go right down to 1 GB with all these chilies."[5] Proving that, when it comes to absurd credulity, the burger-stuffed hordes of the West do not after all have a monopoly.

6

"Red and Incredibly Beautiful"— Chili Goes to China

The precise route of entry—or more likely routes—of chilies into China remains shrouded in historical uncertainty. We have seen that they became established in the Portuguese port city of Macao in the early sixteenth century, but there is no evidence of a gradual branching out from there across the immensities of the Chinese interior. Furthermore, although chilies were absorbed as rapidly and transformatively in certain regions of China as they were in India and Thailand, they achieved only a peripheral presence elsewhere. These patterns of absorption suggest what has become the orthodoxy in food history in recent years: Chilies made their way into China by various unconnected conduits.

If the maritime route, plied primarily by the Portuguese, was the main channel of transmission across much of South and Southeast Asia, it seems highly likely that land routes brought the chili to those zones of

China where it has thrived and played a central role ever since. Of all China's provincial cuisines, those most dedicated to the searing heat of chili are those of Sichuan and Hunan, two landlocked but not contiguous provinces in the southern part of the country. How the chili arrived here has been subject to much conjecture, but the overland route via India and Burma (now Myanmar) remains the favored theory.

In a 1988 study, China historian E. N. Anderson wrote, rather sweepingly, of the chili pepper:

> *Brought to the Orient by the Portuguese in the 1500s, these plants did not remain a minor and local part of the diatom as did tomatoes and eggplants, but swept through the Far East with epochal effect. Perhaps no culinary advance since the invention of distilling had had more effect than the propagation of chili peppers in the Old World.*[1]

They may have swept through Thailand, Korea, and Japan at Portugal's intervention, but not quite through China. External trade contact with Sichuan and Hunan came via Middle Eastern merchants, principally Persian, plying the ancient routes of the Silk Road, exchanging spices for Chinese silks, porcelain, and tea.

As the historian of Arabic food Charles Perry has pointed out, we can be certain that Persian merchants from Khorasan, a region that now incorporates parts of Iran, Afghanistan, and Turkmenistan, introduced chilies to Kashmir and Nepal, because the local word for them there is *khorsani*.[2] The routes they followed continued across the northeastern part of India (now Bangladesh) and northern Burma, and on into Sichuan. In the case of Hunan Province, there is less certainty. It is possible that the overland trail extended there via Sichuan, but from Hunan's geographical position in southeastern China, there is a realistic possibility that it received chilies from the maritime routes. Chilies from Macao could have traveled north through Guangdong Province to Hunan, or even westward across Jiangxi from the port cities of Fujian, which had intensive trading connections with the Portuguese. In a seminal 1955 paper, "The Introduction of American Food Plants into China," Chinese historian Ho Bingdi, although he did not specifically mention chili peppers, outlined the routes by which peanuts and sweet potatoes arrived in China.[3]

Having been expelled from Guangzhou (formerly Canton) in 1522, six years after first making landfall there, the Portuguese moved on around the Chinese coast to the southern ports of Fujian Province, where they continued to trade illegally in defiance of imperial decree. They maintained a trade in cotton along this stretch of the southeastern coastline all the way up to Shanghai, which in itself was not otherwise an international port of call at this time. Ho also points out that Chinese indigenous traders operated between China and the South Pacific islands, where they had been established for a hundred years following the celebrated Chinese naval expeditions of the early fifteenth century (when, as the title of a bestselling work of popular history has it, China "discovered the world"). Perhaps those Chinese traders met with Portuguese commercial ships before the Portuguese had even made contact with Guangzhou on the mainland. In the case of sweet potatoes, Ho argued that they may have come in via the Fujian ports, but there was some local historical documentary evidence from Yunnan Province—south of Sichuan and bordering Burma—that they came via the overland routes from India and Burma. In fact, as food historians now concur, they were most likely to have come from both directions at proximate times, following slightly different routes of propagation. The same is likely to have been true of maize.

That would seem to suggest that some chili peppers may have made their Chinese debut from the maritime entrepôts of the southeast coast, while others came overland in caravan routes from the Ganges plain and Burma into southwestern China. What is tantalizing is that they should have been adopted enthusiastically in some regions, but largely overlooked in others. As a recent historian, Caroline Reeves, has shown, there are references in the so-called gazetteers, China's invaluably rich written local history records, for chili cultivation in Shanyin county; Zhejiang, to the south of Shanghai in 1671 ("*laqie* is red in color and can be

substituted for pepper [i.e. Sichuan peppercorns]");
and in 1682 in Gaiping county, Liaoning, a far northeastern province beyond Beijing, bordering the northern Korean peninsula. Liaoning chilies must have come
from Korea, perhaps originally from Japan, courtesy of
the Portuguese. Each of these citations predates the
first recorded references to chilies for Hunan (1684)
and Sichuan (1749), even though the provinces of Zhejiang and Liaoning are not known for hotly spicy cuisines.
Conversely, if the overland transmission of chilies did
indeed continue from Sichuan eastward toward Hunan,
it must have crossed Chongqing Province, which lies
between them, and whose food culture is often classified as a subdivision of Sichuanese.[4]

We owe the first known printed Chinese reference
to chili, however, to a late Ming lifestyle guide of 1591,
the *Zunsheng Bajian* (*Eight Discourses on the Art of
Elegant Living*) by Gao Lian. Here their use is described
as being very obviously decorative rather than dietetic,
a preference that recalls the first botanical uses of the
chili plant in Spain and Portugal: "The clustered *fan-
jiao* [chili peppers] with white flowers and round fruits
are red and incredibly beautiful." Red has been an aus-
picious color in Chinese culture ever since ancient
times. It denotes life, health, and vigor, and the berrylike red chili fruits, redder even than the reddest autumn berries, must have looked like vivid invitations to
happiness. At around the same time, the great drama-
tist and poet often known as China's Shakespeare, Tang

Xianzu, praised the chili plant for its "middle-level grace," in a botanic ode, one of those eulogies that loses everything in translation, turning from finely calibrated appreciation to clunking faint praise.

Chinese gastronomy has always worked with a broader range of fundamental taste categories than has Western cuisine. It is only in recent years that umami, the concentrated flavor of certain savory foods high in glutamates, has been added to the original basic four of salt, sweet, bitter, and sour. In China, the taste categories, while variant among regions, have always been defined in greater detail, even though some of the categories—such as "strange taste"—may appear to lack precision. Hot or spicy taste has been a constant, though, and the interesting aspect of this is that it did not have to wait until the arrival of chili pepper to appear in the gastronomic canon. Much as with Indian cooking, spicy hotness was already an element in Chinese cuisines as long ago as the sixteenth century B.C.E., when the Shang dynasty minister and court chef Yi Yin expatiated on the five-flavor system (salt, sour, sweet, bitter, and spicy). As with India, much of the hotness was derived from mustard seed, horseradish root, and ginger, and the category would eventually include Indian black pepper, cardamom, cinnamon, mace, and nutmeg, as well as hot radishes and the fruit of the prickly ash tree, known misleadingly in English as Sichuan peppercorns. Indeed, these last were the principal means of achieving spicy hot taste.

In addition to these flavors, there was *shizhuyu*, also known as *yuejiao*, from a plant (*Zanthoxylum ailanthoides*) native to the forests of southeast China and Taiwan, as well as other parts of Southeast Asia and most of Japan. In the Tang dynasty, *shizhuyu* was an indispensable condiment, made into a paste and used to accompany slow-cooked meat dishes, where its overt pungency masked the often suspect smell of the pork, mutton, or beef. Although *shizhuyu* is still cultivated for use in Chinese herbal medicine, as an analgesic and as a specific remedy against excessively moist constitutions, it is now known as a culinary ingredient, if at all, only from references to it in Tang poetry. The fact is that the arrival of chili toward the end of the Ming era rendered *shizhuyu* a quickly forgotten figment of antiquity. Similarly, the dogwood berry, bitter fruit of the deciduous tree *Cornus kousa*, widely used in ancient Chinese cuisine to season pickled fish, meat soups, and bowls of noodles, followed it down the same chute to gastro-oblivion.

The cuisine of Hunan, also known as Xiang cuisine, is the hottest of China's regional cooking styles, hotter still than Sichuanese. It is characterized as *gan la* (dry and spicy), and uses Sichuan peppercorns as well as hot chilies. Liberal use of rice vinegar is thought to offset their respective numbing and burning effects. *Duo lajiao* is an all-purpose relish of salty vinegar-pickled chilies, used to fire up many a noodle dish, and also to dress the inimitably Hunanese steamed heads of freshwater carp from the Xiang River. In Hunan, chili is put through its dietetic paces, added to spicy stews to warm the blood in winter, used to cure and smoke meats that, when eaten, cool the body and open the pores in the humidity of summer. Dried chilies are used either in small flakes as liberally as black pepper is elsewhere in the world, or as whole split pods for soups or dishes such as smoked beef with crisp-dried chilies, which incorporates both dried and pickled chilies with peanuts and garlic.

Hunan's most famous scion was Mao Zedong, who was as sworn to hot chilies as he was to revolutionary strategy, finding even a slice of watermelon a little naked unless it had been liberally showered with chili flakes, and bread a bland bore unless it had chilies baked into it. "You cannot be a revolutionary if you don't eat chilies," the Chairman chuckled to one of the northern neighbors, an official of the cordially despised Soviet Union, a lapidary wisdom that failed to make it into *The Little Red Book*. A dish known as *Mao shi hongshao rou* (Mao's red-braised pork) is still an international Chinese perennial, in which braised fatty pork belly is made fragrant with star anise, cassia, ginger, and chilies. On the other side of the political divide, General Tso's chicken, a stalwart of American Chinese cooking, largely unfamiliar on the opposite side of the Atlantic, was invented in Nationalist Taiwan in the 1950s. Battered chicken with dried chilies in a garlicky sauce based on rice wine and soy, often bemusingly served in the States with steamed broccoli as well as rice, is named for a Qing military leader of the nineteenth century, Zuo Zongtang, who wouldn't have appreciated the gaggingly sweet version now popular in the takeout industry, and wouldn't have had the faintest idea what the broccoli was. Zuo was indeed Hunanese by birth, though the dish is unheard of in its supposed home region, where sweet flavors are not appreciated.

The hotness and dryness of Hunan cuisine is best represented by *ma la gan guo,* a dry hotpot dish that can be based on beef, fish, or tofu, is stir-fried over ferocious heat in a small wok, but is always made with an abundant variety of vegetables such as red and green bell peppers, celery, sugar snaps, bamboo shoots, lotus root, mushrooms, and spring onions, as well as a tumult of spice ingredients, from fresh chilies, chili paste, and Sichuan peppercorns to cassia, star anise, and fennel seeds. It's a drier and less oily version of its Sichuanese cousin, *ma la xiang guo,* which comes in more of a broth that tempers some of the heat.

There are some similarities between the food traditions of Hunan and Sichuan, but the cooking of Sichuan has its own very distinct regional identity. The fertile basin grows an abundance of vegetables as well as rice, while the highland zones are rich in mushrooms and more exotic fungi. Rabbit is an unusual meat preference, only very sparsely eaten in the rest of China, and there is some use of yogurt, which arrived from India and Tibet in the early medieval period. Whichever route in they took, chilies assumed their place alongside Sichuan peppercorns, almost entirely replacing culinary use of the pungent berries of the *shizhuyu* tree. There is also much use of preservation techniques—drying, pickling, and salting, the last using salt from the region's saline springs—and dried meats are traditionally anointed liberally with chili oil at the table. Chilies are correctly thought to produce a different sensation in the mouth than Sichuan peppercorns, which have a tingling and numbing effect like a local anesthetic as opposed to the ardent burning of chili. A fava bean–based chili paste, *doubanjiang*, is another essential condiment. Chili-laced hot pots with plenty of broth are classic main dishes. Sauces that contribute their own specific character to dishes are very important. *Yuxiang*, literally "fish-fragrant," is a blend of *doubanjiang*, pickled chilies, sugar, and rice vinegar that contains no seafood ingredient but is so called because it was once the traditional condiment for fish, leading to applications such as fish-fragrant braised eggplant that seem puzzling to the uninitiated. The famous *guaiwei* ("strange taste") is a more intricate compound of *yuxiang*, sesame paste, black rice vinegar, Sichuan peppercorns, soy sauce, and yellow rice wine that is used for braising chicken or pork tripe, or for seasoning dried fava beans eaten as a savory snack.

Sichuan's most internationally famous production is likely *gongbao* (or *kung pao*) chicken, a stir-fried dish of brown chicken meat, celery or leek, and raw peanuts that are sizzled in oil aromatized with whole dried chili peppers and Sichuan peppercorns. Named for a Qing provincial governor of the nineteenth century, Ding Baozhen (*gongbao* is the phrase for his job title, "palace guardian"), it commemorates the governor's adamant fondness for peanuts, but its hot and numbing spice elements are very much classic everyday Sichuanese fare. Over time, the dish has been refined to require particular varieties of chili, notably the type known in Chinese as *qixingjiao* ("facing heaven pepper"), a middling-hot *Capsicum annuum* variety whose conical red fruits grow in an upward-pointing formation, a feature that would once have made it prized as an ornamental plant. At the time of the Cultural Revolution in the late 1960s, *gongbao* chicken was prosaically renamed *hula jiding* ("chicken pieces with seared chili") to shear it of its lingering connection with the detested imperial era, but the eventual official revocation under Deng Xiaoping of what is now referred to euphemistically as the "period of turmoil" has restored the traditional name.

Other Sichuanese dishes whose names gain in grotesque picturesqueness in the translation include *mapo tofu* (something like "Poxy Granny's tofu"), a bean curd dish alive with chili bean paste, dried chili flakes, chili oil, and Sichuan peppercorns, and *mayishangshu* ("ants climbing a tree"), a dish of ground meat on thread noodles in a sauce of chili paste, rice vinegar, soy, garlic, and ginger.

The great benison that chili peppers brought to Chinese cooking in the regions that adopted them is that, as elsewhere, they were not expensive to produce. They cropped reliably and plentifully, and before long, particular varieties of chili that were suitable to China's spread of microclimates were developed, some of them putting down roots so readily that by the time the Dutch botanist Nikolaus von Jacquin, completing a taxonomy of chili species in 1776, recorded a type he named *Capsicum chinense* (Chinese pepper), he did so under the incautious assumption that it must be native to China, because it was so widely used in cooking. This is the bonnet group of chilies that includes the habanero, but like all other species, it originated in the Americas. The value of chilies to poor people's food is in their effect as much as in their extensive nutritional advantage. Impoverished sustenance tends to be bland and monotonous, and anything affordable that enlivens it in the way of seasoning is readily embraced. The risk is that it, too, then becomes associated with poverty or periodic lean spells. In Hunan, reports *Beijing Today*, they have a saying that anybody without sufficient means is living on "chaffs in chili dressing," the hard seed casings of grain pepped up with a little hot spice to disguise their unpalatability.

These days, in line with the rest of the chili-crazy world, Chinese cooking is developing ever spicier versions of many of its traditional dishes. Sichuan food in particular is getting steadily hotter than its already sizzling historical antecedents. Even the time-hallowed Peking duck has acquired a garnish of chilies in among the cucumber on some menus, or comes with the option of a chili dressing in place of the traditional sweet bean sauce. And, as though to fix the association between spicy tastes and hotheaded youth, according to *China Scenic,* "the 'insanely spicy' chicken wings served at small restaurants, especially near universities, have become an unforgettable reminder of their college days for many graduates."[5]

7

From Piri Piri to Paprika— European Variations

The role that chilies, and spices in general, have played in European cuisines is more complex and more subject to cultural mutabilities than it is anywhere else in the world. If hot spice in particular settled into the regional cooking styles of those parts of the world that it conquered in the sixteenth century, until it radically transformed them, in Europe a different set of culinary values prevailed. Where chili was incorporated into European cooking, at least until the modern era, it happened only at the margins, and in the most cautious ways imaginable. Dried chilies were present in ground and powdered form, but at very low concentrations of spicy heat, and in parts of the continent, such as the Mediterranean littoral of southern Europe, it was principally the entirely innocuous bell pepper that came to be specially cultivated and valued, depending on color, for its sweetish or bitter blandness. Why was this?

Since ancient times, European medical theory had

been based on the system inherited from the great Greek writers Hippocrates and Galen, in which the body's vital fluids comprised four corresponding humors or temperaments, each correlating to one of the four essential elements. These were blood, which was associated with air and was responsible for a sanguine demeanor; yellow bile (fire), which led to choleric or hot-tempered natures; black bile (earth), the bringer of melancholy; and phlegm (water), which produced a phlegmatic or apathetic disposition. In addition to their influence on the emotions, the humors corresponded respectively to the four seasons of the year, from spring to winter, which could be extended by analogy to the seasons of a lifetime, from infancy to youth to maturity to old age. Some of the metaphoric residue of this scheme lives on in the practice of describing people as having a splenetic or choleric nature, while the word *melancholy* itself is formed from the Greek for "black bile." In addition to their temperamental characteristics, each humor was composed of a unique compound of either hot or cold, and moist or dry, aspects in all permutations. Blood was moist and warm, yellow bile warm and dry, black bile cold and dry, and phlegm moist and cold. The system had a zodiacal precision, forming a cyclical model of every human life, and it depended in its application to medical contexts on the supreme classical notion of balance. A sick person was essentially suffering from a humoral asymmetry, which must be treated by administration of foods and drinks from the opposite side of the spectrum, or by more radical treatments such as purging and bloodletting.

The humoral system survived in Europe, and indeed found its adapted way into Islamic medical theory, for not far off two thousand years—at least until the age of the European enlightenment—but it was periodically subjected to revision and rethinking, largely at the behest of new religious currents. In the East, the Christianization of the Byzantine world weakened some of the emphasis of humoral medicine and transferred the causes of sickness to an interventionist God, but it was not entirely abandoned. In western Europe, it enjoyed tenacious traction, being subjected to tireless researches in which wild herbs, minerals, and hazardous toxins were investigated for their possible roles in helping correct the imbalances that led to illness. If willow bark yielded a potent analgesic that would come to be known as aspirin, and the autumn crocus an anti-inflammatory agent eventually identified as colchicine (much used for the relief of gout), both known since the second millenium B.C.E., there were potentially limitless further possibilities throughout the natural world for safeguarding, restoring, and maintaining health, possibilities that continue to sustain a thriving commerce in herbal medicine to the present day.

During the flourishing of the medieval spice trade, when the tables of the rich were extravagantly scented by pepper, cinnamon, nutmeg, cloves, and ginger from the eastern trade routes, every spice was given its own humoral analysis in the medical lexicon of the day. Most were classified as hot and dry, to varying degrees, and therefore generative of yellow bile and productive of quick-tempered impulsiveness. In other words, they were recommended for those who had succumbed to a state of torpid lassitude, but were definitely to be avoided by those with a tendency to flying off the handle in volcanic rages. Cumin was hottish, but not as hot as black pepper. Galangal was hot, but ginger root was hotter still. And so forth.

When a whole array of new foods from the Western Hemisphere arrived in Europe at the turn of the sixteenth century, they were not, as was the case throughout Africa, the Middle East, and Asia, absorbed readily into the diets of even the elites, but remained largely on the fringes. There were exceptions, such as the relatively quick adoption of maize into northern Italian cooking, or of potatoes—after an initial period of bemused incomprehension—in Britain and Ireland, but by and large, new foods remained on the peripheries precisely because nobody could be certain of their status in the humoral system. Thus it is that we look in vain for appearances of American foods in the European cookbooks and dietary treatises of the sixteenth century, as food historian Ken Albala explains:

> *When authors did discuss these foods, their dietary conservatism almost always led to suspicion and rejection, especially when these*

*foods could be readily compared to a familiar food
already disparaged by theorists. Whether these
learned opinions can be held partly responsible
for the long lag before new foods were adopted is
impossible to say. It may be equally likely that
while tomatoes, maize and chili peppers were
admired as ornamentals in European botanical
gardens, people down the social scale began to eat
them anyway, despite all the warnings. Whatever
the case, it was not until after the mid-seventeenth
century, and in many cases much later, that new
foods began to be grown and eaten on a large
scale. And it is not until then that humoral theory
began to lose authority among food writers.[1]*

If Albala's speculation is correct, what helped to pull
the carpet from underneath humoral theory was the
consumption practices of subaltern sectors of European
society, who ate those foods that had not yet been
cleared as safe for the elites and, in the case of chilies,
just because the economics of growing them made them
far more accessible to the poor. Still, this was a very
gradual process, certainly compared to the adoption
across all strata of society of the hot drinks—tea, coffee,
and chocolate—when they made decisive inroads into
European societies in the mid-seventeenth century.

When European powers ceased to be content with
trading with the Asian nations and began colonizing
them, they monopolized the supply of coveted spices,

with the result that both their commercial value and their social status in the home markets began tumbling. A new cult of essentialism took hold of elite cooking in which complex dishes with layers of seasoning lost favor to ones that tasted fundamentally of their principal components. By the seventeenth century, the goal of unadorned transparency in the science of cooking had possessed the upper echelons of French cuisine, triggering a century-long debate about integrity and honesty in the matter of nutrition, as against embellishment and intricacy, the former becoming very much the national standard. It claimed a role at the forefront of speculation on sensuous artifice versus back-to-nature ruggedness among French Enlightenment philosophers, and conversely provided the nationalist mood music for English cultural commentators who raised the banner of roast beef in its ungarnished manliness against the primped-up ragoûts and cassoulets of the ancestral enemy across the Channel.

A secondary impulse in northern Europe came from the rise of Protestant theology after the Reformation. The theory that digestion was a form of fermentation, so that overtaxing the body with rich dishes and complicated seasonings was a matter of making a rod for one's own back (and stomach), became the orthodoxy. On this pseudoscientific reading, the simplest, plainest foods—such as fresh vegetables and herbs, steamed fish and fresh fruits—were the most readily assimilated by the body. The doctrine incorporated not only a strong commitment to the reaction against lavishness in consumption, seen as the decadent preserve of Catholics and other continentals, but also the distant acknowledgment of a literalist interpretation of the Creation myth, in which God had originally given a primordially vegetarian humankind the fruits of the earth to feed on.

The new puritanism in cooking was to be seen in the refined development of the principle of saucing. As Rachel Laudan has shown in her global food history *Cuisine and Empire*, saucing in many world cuisines, such as the various Indian, Chinese, and Mesoamerican models, is a matter of building up layers of flavor, adding spices, herbs, and other flavorings to what are essentially purées of such basic ingredients as tomatoes and onions. In European cuisine, however, the move was toward creating essences of the star protein in a dish, with sauces based on meat and fish stocks that were themselves highly concentrated reflections of the meat and fish they accompanied. Seasonings, while still essential, were expected to play a supporting and emphasizing role, not a divergently complementary one, and even if the final effect was an intensely concentrated richness, it was a richness that underlined the dish rather than calling attention to itself as a discrete element. Classic Indian cooking starts from the principle of making a complex, multilayered sauce from an armory of roasted spices, supplemented by onions, garlic, and ginger, and then tomatoes and chilies, and only when it has comprehensively infused is a main ingredient cooked, to which the sauce then becomes the accompaniment. In classic French cooking, by contrast, a fillet of fish or meat is cooked first, and a sauce is then made by reducing the appropriate stock with some wine, seasonings, and perhaps cream *à la minute*, for pouring over the principal ingredient on the plate.

These overlapping historical currents account for the peripheral absorption of chilies into the various culinary traditions of Europe, where they were absorbed at all. As we have seen, Spain and Portugal took to them with the greatest enthusiasm, incorporating piquant heat into the blend of ingredients in the traditional sausages, chorizo and chouriço, and formulating a multipurpose hot dressing for meat and fish in the guise of piri piri sauce. As such, the only peripheral inroad that the chili made into French cooking was in the deep-south region of the Pays Basque, where in the guise of the *Capsicum annuum* varietal espelette, it lights up dishes such as piperade, a hearty stew of green bell peppers, tomatoes, and onions that comes on a little like the badass older cousin of clean-nosed Provençal ratatouille.

In Italy, other than in parts of the Neapolitan and Calabrian south, chilies were of little or no interest until the twentieth century, when middling-hot peppers—peperoncini—began to be cultivated more widely. Chopped fresh chilies now find their way into pasta dressings and condiments, are available in brine-pickled and oil-cured forms for eating with cured meats and cheeses, and add a manageable sense of frazzle to various salumi and pepperoni. *Sugo all'arrabbiata* (literally, "infuriated sauce") is a simple olive oil, tomato, and chili potion from the Lazio region around Rome that has since become internationally known. Compared to piri piri, it seems less infuriated than mildly grouchy, but the degree of volatility varies from one kitchen to another. In Calabria, strings of red chilies drying on wires trained over the housefronts are as common a sight as they are in Mexico.

In central Europe, chilies appeared very discreetly in the form of the ubiquitous spice, paprika. As a dry spice made from pounding up wind-dried red chilies, paprika has its origins in Mexico itself, and came to the Iberian peninsula in the immediate post-Columbian period, when it became known as Spanish *pimentón*, an essential ingredient of the cooking of the Extremadura region on the Atlantic coast of western Spain. As we have seen, it then followed the eastbound trade routes to the Near East and India, from whence it migrated back overland with the imperial sweeps of the Ottoman Empire, which had briefly laid siege to the Portuguese Indian outpost of Diu, an island off Gujarat, in 1538. By this route, paprika eventually made its way through Turkey and then along the Balkan corridor into southeast and central Europe, passing through Bulgaria and then on to Hungary, where the peppers for it may well first have been planted by Bulgarian migrant herdsmen.

Although it is indelibly associated with the cuisine

of Hungary, where it adds a subtle, sweetly smoky burn to traditional *gulyás* (goulash), and other long-simmered dishes, paprika only became widely popular in Hungarian cooking during the nineteenth century, when it gradually climbed the social scale on a wave of post-Napoleonic nationalist sentiment. That said, it was probably herdsmen out on the southern plain, cooking the meat of cattle in cauldrons over open fires, who first began to substitute the intermittently available black pepper in their seasoning with roughly ground dried red chilies from domestic gardens.

Oddly, in a reverse of culinary evolution with respect to chilies elsewhere, Hungarian paprika has gradually become milder in recent history, rather than fierier. In the 1920s, it began to be made from a specially cultivated sweeter and milder variety of chili, and was processed by a machine that split the pods and separated out the heat-bearing pith as well as the seeds. The result is that in Hungary, the gentlest variant of paprika, vivid red *édesnemes*, is considered the most refined, while the raging brown *erős*, the most pungent type, is the suitable choice for hotheads. Szeged and Kalocsa on the Southern Great Plain of Hungary are the two principal producing regions.

It was only in the 1780s that the first systematic cultivation trials of chilies for paprika were conducted in the botanical gardens at the University of Pest, but the spice itself was already in widespread use in both peasant and middle-class kitchens by then. The German botanist Count von Hoffmansegg, passing through Hungary on a biological collecting trip in 1795, enjoyed one of the local culinary specialties sufficiently to mention it in correspondence home to his wife: "I really liked a Hungarian dish, meat with paprika. It must be very healthy."[2] This measured note of approval was enough to propel paprika-cooked dishes into the echelons of aristocratic gastronomy, both in Hungary itself and back home in Germany. In 1879, no less a figure than the great French chef Georges-Auguste Escoffier began importing Szeged paprika to season his own version of Hungarian cooking, which had suddenly gripped the imaginations of the world of French haute cuisine.[3] Eventually, he would add his own meticulously researched goulash and *poulet au paprika* to the menu at the Grand Hotel in Monte Carlo during his residency there in the 1880s. So familiar would the dish become in the French culinary lexicon that it played a starring role at the Paris World Fair of 1900, and Escoffier's goulash recipe duly found a place in his epochal *Guide Culinaire* (1903) as an international reference dish.

Not only do the meaty soups and stews of *gulyás, pörkölt,* and creamy *paprikás* rely on paprika, but so, too, does *halászlé* or fisherman's soup, a ketchup-red broth of freshwater fish, usually containing hefty chunks of carp, perch, and pike, that uses the hotter grade of paprika and is probably central Europe's fieriest traditional dish.

It is eaten with lots of bread to gentle the burn, accompanied by Riesling white wine spritzers, as a curtain-raiser to the festive season on Christmas Eve.

As tastes have become hotter in response to international trends, the Hungarian market has been invaded by a plethora of red pepper pastes sold in tubes for use as ingredients and condiments, some still replete with seeds. These are also the preferred means of spicing up stews and vehicles for dipping bread into over the eastern border in Ukraine, and versions of paprika chicken and the hot fisherman's soup also turn up in Romania.

From Hungary, paprika migrated into the neighboring states of Germany and Austria, where it came to contribute subtle touches of warmish spice to dishes such as *Paprikaschnitzel,* known to less sensitive earlier eras as *Zigeunerschnitzel* ("gipsy's schnitzel"), a pounded escalope of veal or pork, sometimes bread-crumbed, served in a bright red sauce of bell peppers, tomato paste, onions, and paprika, and local versions of *Gulasch.* Viennese paprika chicken, *Paprikahendl,* inherited from next-door Hungary via Burgenland, usually served with spätzle and salad, also incorporates red bell pepper strips and tomato paste in a fragrant creamy sauce aromatized with sweet paprika and herbs. What English usage knows as "deviled" dishes owe their malevolent natures to dashes of discreet spice—deviled eggs are halved hard-cooked eggs topped with cheesy mayonnaise and paprika, sometimes boosted in these heat-seeking days with a few drops of hot chili sauce—

although more often in Germany this preparation is known by some other ethnic displacer, such as Russian eggs, or just as stuffed eggs. Paprika also plays a starring role in the light cheese and onion spread known in Austria as Liptauer (originally from the Liptov region of Slovakia, once part of the doomed Austro-Hungarian empire), used for topping open sandwiches and crispbreads, and eaten as a side snack in the *Heurige,* or wine taverns, to accompany the just-fermented turbid white wine of harvest time.

Chili expert Dave DeWitt notes that the first appearance of paprika in a printed European recipe is in the *Theoretical and Practical Compendium of Culinary Arts,* published in Vienna in 1817. It was written by F. G. Zenker, court chef to the Austrian field marshal Karl Philipp, prince of Schwarzenberg, and crops up, tellingly, not in any ancestral central European preparation, but in a recipe called "Chicken Fricassée in Indian Style."[4] By 1817, there was a lot more to most Indian cooking than a dash of paprika, but treatments such as this would have helped ease the passage of tingly spice into the culinary repertoire of the *Oberschicht,* the Germanic beau monde.

The take-up of chili in Europe's far north was only ever very limited. It made hardly any inroads into the traditional foods of Scandinavia, for example. While proximity to the Near Eastern trade routes spread hot spice into the central Asian republics of the former Soviet Union, European Russia took to chili pepper in its food only very cautiously. Even paprika appears only fairly sparingly, in meaty soups such as Russian-Ukrainian *solyanka*, in the dressings for salads of diced vegetables, and as a probably belated addition to the sauce for beef stroganoff, the preferred heat source in hotter dishes otherwise being mustard. There was a migratory wave of Korean people into the eastern zones of Russia in the late nineteenth and early twentieth centuries, which made the dressed salads and condiments of Korean cuisine, particularly kimchi, popular throughout Russia, but as Korean food writer Changzoo Song observes in a paper published in the *Journal of Ethnic Foods,* "[Russian] kimchi contains less chili powder as compared to that of contemporary South Korea and, therefore, is less spicy."[5] A cult of delicacy in the Tsarist centuries, by which elite customs were distinguished from those of the peasantry and the serfs and which after all did no more than mirror the earlier development of haute cuisine in western Europe, bequeathed to Russian taste a suspicion of coarse, rollicking seasonings that overwhelmed the palate.

Where chili peppers did find a role was in flavoring vodka. The exact origins of pepper vodka are tantalizingly obscure, although Tsar Peter I, known to history as Peter the Great, who reigned from 1682 to 1725, is reported to have enjoyed seasoning a glass of ultrarefined vodka with black pepper. As with many of the flavoring traditions in vodka, the technique may well have originated in the effort to mask the rank aroma and taste of crudely distilled, unrectified spirit with a distracting aromatic element. However, pepper vodka, *pertsovka*, migrated as a tradition to Ukraine, where the flavored vodkas known as *horilka* include a variant called *horilka z pertsem*, which often has a whole red chili pepper or two bobbing about in the bottle. This style is known as *pieprzówka* in Poland. In most cases, the spice mix in the spirit is a complex blend of chilies, black peppercorns, and paprika with essential oils of pepper and cubeb berries (a close Indonesian relative of black pepper distinguished by the little tails on its peppercorns). If you like it spicy, pepper vodka makes a Bloody Mary to beat the band.

In Great Britain, chili has no more been absorbed into national food traditions than it was in most of northern Europe. There is a huge and growing appreciation for spicy food, reflected in the exponential growth of year-round chili festivals at all levels of expertise, but the British are content to experience chilies off the rack, as it were, in one or other of the multifarious overseas cuisines that have been assimilated into the national culinary imaginary. These include the widespread fondness for Indian cooking, a burgeoning vogue for Thai and Southeast Asian food, including the hotter versions of Chinese, and Tex-Mex, still largely mistakenly thought to be undiluted Mexican so far as the restaurant scene is concerned. Chili con carne is a staple of domestic cooking, in a version that always includes a can of red kidney beans, some chopped red or green bell peppers, and canned tomatoes, their juice often obviating any perceived need for beef stock. The spice range in it has expanded in recent years from standard chili powder (more usually an unalloyed hot ground chili product than the spice mix more familiar in the United States) to dried whole chilies, chili flakes, and a whole pantry full of spice pastes, from American-style chipotle to preparations that are more like North African harissa. TV chefs and food writers have persuaded adventurous home cooks to experiment with adding dark chocolate, coffee, and garnishes such as avocado and slivered radish. I have before me a recipe that suggests adding a can of baked beans in BBQ sauce to the pot, about which the less said, the better.

Prior to the widespread availability of hot chili powder, British spice racks usually included mild paprika and cayenne pepper for a touch of extra sting, but nothing more volatile. Isabella Beeton's canonical *Book of Household Management* (1861) acknowledges something mysteriously called "English chilies," cramming fifty split ones into a pint of vinegar for what would surely be a rocket-fuel salad dressing, and leads one to suspect that whatever the contemporaneous Victorian variant was, it was rather low on the Scoville scale. Otherwise, give or take the odd deviled egg, and despite latter-day supermarket brand innovations such as chili-spiked sausage rolls and all-purpose chili dipping sauces on the east Asian model, British cooking has not felt the need to incorporate chilies into its own repertoire, as has happened elsewhere. In this, the country's culinary habits mirrored its position as a linchpin of the world wine trade. For many centuries, largely for climatic reasons, it had no wine production of its own to speak of, and so it absorbed, and became extravagantly well-versed in, the wines of everywhere else. The same has happened with food. If India and Thailand and Mexico and Texas already know how to use chilies, just eat their food and be damn glad of it.

8

Bowls o' Red and Chili Queens— An American Affair

The early history of North American cooking bears the complex imprints of the various culinary traditions brought across the Atlantic by European settlers from a diversity of backgrounds. There was an obvious English strain, buoyed by the use of standard cookbooks such as Eliza Smith's *The Compleat Housewife* (1727) and *The Art of Cookery Made Plain and Easy* (1747) by Hannah Glasse. These were domestic tracts that retained a link to the cooking of the English aristocracy, theoretically democratized for use in middling households with kitchen staff. Glasse's book found a home in the kitchens of George Washington, Thomas Jefferson, and Benjamin Franklin, and although its ideological heart lay in Anglo-Saxon thrift and economy—its third chapter was entitled "Read this chapter, and you will find how expensive a French cook's sauce is"—it nonetheless applied the glossy veneer of haute cuisine when inspiration demanded. There were daubes and truffled sauces, and a recipe for "French bread," but there was also an attempt at a chicken curry in the Indian style, coyly spiced with ginger, turmeric, and pepper, but with nothing so brash as a chili pepper.

By the time the North American edition of Glasse's book had appeared in 1805, it was a few years behind what is generally considered the first properly indigenous United States cookbook, *American Cookery* (1796) by Amelia Simmons. While her compendium has obvious continuities with the English cookbooks, Simmons diligently adapts many traditional recipes to the seasonal ingredients of New England and the eastern seaboard. Its roast turkey with cranberries is the first such printed recipe, joining cornmeal johnnycakes, Indian pudding, and Indian slapjacks. The more showstopping recipes, such as the dressing of turtle or calf's head, or the round of beef à la mode, are seasoned with thoroughgoing quantities of cayenne pepper, the first suggestions of anything in American cookery with a spicier attitude than regular pepper.

In the nineteenth century, the Scottish physician William Kitchiner's *Apicius Redivivus, or the Cook's Oracle* (1817),[1] which made its way across the Atlantic to become a New York edition "adapted to the American public" in 1830, takes a buccaneering approach to seasonings and dressings for meat and fish that are laden with what today's food science knows as umami, the taste element defined by a concentrated savoriness. A sauce piquante for cold meats, fish, and salads is essentially a well-seasoned mayonnaise, but may be boosted by additions such as "mushroom catchup," horseradish, capers, and cayenne. An all-purpose sauce for grilled meats may be sharpened with "a little Chili vinegar, or a few grains of Cayenne." The book warns that inferior cayenne has been colored red with lead oxide, to disguise the inferior faded peppers in it, and there were directions on making your own from fresh whole homegrown chilies: "Take away the stalks, and put the pods into a colander; set it before the fire; they will take full twelve hours to dry; then put them into a mortar, with one-fourth their weight of salt, and pound them, and rub them till they are as fine as possible, and put them into a well-stopped bottle." For the true aficionado, there was a chili wine, made by steeping about fifty fresh red chilies in half a pint of brandy, claret, or white wine for two weeks, a potion that added instant opulence to soups and sauces.

Those catchups, catsups, and ketchups eventually came to be made with tomatoes, as a result of the Spanish influence on North American cuisine, gradually acquiring an ever sharper edge of spice that linked it back to its Mexican origins in chili-laced tomato sauce. It isn't certain, but it was most likely migration from the British West Indies to the southern colonies of America starting in the late seventeenth century that began the gradual introduction of tomatoes into the North American culinary lexicon. By the time of the Revolution, they were being widely cultivated throughout the

Carolinas, although many people still refused to eat them. While Europeans were warming to them under the romantic nomenclature of "love apples," they were still widely regarded by many people in America as toxic. Others thought they looked disgusting.

In contrast, in the noncolonial southwest, a different attitude was to prevail. Ranchers, wranglers, and cowboys working the Great Plains and Rocky Mountains inherited many of the traditions of Mexican *vaqueros* and their way of life. By the mid-nineteenth century, English- and French-descended immigrants made their way west of the Mississippi and began to mingle with Spanish and criollo people who had settled in the sectors of northern Mexico that would become Texas and California. The original dissemination of chili peppers into what are now the southern states would have been by birds, as in distant prehistory, but they were adopted by Native Americans as far back as the early 1600s and became an important commodity in their trading economy. The berrylike peppers known as chiltepins or chilipiquins can still be found growing wild in Arizona and southern Texas to this day. Various of the Founding Fathers grew chili plants in their private gardens from seeds imported from Mexico, but ornamentally rather than culinarily, much as the Europeans did at first.

Large chilies found their way into American cookbooks of the later nineteenth century in the form of *chiles rellenos* (stuffed chilies). The ways of preparing this dish would become legion, but what they had in common was scooping out whole chili pods of their seeds and pith, and then filling them with a vividly seasoned savory mixture, before either roasting them or frying them in sizzling lard. They were usually battered, often filled with diced meat, tomatoes, and rice, perhaps a little dried fruit. Some American recipes call only for mild bell peppers, but the true Puebla dish is made with poblano chilies, which have some modest heat when green, and considerably more when ripened to red. North of the border, the stuffed pepper eventually acquired a cheese-based filling, and is often little other than molten Monterey Jack oozing forth from a blistered jalapeño.

The deep and pervasive influence of Mexican cooking on the foodways of the southern states produced in due course one of the most significant fusion cuisines of the Western Hemisphere, notably in Texas, where Tex-Mex would become a style eventually recognized the world over, but also in California, New Mexico, and Arizona. Many classic dishes, street snacks especially, have consequently wrongly been thought to be Mexican in origin, but are pure American inventions, among them crisp tacos, fajitas, and nachos. In addition, certain styles of preparation and garnishing have departed from the Mexican template. The liberal use of melted cheese is specifically Texan. There are dry-textured salty cheeses in Mexican cooking, often sold, like añejo, pregrated for sprinkling on enchiladas or refried beans, but the indulgently gooey approach to cheesing a dish, with blankets of bubbling Jack, Velveeta, or Cheddar adding fatty richness to the spicy meat dishes, is Tex-Mex through and through. The same is true of any beans other than black beans—pinto, lima, and red beans are all-American staples. Cumin, only rarely used in Mexican food, is one of the characteristic spice tastes of Texas, probably first imported, according to Texas food historian Robb Walsh, by settlers from the Canary Islands arriving in San Antonio in the eighteenth century.

That other standby of the spice rack, chili powder, originated in its classic form in New Braunfels near San Antonio in the 1890s, most likely the invention of a German migrant café-proprietor, William Gebhardt. Texas Germans from the hill country were almost as influential in the state's culinary history as were Texas Mexicans, and Gebhardt played a key role. He ran the catering arm of a friend's saloon bar, the Phoenix Café, where customers were entertained by such diversions as dueling badgers, while a parrot stood guard on a perch at the door, snapping, "Have you paid your bill?" in peremptory German to departing patrons. Gebhardt's chili-laced dishes were a hit with the locals, but were restricted to being a seasonal food, since local chili production was based on cropping through the summer months only. In order to offer his diners hot food year-round, Gebhardt began importing Mexican ancho chilies from San Luis Potosí, fully five hundred miles to the south. But how to preserve them through the year in a form that took up as little storage space as possible? Passing the peppers several times through a meat grinder was an early fix, but one that soon gave way to a skillfully developed mixture of dried chilies, cumin, garlic, oregano, and black pepper, soaked in an alcohol solution, pounded into a paste, heat-dried and then processed through a coffee mill. Not only did this seem a useful resource for the restaurant kitchen, but the product could be packed in little bottles and sold retail under a proprietary brand name, Gebhardt's Eagle Brand Chili Powder, registered in 1899, the inventor prudently having revised its original name, Tampico Dust.

Gebhardt sold his powder in classic western fashion, from the back of a wagon that rolled through the streets of San Antonio. Before the century was out, Eagle Brand was being bulk-produced in a factory in the city, and by the time of the Great War, it was turning out eighteen thousand bottles a day and accounted for 90 percent of the total importation of chili peppers into the United States. In 1923, Gebhardt authored a pamphlet entitled *Mexican Cookery for American Homes,* a document that enjoyed an influence out of all proportion to its original promotional intent and was still being reprinted in the 1950s. Its author died in 1956, a millionaire many times over. Long since swallowed up by bigger fish, the Gebhardt brand nonetheless still exists today, and the chili powder is still made to the progenitor's original formula.

The other historical figure with a claim on the invention of chili powder is DeWitt Clinton Pendery, whose family firm is still going strong. Pendery began selling a proprietary spice blend, Chiltomaline, to restaurants and hotels in Fort Worth and the environs around 1890. It, too, consisted of ground dried chili pods, cumin, oregano, and other spices, but no garlic, and was sold with more of an emphasis on its physically beneficial properties than Gebhardt's brand: "The health giving properties of hot chile peppers have no equal. They give tone to the alimentary canal, regulating the functions, giving a natural appetite, and promoting health by action of the kidneys, skin and lymphatics."[2]

Rachel Laudan has argued that the use of chili powder has crucially influenced the understanding of chilies in much of the Western world. The Mexican preference for pounding rehydrated chilies produces a fuller, more three-dimensional chili flavor, compared to the use of ready-made powders. To some extent, there are continuities with the use of curry powder in Western attempts at Indian cooking, although there is a more obvious antecedent for that in the production of freshly roasted, ground and blended dry spices, with which the clarified fat is aromatized at the beginning of most Indian recipes. Chili powder, by contrast, is added to Tex-Mex and other North American and European spicy cuisines in the manner of a seasoning, rather than as a whole ingredient. Commenting on the Mesoamerican culinary exchange and its historical reverberations, Laudan writes that "much that had been learned about chilies was ignored. In most places (except perhaps

North Africa) the dried chilies were not rehydrated and sheared to produce a puréed sauce. As a result the color, texture, and fruity tastes they could contribute to dishes were not appreciated. And because they were not eaten in quantity as sauces, they did not add much vitamin C to the diet."[3] Fundamentally, the role that chilies have widely assumed away from their heartlands in Central and South America has emphasized their pyrotechnic effects at the expense of their integrity as a nutritious and versatile component of a dish in their own right. This functional shift, where it has occurred, represents the historical turning point in the story of chilies and their transmission to outlying gastronomic cultures, an observation that brings us neatly to the hot topic of chili con carne.

Declared the national dish of Texas in a decision of the state legislature in 1977, chili con carne—or chili, pure and simple, as it is universally known—probably began life sometime in the mid-nineteenth century as a cowboy's travel provision. This was the theory advanced by Everette Lee DeGolyer, a Texas oilman and studious historian of the Southwest whose published papers contain evidence that, around 1850, an instant meal for use by chuck wagons on the prairies was in circulation. It consisted of dried ground beef pounded together with fat, oregano, and chili peppers and formed into rectangular slabs that became known as "chili bricks." DeGolyer called this "the pemmican of the Southwest," after the fatted dried meat of the Native American peoples, a boon on long journeys when preserved foods were indispensable. The bricks were reconstituted in boiling water over a campfire, providing nourishing and satisfyingly meaty sustenance on the cattle trail.

Among the alternative theories as to its origin, chili might have been formulated by the *lavanderas* (washerwomen) who followed the Mexican and other armies through what is now Texas in the 1830s. According to this account, the meat in the dish was more likely to have been venison or even goat than beef, but fierily seasoned all the same with chili peppers, at least partly to disguise the fact that the tubs in which the dish was stewed every night had been used all day for washing clothes. In place of oregano, the women seem to have used wild gatherings of the related herb, marjoram.

Robb Walsh points up the forceful case that chili con carne, with its Spanish name, is far more likely to have originated among those Spanish settlers lured to San Antonio in the eighteenth century with the promise of riches, land and titles.[4] The telltale ingredient is cumin, which has no business in indigenous food of the Southwest, but comes originally from Middle Eastern food, and would have been imported to the Americas by the Spaniards who had already incorporated it widely into their own cooking. On this account, the tomatoes are something of a giveaway, too. The recipes of the prairie theories do not appear to contain tomatoes, which would again have been an obvious importation accompanying the Iberian diaspora. There are those Texan traditionalists today, hostile obviously to any suggestion of Spanish derivation, who insist that true chili does not contain tomatoes.

Even more than tomatoes, the other now canonical ingredient that true chili does not contain is red beans, or indeed beans of any description. Beans began to appear in published chili recipes around the 1920s, probably out of some conflation of the dish as wagon-train fare with the ranch hand's other favorite standby, pork and beans. More than any issue that rages in the great debate over what goes into genuine chili, the occurrence of beans in a recipe is as incendiary as chili peppers themselves. In a February 2015 article in *National Geographic*, Rebecca Rupp reported:

> *Rudy Valdez, a member of the Ute Indian tribe, won the world chili championship in 1976 with a native recipe that he claimed dated back 2,000 years. The original chili, according to Valdez, "was made with meat of horses or deer, chile peppers, and cornmeal from ears of stalks that grew only to the knee." Tellingly, he adds, "No beans."*[5]

Even in its postulated antiquity, the dish was innocent of beans. The supermarket can of chili con carne may be bristling with kidney beans or navy beans, but if in doubt in your own kitchen, don't. There are no beans in the official Texas state dish.

Heather Arndt Anderson does not scruple over the varying theories as to the origin of chili, boldly declaring that, "[c]ultural integrity aside, chili con carne was invented by Latinos in Texas and began its ascent across the United States by the mid-nineteenth century, along with written accounts of 'The Wild West' and life on the frontier."[6] Certainly, there has to be some historical significance in the fact that a book with the very title *Chile con Carne, or The Camp and the Field,* by an American army surgeon, S. Compton Smith, an account of the Mexican-American War, was published as early as 1857. This was only a decade after the conflict that resulted in Texas being annexed by the United States, and so it seems extremely likely that the dish Compton Smith observed, and which he calls "a popular Mexican dish—literally red peppers and meat," was indeed of Hispanic origin.[7] The point, however, is that, like many another dish that has been transmitted among different culinary cultures, it was creatively retooled in its new home almost from the start. As food writer Andrew Smith puts it, "[i]t is likely that the dish [Compton] Smith identified was consumed throughout northern Mexico and the southwestern United States but that the term itself was an Americanization."[8] Indeed, its Spanish name is less convincing as a marker of ethnic authenticity when one reflects that the more likely description of the dish in that language would be *carne con chile,* meat with peppers, rather than peppers with meat, which seems to recast the meat as an optional incidental. The Spanish name itself is surely a Texan invention.

A stew of red meat with chili peppers and other spices was undoubtedly a regular source of sustenance in the saber-rattling period that led to the territorial war, whether it had a name or not. In 1845, the year before formal hostilities broke out, a Yankee journalist, his classical education and northern manners getting knocked about good and proper on the volatile border, sat down to dine with an American officer: "Our frontier meal of beef, sauced with appetite and the 'grease' of fried pork, and seasoned to scalding heat with red pepper [chili], with milk to neutralize its blistering effects upon our throats, and thin Mexican cakes, called 'Tortillias' [sic], was brought in by the Col[onel]'s Mexican 'woman.'"[9] This is clearly nothing other than chili con carne. Note the innovative realization that milk is a better recourse for cooling the mouth than the cold water more often drunk with hot chili in this era.

If its origins are distantly in Mexican foodways, no self-respecting Mexican now recognizes Texas chili as having anything to do with them. Food is so often the vehicle through which rivalrous antipathies between neighbors are expressed—what could be more contemptibly indicative of an inferior people than the foreign muck they eat?—and the Mexican disavowal of chili reached a lacerating pitch, from which it has scarcely mellowed, in the last century. In the *General Dictionary of Americanisms* (1942), Francisco Santamaría declared chili con carne "a detestable food which, with the false title of Mexican, is sold in the United States from Texas to New York."[10] Its detestability probably only increased the farther north it got from the Mexican border, that migratory journey that undoubtedly added the beans to it and, among other convulsions, produced the Cincinnati variant, in which the chili is layered with beans and spaghetti. This latter was a formula perfected by Macedonian émigré restaurateurs the Kiradjieff brothers in 1922, and sold originally from a hot-dog shop next to the Empress burlesque theater on Vine Street. It is now the region's preeminent "traditional" dish.

Amid all the nationalist wrangling, the story of Texas chili is untellable without paying due homage to the Chili Queens. Exactly when these redoubtable Mexican ladies began regularly plying their wares on Military Plaza in San Antonio is unclear—they were certainly there by the 1880s, and perhaps a good twenty years before that. They were glamorously dressed street-food vendors who operated from decorated open wagons hung with ornate colored lanterns that they set up each evening around dusk. They rewarmed their chili in pots hung over mesquite fires on the square, and sold it in individual ready-to-eat servings to passersby. Each had her own recipe, and regulars would delight in comparative tasting of their products to find which one they liked best. Laborers were extremely grateful for the hearty, spicy sustenance they offered at prices everyone could afford (an average ten cents, including bread and a glass of water), although the San Antonio gentry looked distinctly askance at the vendors, trying various legal ruses to get the stands shut down, to very little long-term effect. In the early 1890s, the city mayor Bryan Callaghan had the stalls in the vicinity of the Alamo evicted, but they soon inveigled themselves back again, and carried on trading unlicensed. A photograph from January 1933, taken at a chili stall staffed by three women on Haymarket Plaza in the city, shows customers, including a boy with a mariachi guitar providing the musical accompaniment, still crowding around the counter, hungry for the Chili Queens' wares a good half century after their tradition was established. It was only when they were required to sell their wares from screened-off tents in the period leading up to World War II, a legal recourse that more than any other dented the popularity of their business, that they finally disappeared.

As well as open-air sales, many humble homes transformed themselves into public eateries in the impoverished Laredito district of San Antonio, as was described by the journalist Edward King in a Texas travelogue piece for *Scribner's* magazine in 1874.[11] Inside the house he looked into was a long table flanked by benches and set with bowls and glasses, dimly illuminated by a single candlestick. On the earth floor, chickens were settling themselves for the night. "The fat, tawny Mexican materfamilias will place before you various savory compounds, swimming in fiery pepper which biteth like a serpent; and the tortilla, a smoking hot cake, thin as a shaving, and about as eatable, is the substitute for bread." It seems likely that these home catering operations were the precursors of the outdoor chili stands, which became a means of reaching a wider potential clientele than were prepared to venture into the homes of the poor. By the time the stands had themselves spawned a network of chili parlors, or simple restaurants—the earliest Mexican restaurants in the United States—the appeal had spread to all sections of society, and the moneyed and the mighty mingled with the indigent even in the most louche quarters of the city.

It was in 1882 that a Confederate Army veteran, William Tobin, was awarded a contract to supply the U.S. Army with chili. Long before chili reached the bulk production mass market, Tobin was the first American to produce a canned version of the dish. His earliest recipe used goat meat rather than beef, perhaps in homage to the Mexican washerwomen's chili, perhaps instead through simple economy. And as to the washerwomen themselves, perhaps they don't so much underpin a rival theory as to the development of chili con carne, but are an integral, indistinguishable part of the principal narrative. Writing in the *Texas Monthly* in August 2017, John Nova Lomax suggests: "It's easy to imagine that the *lavanderas* and the Chili Queens were one and the same. San Antonio has always been a garrison town—it remains one today, to some degree—and it's easy to imagine the nineteenth-century Chili

Queens packing up their pots and pans and hitting the road when the soldiers, the mainstay of their business in peacetime, marched out to war. Why wouldn't they?"[12]

In 1893, chili made a seminal appearance at a World's Fair in Chicago known as the Columbian Exposition, a gigantic celebration of the quadricentennial of the European discovery of the Americas. As well as introducing the world to Shredded Wheat and Juicy Fruit chewing gum, the exposition featured among the Texas exhibits a "San Antonio Chilley Stand." Once again, the dish proved an instant hit with most who were trying it for the first time, in spite of how its outrageously hot spice was a jolting shock to the untutored palate. This single event appears to have lit the fuse that spread chili to the northern states, and before much longer, cookbooks began to feature recipes for it. By the time it had acquired its beans and tomatoes and become thoroughly *agringado* (Americanized) in the disdainful estimation of Mexican commentators, it had become not just a Texan but a national staple.

Although Texas has proclaimed chili con carne the state dish, there isn't anything as crushingly bureaucratic as an official recipe, only a few straightforward guidelines. Nonetheless, we can be crystal clear about those guidelines. No beans. Tomatoes (or canned tomato sauce) only if you think you should. No fancy outré additions like chocolate, cilantro, craft beer, whiskey, bacon, sausage meat, goat cheese, or avocado. The authentic Texas "bowl o' red" is coarsely chopped beef chuck, onion, beef stock, garlic, cumin, and an avalanche of chilies in whatever form or forms you think best—whole, flaked, fresh, dried, powdered. Long, patient simmering is key. Do not serve over or under spaghetti. Do not serve on a bed of rice. Do not serve with fries. Do not serve in a goddamn baked potato. What were you thinking? Baked potatoes are for shredded cheese, sour cream, and chives, not chili. A big enough bowl is a meal on its own, without the need for anything on the side. If you're from New Jersey or Pennsylvania, you may rejoice in something called a Texas chili dog, a wiener in a bun topped with chili sauce. It may be a beautiful thing if you're sitting in a beer garden in Philly in the fall, but it was invented by Greek people around the time of World War I. And that ain't freakin' Texas.

9

Pepper Sauce—
A Global Obsession

The unprecedented international success of chili peppers, exported around the world since the sixteenth century, has made them truly the global spice. Either assumed into regional culinary traditions or valued as an interesting adjunct to blander and more resistant food cultures such as those of northern Europe, they have taken root in a diverse range of climates and geographies, adapting themselves happily to local conditions and finding aficionados among bold and adventurous eaters of all ages. The result is that the chili on its own has become, culturally at least, interestingly rootless. If certain spices, or combinations of spices, instantly recall certain national culinary modes, so that lemongrass suggests Thai food, Sichuan peppercorns that of southern China, wasabi Japanese, and the protean ground spice blends we know as curry powder any of the regional cuisines of the Indian subcontinent, where in the world does the taste of a hot chili evoke? It ought to be Mexico, or more widely, Central and South America, and yet there is something entirely cosmopolitan about the chili. When European colonialists first sailed home with their seeds, they were unwittingly scattering them across the face of the earth.

What helped drive the development of chili as an all-purpose taste in the course of the nineteenth century was the rise of proprietary chili-based products, principally the bottled hot sauces that began to appear on the American market in particular as condiments and seasoning ingredients. These in turn probably derived from the British tradition, extending back to the seventeenth century, of trying to produce a rough-and-ready cheap imitation of Asian liquid condiments. By the onset of the Victorian era, these recipes had risen in dignity to the original formulation of Lea & Perrins Worcestershire sauce, a dark brown fermented brew of barley malt and spirit vinegar, molasses, anchovies, tamarind, onion, garlic, and spices. It was used to pep up Welsh rarebit, devil a hard-boiled egg, or add the finishing kick to a Bloody Mary. Prior to this, however, fermented liquid condiments that distantly suggested soy sauce, Indochinese fish sauce, or Cantonese *kê-chiap* contained whatever was near to hand and capable of spoiling productively. The earliest known record of a commercially produced homegrown American hot sauce appears in an advertisement in a Massachusetts newspaper of 1807, and was probably a homemade commodity based on cayenne pepper. Whether these early versions of cayenne sauce were particularly spicy-hot is open to question, however, as argued by one prominent U.S. culinary historian: Charles Perry disputes that the early Massachusetts cayenne pepper sauce, and other early bottled sauces like it, were truly spicy. "Number one, Massachusetts: home of the fish cake and boiled New England dinner. It was as allergic to hot spices as old England was at that time," he says. "Another reason: they would have been making it with vinegar and so they would not have extracted much if any capsaicin from the chilies and they would have had basically a vinegar that had kind of the aroma of chilies. And that may have been just what they wanted."[1]

In either the 1840s or 1850s, a New York City manufacturer called J. McCollick & Co began marketing a product called Bird Pepper Sauce, probably made with wild chiltepins (also known as bird peppers), which came in a grandiose container called a cathedral bottle. These were very tall ornate vessels of the Gothic Revival period, so called because each facet of the square-based, narrow-bodied bottle had the outline of a churchlike window with pointed arch. The McCollick bottle was nearly eleven inches high.

Bottled pepper sauces had already become a minor industry in the United States in the period before the Civil War. The excavation in 1968 of the wreck of the *Bertrand,* a steamboat that had sunk in the Missouri River in 1865, salvaged a substantial cargo of provisions that nobody was quite expecting, as hot sauce author Jennifer Trainer Thompson reports: "Riverfront folklore long held that the ship had carried whiskey, gold, and flasks of mercury, so when the archaeological dig excavated more than 500,000 artifacts, workers were surprised to find among them 173 hot sauce bottles from Western Spice Mills of St. Louis."[2] Already in 1850, Maunsel White, who arrived in America as a penniless thirteen-year-old Irish orphan and rose to become a member of the Louisiana state legislature, was producing a proprietary hot sauce that came to the attention of the local press. It was made from a chili variety known as "tobasco," according to the *New Orleans Daily Delta,* and was made by producing a boiled mash from the peppers and adding strong vinegar to it, resulting in what the paper called a "pepper decoction" for distributing statewide. It was sufficiently potent that only a single drop of it could wake up a bowl of bland soup in an instant.

The intriguing aspect of White's story is that he might—though there is no concrete evidence to clinch it—have known another distinguished Louisiana resident, Edmund McIlhenny, progenitor of what would become one of the most widely recognized hot sauce brands in the world. McIlhenny planted out his first crop on land at the family home in 1868. That resulted in 658 bottles, retailed the following year at a dollar a pop. In 1870, he applied for a brand patent, and Tabasco entered the culinary vocabulary. Like White, McIlhenny used the tabasco variety, a *Capsicum frutescens* named for one of the Mexican states where it was widely cultivated, but his recipe raised the production of hot pepper sauce to a new pitch of refinement. To begin with, prior to the harvest, he went around the plantation with a red color stick known in Louisiana French as *le petit bâton rouge,* and only when the ripening peppers were precisely the same shrill shade as the stick were they declared ready for picking. On harvesting, they are ground into a fine mash, salted, and packed into repurposed white oak barrels obtained from a whiskey producer. The mash is fermented and aged in this way for three years, after which it has the seeds and skins strained out of it, and distilled vinegar is added. It is held for a further month, with occasional stirring, before being bottled and released.

McIlhenny was a Maryland banker who had moved to New Orleans around 1840. Despite being extravagantly successful in finance in the antebellum period, he was ruined like so many others by the Confederate defeat, and had retired hurt with his large family to live with his in-laws at their plantation house on Avery Island. There, he looked after the garden, where he probably grew a small patch of tabasco peppers among other fruits and vegetables, and it was during Reconstruction that he hit on the idea of going into commercial production with a pepper sauce. He initially sold it in retooled perfume bottles, graduating to a regular supply of new bottles from a New Orleans glass company that specialized in supplying the cologne market. The present-day Tabasco bottle is very little different from its 1860s forebear.

It seems highly likely that, even if they did not meet, McIlhenny was influenced by White's formula, but Tabasco, largely owing to the winelike precision of its maturation process, is very much its own product. The founder helped its early reception by authoring a little book of recipes with suggestions for using it. It eventually found its way on to dining tables as a condiment, and into U.S. soldiers' ration packs (starting in World War II and continuing ever since), and became virtually as indispensable in a decently spicy Bloody Mary as Worcestershire sauce. Compared to many of the more recent pepper sauces, Tabasco is on the gentler side of hot. It's hot, without being red-hot, but that finely honed balance—and the absence of any other ingredients than peppers, vinegar, and salt—are exactly the key to its global preeminence. Originally, McIlhenny intended to give the product the name of the family's island plantation, but his father-in-law objected, and it was named instead for the peppers that went into it, which was all to the good. Tabasco sounds like a brand name; Petite Anse Sauce just doesn't.

Despite its enduring legacy, Tabasco was so incidental to McIlhenny's own self-fashioning that it did not merit a single reference in his autobiography, which presumes the diligent student of his life will be much more interested in his banking exploits. Notwithstanding that, its commercial success in the 1870s and after was such that it began to spawn a burgeoning band of emulators and tribute acts. The most audacious of these was Bernard Trappey, a former McIlhenny employee who lit out on his own in the 1890s, equipped with seeds from the Avery Island plantation. Very much a family concern, B. F. Trappey and Sons (of which latter there were ten, clustering protectively around one very outnumbered daughter) initially marketed its product as Trappey's Tabasco Pepper Sauce. There was no nefarious intention in this. Trappey considered, not unreasonably, that the name referred to the pepper variety itself, not to a specific rival brand. Indeed, this was the effect of legal judgments in the matter of 1910 and January and February 1922. The McIlhenny family pressed on with its appeal and succeeded in having the earlier determinations overturned. Tabasco was held by the Circuit Court of Appeals to have had the market to itself for the first thirty years of its career, such that the name had gained a secondary association over its generic application to tabasco peppers, qualifying it to enjoy precedence as a brand name. Although secondary association has long since been overturned in U.S. law as a legal principle, it was sufficient in 1922—and again on a subsequent appeal in 1926—to induce Trappey's not only to pay compensation to the McIlhenny corporation, but also to rename its own brand Trappey's Louisiana (now Louisiana-Style, since it is actually made in Colombia)

Hot Sauce. In one of commercial history's resonant ironies, McIlhenny acquired it in the 1990s, but sold it on again in 1998 to the recently founded multibrand corporate, B&G Foods of New Jersey.

Trappey's, too, is on the milder end of the hot sauce spectrum, gentler still than Tabasco. It's vinegar based, but also includes thickening gums and a red colorant. Many of the early American hot sauces were relatively tame compared to the turbo-charged era of today. Frank's RedHot was first marketed in 1920, from a long-worked recipe that its founder, Jacob Frank, had first formulated at about the time that Trappey was getting started. In 1918, he went into partnership with Adam Estilette, proprietor of a pepper farm in New Iberia, Louisiana. Their sauce was an aged blend of cayenne peppers in vinegar, garlic and other spices, bottled at a very modest 450 SHU. Now produced in Springfield, Missouri, it has been inextricably associated with Buffalo chicken wing sauce since the original prototype of that dressing was created by Teressa Bellissimo at the Anchor Bar and Grill in Buffalo, New York, in 1964, using Frank's RedHot and butter.

Baumer's Crystal Hot Sauce, still produced by the Louisiana-based Baumer family firm, was launched in 1923, as a middling-hot relish made from aging cayenne peppers with distilled vinegar and salt. The Bruce family of New Iberia followed in 1928 with its Louisiana Hot Sauce, the first to use the name of the state in its brand

ID. It was sold initially to neighboring households, but soon found a niche for itself in a rapidly crowding market. The slogan "Not too hot, not too mild" made a heroic attempt to appeal to everyone, and it, too, was made to what was now established as the regional formula, from ground cayenne peppers mixed with vinegar and salt and allowed to ferment during the maturation process. It was sold to a Georgia-based combine in 2015, although its production is still located in New Iberia. Outside Louisiana, the Garner family of North Carolina created their hot sauce in 1929, and named it Texas Pete after the founder's youngest son (whose name was actually Harold). The business began life as a barbecue stand in Winston-Salem, its flagship product being barbecue sauce, but customers whose taste buds had been weaned on the new, more piquant products requested a spicier sauce. As they used to say, the customer is always right: Garner's Texas Pete Hot Sauce grew to become another of America's top-selling brands and is still family owned. All of these brands have since generated much hotter variants that have taken their places alongside the original recipes, to keep up with a chili scene that is permanently aflame.

Beyond the borders of the United States, bottled hot sauces are legion. Mexican producers got in on the act relatively late, which is less surprising when one bears in mind the fact that hot dressings and salsas were a standard production of the Mexican domestic kitchen for centuries. Nobody who knew how to handle fresh chili peppers needed to buy a bottled sauce. Then again, there were potential killings to be made north of the border. Having a geographical foot in the door also helped. Tapatío Hot Sauce was launched in 1971 by a Mexican entrepreneur, Jose-Luis Saavedra Sr., out of Maywood, California. Hailing from Guadalajara in Jalisco state, Saavedra gave his sauce the name by which the inhabitants of that city are known. With its sombrero-clad mariachi man logo, Tapatío could be said to have helped inaugurate the taste for Mexican salsa in the modern era. Now made in Vernon, California, it is an instantly recognized brand throughout the United States and Central America.

Valentina, by contrast, is an indigenous Mexican brand, established in 1954 by a Guadalajara company, Salsa Tamazula. It is made from the *puya* variety of chili, grown in Jalisco, and has a relatively thick consistency for a pouring condiment. The Cholula brand was licensed by the José Cuervo tequila manufacturer in 1991, having been under small-scale production to an old recipe for most of the preceding century as an ingredient for sangrita, the chili-spiked pomegranate and citrus drink traditionally imbibed as an accompaniment to shots of tequila. It is made from a combination of chipotle, arbol, and piquin peppers. The name Cholula references the oldest continuously inhabited city in Mexico, which began to grow from a pair of small villages around 500 B.C.E., but the sauce is produced in Chapala, Jalisco. It comes in a bottle with a distinctive traditional round wooden top, and a beguiling white-clad lady standing before her arched stone kitchen doorway on the label.

The Caribbean region has long been one of the happiest hunting grounds for hot sauces. From island to island, markets sell privately produced bottled hot sauces often made to closely guarded family recipes. These are the real thing, a more adventurous proposition than the many fine commercially produced brands, and since the region is home to some of the hottest chili varieties on earth, an explosive experience is to be expected. Like the North American sauces, many of the Caribbean concoctions are vinegar based, but mustard also plays an essential role, adding complexity to the heat of the chili. Moruga scorpion peppers, so called for their little curly tails and among the world's most incendiary, are used to telling effect in Trinidad and Tobago's sauces, adding fire to traditional dishes such as callaloo, a thick green stew of taro leaves, okra, garlic, and coconut milk, eaten as a versatile side with fish or meat. A proprietary brand, Matouk's Trinidad Scorpion Pepper Sauce, produced on Trinidad from aged morugas and Scotch bonnets, is chunky in texture and aromatic with West Indian herbs. It offers a hit somewhere to the north of one million Scovilles.

Fruity hot sauces are the specialty of Jamaica, where mango, pineapple, tamarind, and papaya are often blended into the base of Scotch bonnet peppers and vinegar. The colors alone can be delirious, with orange, yellow, and green sauces muscling in among the red tones predominant almost everywhere else. Pickapeppa Sauce, founded in 1921 and made at Shooter's Hill near the town of Mandeville, is a gentle vinegar-based, tomato and chili condiment that is traditionally mixed with cream cheese for spreading on crackers. It, too, has fruit notes, from mango, tamarind, and raisins. For the full scorch experience, the company also produces Pickapeppa Hot Pepper Sauce made with Scotch bonnets and just enough sugar to act as a seasoning for the fiery chili flavor.

Bajan pepper sauce is also generally made from bonnet peppers with vinegar and mustard on Barbados and is widely used as a cooking ingredient in meat, fish, and vegetable dishes. Lottie's Barbados Hot Pepper Sauce is a mustard-laced blend of bonnets, onions, and garlic. The pride of Saint Kitts is Mrs. Greaux Hot Pepper Sauce, a virulent red blend spiked with curry leaves, while its companion island, Nevis, is home to Llewellyn's, which combines red bonnet peppers and Caribbean thyme for a fragrant potion made by an émigré from Manchester, England. Erica's is one of the longest-established brands in the Grenadines, made at Kingstown on Saint Vincent from locally cultivated habaneros. Elsewhere in the British Virgin Islands, Caribbee Hot Sauce, made on Tortola, comes with a jaunty wicker hat in both red (pepper-based) and yellow (mustard-based) variations.

On Saint Croix in the U.S. Virgin Islands, Miss Anna's is made to a century-old family recipe from habaneros, mustard, curry leaves, and other local spices. The Haitian specialty, for which everybody has their own preferred recipe, is Sos (Sauce) Ti-Malice, a kind of sofrito of habaneros with onion and garlic, simmered in lime juice and perhaps a little tomato paste. Bell peppers are sometimes added for their color, and the sauce is served as a condiment for grilled meats or fish. Legend has it that it originated as an ambush recipe by a host who was trying to put off a greedy guest from eating too much. The trick backfired, and the lacerating relish only made everything more delicious.

Perhaps no other eminent branded product is greater proof that chili and its traditional hot sauces are no respecters of boundaries than Huy Fong Sriracha Hot Chili Sauce. Produced in enormous quantities in Rosemead, California, the Asian-style chili dipping sauce in the instantly recognizable green-topped squeezy bottle comes from a company founded in early 1980 by a Vietnamese refugee named David Tran. Tran fled Vietnam after the U.S. disengagement, arriving in the States on a Panamanian-registered Taiwanese freighter and being granted political asylum. The company name, Huy Fong, is taken from the name of the ship on which Tran traveled. Barely pausing to catch his breath, he founded his sauce business straightaway, delivering his first products to Asian markets and restaurants in Los Angeles and San Diego in a Chevrolet van, on the sides of which he had painted his own rooster logos (the symbol of Tran's birth year in the Chinese calendrical system). There was a range of sauces, but it was the sriracha, made from fresh jalapeños, that really set the market alight. Tran's sriracha is a medium-hot condiment with an appealing blend of sweet and sharp notes in the flavor. A standby of Asian and other restaurant kitchens worldwide, it has been supplied to the NASA International Space Station, which is not bad going for a product that started life in a very humble domestic kitchen in Vietnam in 1975.

From the keynote ingredients in sauces and relishes such as these, chili has branched out to become a flavoring and heating element in many types of food and drink. Chili chocolate has enjoyed a connoisseurial surge in recent years, and has on its side the impeccable antique pedigree of matching two ingredients that found themselves side by side in chili's lands of origin. Allied to quality chocolate with high cocoa values—70 percent or more—chili blends into its luxuriously silky medium with graceful ease, adding a strong smoldering aftertaste to the richness of the cacao. Picking up on the craze, Mexico's celebrated coffee liqueur Kahlúa now has a chili-chocolate version, while chili beers, and of course chili-chocolate beers, have claimed a niche on the spicy alcohol shelf alongside the many brands of spiced rum. The House of Chilli on the Isle of Wight, off England's south coast, makes a chili cider, as does the Finnriver Cider Company based on the

Olympic Peninsula of western Washington State, a strong, semisweet brew of local apples and habaneros.

Chili has lent its fire, it would seem, to virtually anything consumable. But why?

10

Taste and Touch—
How Chili Peppers Work

No other edible natural commodity has undergone the journey that the chili pepper has in its long and dazzlingly colorful history. It has progressed from being a nutritional staple in its regions of origin to a global food fashion, to a centerpiece of cultural bravado, a trajectory in which its most noticeable attribute—its hotness—has evolved from a necessitous virtue into an index of adventurous gustatory heroism. Like no other spice or seasoning, its incorporation into a dish does not simply offset a preexisting recipe but remakes it in its own image. This has resulted in a functional ambivalence in the use of chili peppers, at least in the West. In one sense, the taste for chili-hot cuisine answers a predilection for brash overstatement in food, for strong, uncompromising flavors that leave long aftertastes and are richly alluring to the point of obsessive overuse. In this model, chili is the quick-fix antidote to an otherwise bland diet. On the other hand, subtle refinements in combining chili with other flavors, in the contexts of Indian and Southeast Asian cooking in particular, produce intricate and alluring new dimensions to dishes, their taste elements deepened by the extra levels of flavor that chilies contribute.

These multiple applications, which are hardly matched in their complexity in the stories of any other ingredients that have traveled around the world, with the possible exception of sugar, can be traced to the unique properties of the chili. What it bestows on food is not just a category of flavor, but a haptic sensation on the palate, technically known as chemesthesis. All food obviously mobilizes the sense of touch, as soon as we put it in our mouths but, once swallowed, that sense is mostly gone. Chili continues to work on the tongue and palate long after its consumption. That is because its active components, the capsaicin and similar compounds in it, stimulate the chemical sensitivity of the skin and—especially—the unprotected mucous membranes. Activating the receptors that mediate the body's perception of heat and pain, chili has an impact on the organism that goes beyond the two principal external senses involved in the consumption of food, namely smell and taste. Chili is not the only chemesthetic food. Think of the stinging and streaming eyes provoked by chopping onions and shallots, the prickling in the nose caused by mustard, horseradish, and wasabi, or the cooling, refreshing feeling that herbal mint or menthol leave behind. These effects have applications beyond food, as we saw in part 1. Just as menthol is added to topical analgesic creams to assist the sensation of relief from muscular pain, so capsaicin is added to anti-inflammatory ointments for the soothing endorphin response that it stimulates. None of these other foods has quite the intensity and sustained palatal activity that even relatively milder chilies produce.

Chilies have a nongastronomic effect in addition to their more obviously culinary one. They leave the palate energized (or, eventually, exhausted), and leave the consumer intensely alert and uplifted, rather than ordinarily satiated. There could be a bundle of benefits to this. First, chilies make food more interesting. No matter how many times you have experienced it before, the impact of chili on the palate is always newly shocking, especially for the first mouthful or two. Combined with their relative cheapness, this made them the ideal ingredient to enliven a bland diet organized around the daily consumption of the same small handful of staple foods. Chilies turn a bowl of Chinese rice congee from an easily assimilable breakfast gruel, the food of ill people, distantly derived from the bitter recourse of periods of scarcity, into something explosive and challenging, a proper wake-up call to the bleary morning palate. Tibetan cooking, possibly the world's most upsettingly peculiar cuisine to Western sensibilities, would be altogether drearier without *sepen*, effectively a chili salsa that can be applied to anything from *tsampa*, roasted clods of yak-buttered barley flour, to the slow-cooked dishes of sheep's heads and lungs that sustain high-altitude communities through the unforgiving winters. Chili takes up the slack that the widely used seasoning monosodium glutamate leaves in its wake. By the same token, cultures that were jealous of the blandness of their food, often because spice was seen as directly provocative of flaming temper or carnal concupiscence, would have no truck with chili or, at the most, allowed it a place only in its most housebroken manifestations. If the older hot sauces seem anything but incendiary to today's gastronomic fire brigade, it is because they were first formulated in a period—the mid-to late nineteenth century—when chili was thought to need a responsible restraining hand if it was to gain a foothold in the cultures of temperance and late puritanism.

Second, chili has a climatically related effect. This may be easier to see in cold weather, when a bowl of sizzling-hot chili con carne or a chicken vindaloo is a rapidly efficacious way of reaching the body's frozen extremities. Less intuitive to consumers from northern climes is the idea that chili heat can cool you down in torrid conditions, but precisely because it deceives the body into thinking it is being burned, it promotes the release of sympathetic responses such as dilation of the blood vessels and, most effectively, perspiration. The film of sweat that comes over the skin in response to spicy food cools the body down as it evaporates. One only has to recall that chilies have their natural origins in some of the hottest regions of the planet, in equatorial South America and the tropical zones of Mexico, to understand why they were so readily adopted in countries occupying the same climatic belt around the world.

Third, chili has a now proven effect on mood, contributing the same kind of emotional sustenance that is famously claimed for the theobromine and caffeine in chocolate. The pain-relieving endorphins that the brain releases in response to the assault of hot spice have, like many a chemical analgesic, a mood-altering effect, as well. They stimulate production of the neurotransmitter dopamine, which plays a key role in maintaining a buoyant state of mind, and the deficiency of which is what, conversely, leads to many cases of endogenous depression. These are relatively subtle and short-lived effects, to be sure, compared to other ways of triggering dopamine (the contributor to an online forum who complained that the much-vaunted chili lift was nothing compared to what he used to get in his days as a cocaine user might have been missing a point), but they are nonetheless definite. It isn't difficult to see, in the light of this, why impoverished peoples living lives of grueling indigence—still the greater part of humanity even in the era of globalization—would value a type of food that cheaply and reliably made the world look a little better.

There are also sound alimentary reasons for consuming chemesthetic foods like chili peppers. The effects of hot spice on internal tissue help increase the flow of saliva and also promote the secretion of gastric juices, both of which are aids to digestion. "In addition," report food science researchers Pamela Dalton and Nadia Byrnes, "studies have shown that several types of pungent spices (ginger, piperine, capsaicin) stimulate bile flow, which leads to enhanced fat digestion and absorption, but without fat accumulation."[1] Enhanced digestive capacity is clearly going to be a benefit to those cultures that subsist on largely grain-based diets, as psychologist Paul Rozin has shown. "Digestion of the bland, high complex carbohydrate diets characteristic of the cultures that use chili as a flavor principle may well be improved by the capsaicin stimulant. It is surely true that mastication of these often dry and mealy diets is facilitated by the copious flow of saliva induced by chili pepper."[2] In other words, it isn't just that chilies are highly nutritious in themselves, it's that there are nutritional benefits that are derived precisely from their irritant effect in the mouth and in the digestive system.

And what of the adaptive process by which a liking for the burn of chili peppers is acquired? This is, in gustatory terms, very much a journey from innocence to maturity. Not everybody undertakes the whole itinerary, but those who do are not, despite what is sometimes believed, more adventurous eaters with less sensitive palates. Rozin explains the process: "[T]he same central input, once judged to be negative and painful, becomes pleasant after some substantial experience, often spreading over months or years. It is the very same sensory features of irritation that initially promote rejection, that later become attractive."[3] Nor is the acquisition of a chili taste necessarily confined to the most obvious transitional stage from immaturity to adulthood in the teen years. In Mexico, children regularly develop a tolerance and taste for chili between the ages of four and seven years old, as they see elder members of their families enjoying it. The same is true in the chili-fired cuisines of southern Asia. A process known as hedonic reversal, by which pain is converted into a source of pleasure, the same mechanism by which, more inimically, addictions such as those to tobacco or opiates are acquired following early strongly aversive encounters with these substances, is seen at its most graphic—and most benign—in the development of an affinity for chili. Successfully undergoing an initiation of this kind, in the presence and under the influence of close kin and social peers, creates a particularly binding form of group solidarity. If Western children whose lives are currently consecrated to the consumption of sugar and trans fats developed the taste for hot spice much earlier than they do, it could be that the process of their social development and emotional maturation might be significantly advanced.

Finally, if hedonic reversal is about the conversion of pleasure to pain, there is also such a thing as the enjoyment of unconverted pain, what Rozin calls "benign masochism." The theme park thrill ride may be utterly terrifying to experience, but the pleasure comes from knowing that, barring some unforeseeable disaster, it will not kill us. Compare that to a game of Russian roulette, where every next spin of the gun chamber might blow your brains out. Not so enjoyable. Containment is all. In the present context, Rozin notes that "the peak burn intensity preference for chili likers is often just below the level they claim is overtly painful and negative."[4] The psychology of this is even more complex, but is undoubtedly rooted in the contiguity that there is between the zones of unalloyed pleasure and unmitigated pain. Each depends on the other for the borderlines of its definition, to the extent sometimes that the absence of one precisely counterbalances the presence of the other. Their mutual interdependence therefore creates occasional conduits between the two precincts, such that the consciously willed incurring of pain constitutes a paradoxical assertion of subjectivity. I want this to happen. It will be exciting. An indication of the negotiation that takes place between the two zones lies in the trajectory that confirmed chiliheads find themselves undergoing in pursuing their passion. "There is almost always a level of burn beyond which someone finds it aversive," says Rozin. "One tends at the beginning to like it hotter and hotter, but then it tends to level off."[5] To those not so disposed, benign masochism may look like an urgent case for treatment. There is especially something surreal about it occurring in the food context. It is, however, one of the many physical and emotional competences that separate us from the animals.

With these thoughts in mind, we can proceed to considering, in part 3, what the cultural meanings and psychological significance of chili might be in today's postmodern world. It is clear that, in the advanced industrial societies, chili has become much more than just a gastronomic predilection, but has been transformed into a tool of self-definition, and an often competitive self-definition at that. If, to quote the eternal verity of the nineteenth-century French gastronome Jean-Anthelme Brillat-Savarin, we are what we eat, what might the taste for superhot spicy food say about who we twenty-first-century beings are?

Part

THREE

CULTURE

11

The Devil's Dinner—Discovering the Dark Side of Chili

The preeminent cultural association that hot, spicy food has carried with it since ancient times is with devilry, demonology, the wicked, and the illicit. If the Devil himself sits down to dinner each evening in Hell, it is surely a plate of raw chilies on which he feasts. Not only would these suit his own fiery and rebellious temperament, but if they are also fed to the infernal region's denizens, they would be an appropriately tormenting sustenance in a neighborhood permanently in flames. The drop of water for which the chastised plead in vain would therefore not be particularly helpful to them, compared to the offer of a drop of milk or yogurt.

These symbolic meanings are at work in many different cultures. English-speaking cooks enjoyed their deviled eggs, deviled ham, and deviled whitebait in times gone by, a usage mirrored in some of the European languages, too—*au diable, al diablo, al diavolo*. The logo on Underwood Deviled Ham Spread, a brand exactly coeval with Tabasco, is a little red devil with a pitchfork, albeit an amicably grinning one, compared to the original with his raking fingernails and swishing tail. "Deviling" a dish is terminology that dates back to the late eighteenth century, and refers, as *The Oxford Companion to Food* puts it with elementary clarity, to "the devil and the excessive heat in Hell."[1] The French *maître cuisinier* Alexis Soyer's deviled seasoning recipe of the 1850s is compounded of cayenne and black pepper, horseradish, mustard, and vinegar—in other words, everything one could lay one's hands on that would make the taste buds sizzle. In Italian usage, a dish cooked *al diavolo* can refer either to hot seasonings such as chilies, pepper, and vinegar, but also to meat grilled over open flames or hot coals, like the damned in Hell.

That deviling had seeped fully into the British culinary demotic by the nineteenth century is evidenced by Charles Dickens's Mr. Micawber, who regales David Copperfield with a hastily improvised repast of half-cooked mutton seared on a gridiron, heralded with a bold philosophical entreaty: "[A]llow me to take the liberty of remarking that there are few comestibles better, in their way, than a Devil." He proceeds to coat the mutton slices prior to cooking with a mixture of pepper, mustard, salt, and cayenne, while Mrs. Micawber warms up some mushroom ketchup in a small saucepan. The recipe works, and David, previously repining from amorous anxiety, confides that "[m]y own appetite came back miraculously."[2]

Although deviling was to fall from favor in the century gone by, it excited a certain amount of appropriately heated debate when it was all the rage. The Scottish writer Eneas Sweetland Dallas, in his pseudonymous *Kettner's Book of the Table, a Manual of Cookery* (1877) pleads, none too serenely, for a measure of self-restraint amid all the hell-raising:

> *It is the great fault of all devilry that it knows no*
> *bounds. A moderate devil is almost a contradiction*
> *in terms; and yet it is quite certain that if a devil*
> *is not moderate he destroys the palate, and ought to*
> *have no place in cookery, the business of which is*
> *to tickle, not to annihilate, the sense of taste.*[3]

Dallas allows two types of devil, the dry and the wet, the latter typified by the French tradition of cooking the members and entrails of game birds at the tableside over a spirit lamp before the delighted eyes of diners and dressing them in mustard and mild-mannered spices. In a grudging cosmopolitan temper, he goes on to give a short recipe for French *sauce à la diable,* prefacing it with a trigger warning: "The French cooks' idea of the devil is that he has a passion for shalots [sic]." The formula that follows involves mincing the said shallots with herbs and "as much pepper as may be dared," which may be presumed to include cayenne, simmering them in an espagnole brown sauce and red wine and then straining through a tamis sieve. As a parting shot, Dallas advises readers that they may "know of a surety that this will much rejoice all French devils."[4] Still, it doesn't exactly sound like hot stuff.

At the zenith of Victorian discernment, deviled kidneys were a sine qua non of a civilized breakfast, much celebrated in the tales of the Dublin popular novelist and raconteur Charles Lever. The eye of the narrator of his *Charles O'Malley, the Irish Dragoon* (1841) fairly brightens at the prospect of a breakfast spread comprised of "the mutton and the muffin, the tea-pot, the trout, and the deviled kidney."[5] For what amounted to something of an obsession, less for the gastronomic value of the dish than for its instant hint of the *bonne bouche,* he was roundly satirized by Edgar Allan Poe. "The unction and pertinacity with which the author discusses what he chooses to denominate 'deviled kidneys' are indeed edifying to say no more. . . . Never in the whole course of his eventful life does Mr. O'Malley get two or three assembled together without seducing them forthwith to a table and placing before them a dozen of wine and a dish of 'deviled kidneys.'"[6] Similarly, Anthony Trollope's Archdeacon Grantley in *The Warden* (1855) is able to gaze contentedly over a breakfast table where, among the teeming bounty, are "deviled kidneys frizzling on a hot-water dish; which, by the bye, were placed closely contiguous to the plate of the worthy archdeacon himself."[7] A particular favorite, then. There was something of the gilding of lilies about deviling kidneys. The organs themselves are so rich and densely textured that applying a hot piquant seasoning to them seemed as overly luxurious to its critics, especially at breakfast, as thermidoring lobster might be at the opposite end of the day. By the Edwardian era, it had become a central pillar of the gentlemen's club, prepared with the full folderol in a chafing dish at the breakfast table while one rustled through *The Times*. Old India hands might well stipulate that the hottishness of the sauce, which was traditionally mustard with a good shake of cayenne, might be boosted with curry powder.

At the extremities of the journey that chili peppers undertook in the sixteenth century, diabolic connotations may have been derived from the Christian cosmology of their exporters. The Kristang culinary tradition of Singapore and Malacca (now a constituent state of Malaysia) is a hybrid cuisine marrying Southeast Asian foodways with Portuguese influence. Its *nari ayam,* or devil's curry, is a raging-hot festive dish incorporating a spice paste of red chilies, galangal, lemongrass, ginger, garlic, and turmeric, along with chicken, potato, and candlenuts cooked in mustard seeds and vinegar, in the manner of Goan vindaloo. A deviled chicken dish served in restaurants throughout Sri Lanka consists of deep-fried chicken in a spicy batter, with a dressing of ketchup, chili, and soy sauces mixed with onions, whole chilies, garlic, and ginger.

Portugal's influence is also palpable in the West African Cape Verdean dish of *pastel com o diabo dentro* (pastry with the devil inside), a savory cornmeal turnover usually filled with tuna and tomato and hotly spiced with red chilies. Even in their region of origin, though, where chilies come with just about everything, the devil is still invoked for certain recipes. Mexico's *camarones a la diabla* are fried shrimp in a sauce of blended red-hot guajillo and arbol chilies, tomato, onion, and garlic.

The paradoxical aspect of the demonizing of chilies is that, in ancient popular lore, they performed precisely the opposite function. Because of their searing potency, they were used to ward off evil spirits and ill luck. The *ristras* of drying chilies hung over the adobe houses of the Mexican pueblo not only helped preserve the peppers themselves, but were held to deter any malevolent presences bearing hostile intent toward the inhabitants. Even more effective was the action of burning chilies, which as anyone who has ever been a little too enthusiastic with them in the stir-fry knows, produces an acrid smoke that catches repeatedly at the back of the throat, and reduces anybody in the vicinity to remorseful streaming eyes and coughing fits. Whether burning or not, chili has a purgative and exorcizing function. Far from being the Devil's dinner in these contexts, it is one of the weapons in humanity's armory against him. To this day, a bunch of dried chilies, and often a lemon, too, are hung above the front doors of Mexican houses for their protective benefits. In India, they can be seen attached to the fenders of cars to protect their drivers.

The ancient tradition of wearing a *corno*, or *cornicello* (little horn), in Italy as a talisman against evil probably derives primordially from the mythical figure of Selene, the Greek lunar goddess, whose horns were a transfiguration of the crescent moon she wore on her brow. Worn on a chain around the neck, the *corno* was originally a male custom by which a man sought to guard his virility from the assaults of the evil eye, typically the covetous eyes of other men with designs on his wife. In pagan folklore, the *malocchio* (evil eye) is a source of grievous misfortune, the revenge of envious malcontents against the blessed, manifesting itself as a jaundiced glare, often unseen, at those whom one wishes ill. By means of its strength and its power to bestow fertility, the *corno* kept its wearer inviolate. It could be made of precious metals, terra-cotta, or bone, but was classically fashioned from red coral, in which form it looks uncannily like a chili pepper. This resemblance has eventually suggested a cross-pollination of two mythologies. In Southern Italy, Calabria in particular, it is even held that the chili pepper might be the quintessential form of a *corno*, a proposition that loops the ancient European tradition of the charmed horn back to the even older spiritual efficacy of Mesoamerican chili.

Up to the most recent era, the satanic influence entered the nomenclature of chili pepper varieties surprisingly rarely. Devil's Tongue is a *Capsicum chinense* pepper that appears to have mutated spontaneously in the United States on an Amish plantation in Pennsylvania in the early 1990s. It originally surfaced as a wrinkly-skinned yellow variety similar to, but smaller than, the southern African Fatalii, but has since been bred into an even hotter red manifestation. The shape is precisely like a bumpy-surfaced tongue, with a central groove and a provocative pointed end. In southern Italy, the C. *annuum* variety Satana, known in English as Satan's Kiss, is a cherrylike red chili that fruits copiously and is enjoyed in its locality when stuffed with pounded anchovies and mozzarella and grilled. It's a medium-hot pepper, much gentler than the Devil's Tongue, even though its name suggests something of the same infernal amorousness. Another C. *chinense* variety is the Caribbean Red Habanero, also known as Lucifer's Dream, though that name has also been applied to a milder orangey-red *annuum*. A pair of other long thin *annuum* varieties that produce prolific quantities of assertively hot pods are the Demon Red and the mustard-yellow Devil's Brew. And another of the synonyms of the piri piri (or peri-peri, or birdeye) chili that spread rapidly throughout Africa after its introduction from Portugal is the African Devil or Red Devil.

The number of modern chili products—pastes, relishes, chutneys, sauces, salsas, and extracts—that have diabolical references in their names is now legion. A brisk tour of the market yields, in no particular order: Satan's Blood, Satan's Sweat, Satan's Spit, Satan's Shit,

Satan's Spawn, Satan's Revenge, Saint Lucifer, Chili Devil, Devil's Chilli, Devil's Delirium, Red Devil, Devilspit, Devil's Dynamite, Kiss the Devil, The Evil One, Hell Fire, Hell Raiser, Hell Unleashed, and so forth. Riffing on the theme of evildoing, curses, maledictions, and mischief, there are products that offer to kill you, poison you, give you diarrhea, blow out your colon, make you puke, burn your ass, kick your ass, make you cry, make you hurt, and reduce you to a state of submission. There is frequent recourse to the F-bomb. Holy Fuck, exclaims one label on your behalf. There is a sauce that is for adding One Fuckin' Drop at a Time. The Hottest Fuckin' Sauce may well be the hottest sauce you have ever tasted, until you taste an even hotter one. The raging injunction on the label of Man the Fuck Up!, Ultra Mega Hot Carolina Reaper Purée already makes me wonder whether I have what it takes before I have even taken a knife to the seal. Meanwhile, if Hell can be conceived as a vale of physical as well as spiritual pollution, we have reached a point where chili products called Acid Rain and Toxic Waste gleefully use the counterintuitive language of virulent hazard not in order to warn customers off but to tempt them in. Which leads us to another extraordinary analogy that the modern chili movement has very consciously taken on from the unofficial world of the forbidden, the illicit, and the plain wrong.

There are resonant continuities all through the hot sauce scene with the semantic atmosphere and argot of controlled substances. Without suggesting that anybody involved actually has a finger in both pies, the language used to describe the reputations of the hottest cultivars of chili, and the products manufactured from them, are strikingly similar to those I have encountered during my years as a researcher in the field of proscribed intoxicants. At the most cautious, all the talk of endorphin rushes and dopamine triggering bears obvious parallels with the known psychoactive effects of both opiates and stimulants, and while some scientific authorities dispute whether the consumption of chili peppers actually stimulates these responses in the body, others—and a mass of perhaps suggestible consumers (or should we call them users?)—insist that they do, albeit at much less dramatic levels of intensity. "As a leisure activity," reported Lauren Collins in *The New Yorker* in November 2013, "superhots offer some of the pleasures of mild drugs and extreme sports without requiring one to break the law or work out."[8] Lest it be thought that this is a first-world twist on the chili experience, Denver Nicks, in an article in January 2017 for *National Geographic*, discovered the same sentiment expressed among Bolivian people with reference to their all-purpose chili relish, *llajwa*, a pounded blend of locoto peppers, tomatoes, and the indigenous cilantrolike herb *quirquiña*:

> "We do not eat without llajwa," Garrado tells me, a phrase I will hear repeated many times on my journey. "It's like a vice. It's something that hurts you, but you also like it. Like a drug. Some people

*take drugs and can't stand to be without them.
We here in Bolivia? We're addicted to* llajwa."

Danish chef Kamilla Seidler, chef at Gustu, a fusion restaurant on the south side of La Paz, where the *llajwa* is incorporated into a brandy-based cocktail, concurred: "'I love spicy food,' she says. 'I think it's like a drug a little bit. You get happy.'"[9]

Underlining this allegedly psychotropic connection is the tenacious notion among some commentators that the taste for hot chili can become an addiction. This is physiological nonsense, but is predicated on the undoubtedly sound notion that, as with opiates, alcohol and many banned recreational drugs, a tolerance develops with continued use. The chili sauce that seemed intolerably, painfully hot on first tasting ten minutes ago, or last week, tastes decreasingly acerbic with each fresh encounter, freeing the palate for investigation of something hotter next time. As with any other category of taste, the palate can be trained to appreciate caustic heat, which in the case of capsaicin-laden peppers means to become more robustly ready to withstand it. In 1992, an Australian research team already suggested that the triggering of endorphins is what leads certain people to become "addicted" to capsaicin. As was reported in *New Scientist* at the time, "Because people get a definite buzz from capsaicin and because they become used to exposure to increased levels of the endorphin it stimulates, eating spicy food can be addictive."

Project leader John Prescott of the Commonwealth Scientific and Industrial Research Organisation (CSIRO) stated in a warning that reverberates in stark homology from the gateway theory of illicit drug use, "[t]he first bite of mild curry leads on to the vindaloo."[10] This does not mean, though, that the body now actively needs a gradually progressive daily dose and will go into some kind of catastrophic shutdown if it fails to get it. It isn't that sort of tolerance. While pure capsaicin itself is a toxin, the amounts found in even the hottest pepper varieties are not in themselves harmful to the organism, although their incendiary burn may prompt an effluxion at either end, or both ends, of the alimentary canal.

A celebrated episode of *The Simpsons*, "El Viaje Misterioso de Nuestro Jomer" (1997), sees Homer disdainfully tasting and critiquing the products on show at a chili cook-off. Police Chief Wiggum dares him to try his own monstrous brew, made with a legendary pepper variety known as the Quetzalacatenango, grown deep in the Amazonian jungle by the inmates of a Guatemalan insane asylum. Having coated his mouth beforehand with a protective sealing of candle wax, Homer swallows several of these whole red-and-yellow-striped peppers from Wiggum's bubbling cauldron. He is thrown instantly into a hallucinogenic state reminiscent of the earliest onset of psychotropic flora such as peyote cactus or psilocybin mushrooms, with full-blown visual and auditory disturbances. As he wanders off into the fields, he is met by a talking coyote, voiced by Johnny Cash, who acts as his spirit guide during an initiatory odyssey of self-discovery. The lesson of the experience turns out not to be, as Homer first suggests, never to eat the Guatemalan insanity pepper again, but to find his soul mate, who of course turns out to be Marge.

The reported hallucinogenic effects of very hot peppers are to be taken with a healthy dose of skepticism. There is no evidence that capsaicin has such an action on the brain, but certain reported subjective experiences, and inadequately referenced medical accounts, suggest otherwise. The peculiar state into which NPR reporter Marshall Terry was thrown on tasting Ed Currie's Carolina Reaper in South Carolina in 2011 led to an episode of several minutes of very erratic behavior and strangely trippy-sounding pronouncements, following an initial episode of convulsive vomiting, exactly as can happen with peyote. According to Stephanie Butler of the History Channel online:

> Truly hot chilis can also have mildly hallucinogenic effects. The Mayans used them as stimulants in ancient Mexico, and humans have enjoyed their titillating effects for over 8,000 years. Modern day chili eaters have reported seeing objects that aren't in the room and losing feeling in limbs, among other mind-numbing effects.[11]

An intrepid psychonaut with the nom de guerre of Fer cautiously nibbles at, and then wolfs down the rest of, a blinding-hot dried red chili in Oaxaca in a report for Erowid, an online resource of information on intoxicants of all kinds:

> *Everything shimmered, the world a chimera, like watery-looking heat rising off midsummer too-hot-to-walk-on concrete. My consciousness undulated painfully, and the raucous, festive scene, my friends' conversation, and the bustling restaurant faded into the distance, there but not there. With the edge of my awareness, I knew that my friends watched and laughed, knew the revelry continued around me, knew a world existed outside the inferno in my mouth.*

She makes a vain attempt to ventilate her scorched mouth by breathing quickly in and out. "After several minutes (or was it years?), I felt the outside world returning in slow, pulsating, burning waves. Almost as painful as leaving my body, returning meant feeling the chili's full force again."[12] She confesses, however, that she had also drunk a fair quantity of mezcal.

So we have the alleged effects of chili positioned according to taste somewhere along the range from stimulants or opiates to hallucinogenic agents like peyote or LSD. Pick your poison and set your suggestibility receptors to high. The manner in which chili aficionados talk about their hottest experiences has distinct overtones of drug users comparing notes. The never-ending competitive arms race to breed the hottest chili in the world has seen Carolina Reaper challenged by another C. *chinense* bred at Saint Asaph in Wales and given the name of Dragon's Breath. It claims to be more than half as strong again as the Reaper, prompting Ed Currie to produce a pepper fully double the strength of his Carolina Reaper (over three million SHU). This new chili's mystique is only deepened by its name, Pepper X.

The imaginative observer might compare all this to the rather more sinister business of trying to formulate the most violently potent stimulant in the world, or the strongest strain of grass, were it not for the fact the users themselves, "chiliheads" in their own parlance, quite widely talk about the chili phenomenon as though it were a matter of squaring up to an illicit, and potentially terrifying, experience, a rite of passage. "The heat is just a big plus and makes this wonder stuff last even longer." "Extreme heat and discomfort last for about 30 minutes (for me), but the worst is over in about 15 minutes. The usual eyes watering, nose running, etc. that you would expect from jalapeños, but much more amplified and intense." "I thought the Primos tasted good, as did the Brains, both sweet out of the gate, but you don't get to enjoy it very long because your whole face is on fire. The Barrackpore tasted terrible, like dish soap to me, but I grew them again anyway, because they kick my ass worse than the rest and make some of the best powder."[13]

The search for foods that imitate, or directly mobilize, the effects of psychoactive substances never fails to include chili peppers in its remit. There is an established chili discourse that compares the physiological effects of eating them to the experience of undergoing a chemically altered state of consciousness. While the wilder rhetorical flights that this tradition has disgorged may be fanciful enough, it has undoubtedly captivated many of the more seriously committed chiliheads around the world, and its overtones of the forbidden tie it back to the long tradition of hot peppers as the food of the infernal. I particularly like this description from self-proclaimed Medicine Hunter Chris Kilham:

> *The Devil's own vegetable woos the faithful with a seductive religious experience of chapped and burning lips, a spanked and swollen tongue, a mouth that aches with heat, a searing swallow, a boiling gastric churning, sweat drooling down a sizzling brow, the face and brain flush with hot pounding blood, and a wave of pain-quenching endorphins, which surge in the brain like firemen in a city aflame. In the grip of chili fever, the mind swoons in ecstatic pain, like an acolyte with stigmata.*[14]

Man, that's good chili.

12

Hot Stuff—Chilies and Sex

If hot peppers can be compared to drugs, and their connection to rock and roll is forever sealed by the long abiding of Los Angeles funksters the Red Hot Chili Peppers, it has to be a cinch that the eternal triumvirate can be completed by connecting the world's hottest spice to sex. Sexual allure has been metaphorically related to heat for many centuries, all the way up to the present habit of referring to somebody physically appealing as "hot," a direct shorthand synonym for the sizzling, smoldering, sultry qualities that previous generations found in their objects of carnal desire, those for whom they had "the hots." Your latest date may be "hot stuff," but the ones you have left behind are still "old flames." The idea derives from the association of sexual recklessness and hot-bloodedness, the fiery temperament of people who live in tropical zones, and probably also from the idea of fertility as being "in heat." The condition of being in the heat of sexual frenzy was applied specifically to women at the stage of the estrous cycle (from the Latin *oestrus,* "frenzy") when they are teeming with reproductive hormones.

Sexual desire is a hot state by the lights of the most ancient metaphors. The Old Testament Song of Songs says of passion that "it burns like blazing fire, like a mighty flame" (8:6). Classical literature is full of references to "the fire of love," and the metaphor is broadly transcultural. The late Ming *Gujin Xiaoshuo* (*Stories Old and New*) of the vernacular poet Feng Menglong (1620) relates of a bibulous pair of lovers that "[t]hey drank more than ten glassfuls, and their desire burned like fire." This last example implies that the fire of passion can be stoked by acts of consumption, classically alcohol but also any of a number of foods posited as aphrodisiacs over the centuries. It is no use pointing out that modern science has dismissed the very idea of an aphrodisiac; vernacular belief clings fast to them. Certain foods were held to be provocative of lustful desire because their shapes suggested either the male or female generative organs— asparagus, cucumbers, oysters, figs, and so on. Others are held, like alcoholic drinks or chocolate, to work simply by making their consumers feel good, and therefore more likely to slip into the amorous mood. In the case of chili peppers, the irresistible link between their spicy hotness and the heat of arousal has been so obvious that it has been put to use in all eras.

In the present day, the pseudoscientific claims made for chilies as aphrodisiacs rest on their action in releasing endorphins, which are guaranteed to put the user into a mellow and receptive frame of mind. And then some. According to eatsomethingsexy.com: "even a tiny nibble can have an aphrodisiac effect. A pinch of chili pepper can raise body temperature and get you in the mood to tear off your clothes. It also makes lips plump up with kissable softness and desirability. In fact, it is said that all the heat can telegraph the visual cues of a sexual flush."[1] In fact, capsaicin is more likely to lower core body temperature than raise it, while the swollen lips are a subjective mirage caused by the burning sensation and would be anything but kissable if they were truly painfully tumescent in both participants. On the other hand, we can allow that, seen in the right light, any facial flushing might look like broiling ardor, which could be enough to prompt the tearing off of clothes. This advice is repeated widely in newspaper and magazine articles around Valentine's Day, often with a spurious veneer of expert authority, and represents one of the transmutations that medieval and early modern superstition and folk belief have undergone in the postmodern age. It is not, however, without its historical antecedents.

Those European cultures that only took to chili peppers very cautiously and apprehensively in the sixteenth century did so precisely because they were wary that ingesting a food from distant lands, where the climate was extreme and the habits of the indigenous peoples, from wandering about butt-naked to eating their dead, were enough to cause moral palpitations in the civilized societies of the colonialists, might induce similar laxity in the unsuspecting. They arrived in Protestant northern Europe just as urgent spiritual alarms were beginning to be raised there over the corrupting effects of rich food and high living in the Catholic south, especially among the clergy. If the diet of early Puritans and Lutherans was the pared-back Lenten subsistence regimen of grains and vegetables, with undressed fish and meat on the high days and holidays, a dietary system that was explicitly suspicious of spices, then fiery peppers were hardly likely to be welcome. Indeed, their pyrogenic effect was just what prompted the cautionary note among naturalists, herbalists, and physicians of the day. There was always more to it, though, than an intuitive nervousness at playing with physical fire, a trepidation that extended to the Catholic heartlands as well. María Paz Moreno's culinary history of Madrid notes that "Spanish Jesuit missionary and naturalist José de Acosta, though he recommended [chili peppers] as a digestion aid, cautioned against their abuse, stating that 'much use of it in the young is prejudicial to health, especially to that of the soul, for it heightens sensuality.'"[2]

The suspicion of spices as spurs to concupiscence stretched back to Roman times and was sustained in the Christian era by Galenic medicine. Long before the arrival of chili, the eastern spices—peppercorns, cinnamon, ginger, cloves, and nutmeg—were classified as hot and dry in the humoral system, naturally provocative of carnal urges in those so disposed. The lovers' milieu of the Song of Songs is pungent with spicy aroma, and exotically scented foods awaited arrivals in the Islamic paradisal garden, so that, as spice historian Jack Turner writes, "to point out the sexiness of spice was to state the obvious."

> *To the Franciscan encylopedist Bartholomew the Englishman, writing early in the thirteenth century, the erotic effects of spices were part of the cosmic order, inextricably linked to and explicable in terms of the larger schema of medical science and astrology. The spicer was one of several libidinous professions born under the sign of Venus, along with singers, jewelers, music lovers and tailors of women's clothing.*[3]

A little cinnamon and nutmeg might go a long way in the bedtime posset of a newlywed pair on their nuptial night, a customary recipe still going strong in eighteenth-century England. Indeed, a decoction of honey and ginger, smeared onto the carefully prewashed organ, was thought in the Middle East to be an infallible way of enlarging the penis. This was all very well, but the consensus was that general daily indulgence in spices could only be ruinous to the soul. It is not hard to imagine how chili peppers, with their raucous levels of the kind of warming glow that previously only pepper and ginger provided, fitted into this spiritual scheme on their introduction to European shores.

Over the ensuing centuries, the humoral system, which at least pretended to a kind of scientific rigor, gave place to the dietetic imaginary of Presbyterian ranters such as Sylvester Graham, one of the nineteenth century's most monomaniacal fulminators against the physical causes of spiritual pollution. Graham was obsessed with the deleterious effects of masturbation in the developing male, but he linked its weakening and maddening effect to the ingestion of gruesome stimulants such as tea and coffee, alcohol, meat, and—inevitably—spicy dishes. To underwrite a diet of bland wholesomeness, he invented the Graham cracker, a plain biscuit baked of coarsely sifted wholegrain flour, to be eaten ungarnished. The monitory tones of his disquisition on chastity, addressed as always to young men, are a masterpiece of the categorical utterance:

> *All kinds of stimulating and heating substances, high-seasoned food, rich dishes, the free use of flesh [for eating, that is], and even the excess of aliment, all, more or less—and some to a very great degree—increase the concupiscent excitability and sensibility of the genital organs, and augment their influence on the functions of organic life, and on the intellectual and moral faculties.*[4]

For pathos' sake, if nothing else, we may imagine that Graham's youthful reader, while paying due heed to its ghastly effects, sometimes found himself instinctively tipping a little too much red pepper on his steak, prior to an unsupervised evening constitutional with his girl.

With regard to what can be observed of the science of this, it seems likely the association of capsaicin and the rampant male libido is not causative in that order, but constitutive in the opposite direction. In other words, it isn't that chili will provoke sexually predatory behavior, it's more that it happens to be one of the obvious food preferences of men who are already predisposed that way. This at least was the finding of a team at the Université Grenoble Alpes in southern France, which tested a group of 114 young to middle-aged men by offering them a choice of salt and hot pepper sauce for seasoning a bowl of mashed potatoes: "A positive correlation was observed between endogenous salivary testosterone and the quantity of hot sauce individuals voluntarily and spontaneously consumed with a meal served as part of a laboratory task. . . . This study suggest that behavioral preference for spicy food among men is related to endogenous testosterone levels."[5] The study was widely interpreted to mean that consumption of capsaicin will raise testosterone levels, conferring greater potency on the male sexual impulse and promoting self-assertive and competitive social behavior, although its principal author said at the time of its publication that that effect had been observed only in rodents. There is also the possibility that it is precisely because a certain male social type enjoys being seen as a reckless adventurist and risk taker, an alpha male in all departments, that he has cultivated a taste for challenging food. Correlation does not automatically equate to causation, but the implicit belief that it must is a watchword of many a journalistic interpretation of what are essentially ambiguous findings.

For every piece of research action, it seems, there is an equal and opposite reaction. Thus *The Textbook of Clinical Sexual Medicine* throws a pail of cold water over the whole topic: "Although beta endorphins act as analgesics and pleasure inducers there is little evidence that they enhance libido. To the contrary several rat studies have shown that increased B-endorphins suppressed mating behaviors."[6] Meanwhile, Rita Strakosha, in a scientifically unverified, self-published 2017 paper entitled "Modern Diet and Stress Cause Homosexuality," which sets new standards in the hapless confusion of correlation and causality, claims that gay people are the victims of dietary imbalance, a condition that can easily be corrected by eating the right foods and eliminating the wrong ones. Among the latter are "heavy or rich foods, fatty or fried meals, spicy dishes [uh-oh], citrus fruits and carbonated drinks,"[7] which only leaves one wondering why what she thinks of as correctable sexual variance is not a first-world international epidemic.

Latter-day supporters of the doctrine of signatures, the medieval view that if a plant's fruits or leaves resembled a particular human body part, it would be medically useful in treating ailments of the same organ, will not need much encouragement to see the Peter pepper as a blaringly obvious invitation to sexual dynamism. A *Capsicum annuum* variety whose origins remain obscure, it is grown in the southern states and Mexico, is of medium Scoville intensity, but—most tantalizingly—has the precise shape and proportions of a penis. That is, it has a glans end complete with meatus and, depending on how you look at it, either a retracted or absent foreskin. It comes in tempting red, or an even more anatomically unimpeachable, if exotic, golden yellow. Its form has clearly been perfected through selective breeding from a naturally biomorphic original. Writing in the era before the superhot movement, pepper expert Jean Andrews said of it: "This blistering berry is too hot to eat; therefore, it is classed as an ornamental, or should we say as a conversation piece for the gardener who has everything?"[8]

It may well seem too much of a stretch to see the obvious contiguity between finding your mouth on fire with tormenting heat and being serenely in the mood for love. There is something more enraging than arousing in too much chili burn. If we are to see the homology at all persuasively, if it rests on anything more solid than the metaphorical continuities between the hotness of capsaicin and the hotness of sexual desire, it should probably be looked for in the sense of alertness that assertive spice promotes. The function of all spice in the diet, not just the piquant kinds but the gentler aromatic agents, too, is to raise ordinary protein and carbohydrate, even ordinary sugar, above the level of the humdrum. It adds deeper dimensions to taste, dimensions that become all the more complex when different and complementary spices are combined. Chili in particular, though, transforms that which might be perfectly delicious in itself into something more proactive on the palate by engaging the senses in a way that goes beyond that of taste pure and simple. It creates an awakeness, an acute responsiveness, a sharpened perceptiveness that rises above the principle of straightforwardly satiating oneself through eating. And in that state, the body may be reminded of the other registers of physical stimulation to which it can be subject. It depends, I would suggest, on the precise level of chili heat that any individual user can tolerate. Too much will be inimical to passion for most, but the zone of almost-too-much that the most dedicated aficionados classically reach for is surely the optimal preamble to the exploration of related kinds of sensuality.

The literature on chili as an aphrodisiac tends to focus primarily on what goes on internally after its ingestion, the release of endorphins and neurotransmitters creating a sense of well-being and pleasurable analgesia that then furnishes the stage for erotic activity. Prior to that, though, is the more immediate physiological effect of capsaicin on the soft tissues of the tongue and palate, and it is this that suggests its use as a sexual aid.

Flavor theorist John McQuaid reports that "native Americans rubbed hot peppers on their genitals to dull sensation and prolong their sexual pleasure—something early Spanish settlers also tried, to the dismay of prudish priests accompanying them."[9] This would seem to put it on a par with today's "delay sprays," but whereas the sprays function only through mild topical anesthetic agents such as benzocaine and lidocaine, capsaicin would have caused a certain amount of localized pain before blocking it through the systemic release of endorphin. Initially, the male user would have been hard put to it to use his genital organs at all, after which its benumbed state would have enabled him to sustain a longer performance. A 1997 patent application filed by a Danish inventor was for a capsaicin-based cream that could, it was claimed, produce erection of the male sexual organ within two minutes, and had prompted in experimental conditions an erectile response in an elderly man who had been impotent for many years.[10] Prior to that, in a research paper of 1994, an Italian team at Ferrara University reported in the *Scandinavian Journal of Urology and Nephrology* that an erectile response was induced in male subjects receiving an infusion of capsaicin in the urethra.[11]

Just as there is a legendarily thin line between love and hate, so there is also between the sensual enjoyment and utter torment of chili. Stray over that line, and the fire of chilies becomes something much more menacing, as we shall see next.

13

Fighting Talk—
Weaponized Chili

The fact that chili peppers create a sensation of pain or discomfort when eaten has made them one of the foremost acquired tastes in the history of world gastronomy and has variously conferred on them the reputations of daringly devilish or straight-ahead sexy, depending on your temperamental inclinations. Before their abrasive heat was enjoyed for its own sake, however, it occurred to the earliest consumers and cultivators of chili that their innate aggression against mammalian predators could be put to use as a tool of actual aggression. Throughout history, chili has been pressed into the service of hostility, alongside its benign and nutritious place in the human diet. Human history being what it is, if something has the power to hurt, it is sure to be used in that capacity.

We do not know exactly when chili was first used offensively, but when Spanish and Portuguese adventurers arrived in the Americas, they were frequently met with a practice that appeared to have ancient roots. In

1494, a war broke out between indigenous Taino people and the Spanish colonizers on the Caribbean island of Isabela, triggered by the disastrous collapse of the commercial entrepôt established there. Having mounted serial raids on Taino food stores in order to supply the shortages brought about by their own incompetence, the Spaniards, besieged in their fort, found themselves subjected to a prototype form of chemical warfare. Lacking anything to match the state-of-the-art Toledo steel swords of the Spanish, the Taino forces attacked by launching grenades of ground chili peppers at them. Packed into gourds, the pulverized chili was rendered cleverly airborne on impact by being mixed with ash, which carried it into the eyes and throats of the startled Spaniards, many of whom, blinded and choking, were then mercilessly cut down by advancing attackers who had protected themselves with bandanas worn like surgical masks.

In an apparent refinement of the grenade technique, ballistic chili took the form, among the Aztec and Maya, of gourds filled with peppers in water. The water caused the chilies to ferment, so that when the missiles were launched, their bursting on impact would release the noxious fermentation gases, reducing their victims to spluttering breathlessness.

Where it was impracticable to launch missiles of solid chili, the stinging fumes of smoke from burning chilies was deployed. This was the tactic used against Portuguese invaders in Brazil, and by the Inca against the Spanish in what was to become Peru. It, too, had pre-Columbian antecedents. During one of the periodic revolts against Aztec rule and its tribute system in the 1450s, the people of Cuetlaxtlan in modern-day Veracruz, in the northeastern zone of the empire, rose up against the local governor and assassinated him. When emissaries arrived from the court of Montezuma I to find out why the regular tribute payment was not forthcoming, the local chieftains responded by sealing all the air vents in the Aztecs' sleeping quarters and then setting fire to a carefully constructed pile of chilies. Subjected to what might well have been history's first gas chamber, the imperial messengers were asphyxiated and killed.[1]

We recall also the apparently savage use by Aztec parents of burning chili smoke as a means of chastisement for recalcitrant children, as depicted on Folio 60r of the *Codex Mendoza*. The gloss on the illustrations provided by contemporary Spanish authors notes that children of both sexes might be introduced to this extreme disciplinary practice at the age of eleven. For persistently ignoring his parents' instructions, the boy is being punished with dry chili smoke. "The father holds his naked, weeping son over a fire of burning chilies; the inhaling of the acrid smoke was considered a cruel torment" (in fact a potentially lethal one, as the example of the asphyxiated imperial messengers shows). The girl is only threatened with the fire, receiving a preliminary prickle of it in her nostrils. "The weeping child . . .

kneels, hands bound, confronted with the chili fire as a threat to reinforce conformity."[2] Even if the children were exposed to the chili fumes for only a few seconds, perhaps repeated at short intervals, this seems a particularly draconian recourse, until we turn to the next register of the folio and discover that, once he had turned twelve, a son's punishments might include being bound hand and foot and left stretched out naked on wet ground for a whole day, crying piteously according to the illustration.

Use of smoke asphyxiation from chilies was still being practiced by Native Americans in the so-called Indian Wars of the late nineteenth century. In an audacious raid to free kidnapped Apache women and children in the 1880s, the warrior Fun, second cousin of the great war leader known as Geronimo, employed chili fumes against a group of Mexican miners barricaded inside an adobe church, into which he dropped a bomb of ground chilies mixed with burning wood and pine sap. In the ensuing panic, the miners were sufficiently incapacitated that the prisoners they had press-ganged into working for them could be released.

From mustard gas to nuclear fission, the twentieth century elevated weapons research and deployment to a pitch not seen before in human history. There is seemingly no method of killing and injuring that has not been deployed at one time or another by the advanced industrial nations against each other. Some of these were so gruesome in their effects that they became subject to international treaty strictures forbidding them. Others, many in tottering stockpiles, lie in wait for their moment. At what is known as the "less-than-lethal" end of the spectrum, irritants used in crowd control, to disperse riots, and as personal self-defense agents draw on a wide range of laboratory-formulated chemical substances and natural plant materials, the latter often in synthesized or highly concentrated form. Among these, capsaicin has played a significant role, and is available to the arsenals of police and security forces, and private citizens, too, in many jurisdictions, as an instantly effective means of disabling a potential attacker.

The modern use of lethal and irritant gases dates from World War I, which saw phosgene and chlorine, among other materials, used against troops on the battlefield. Capsaicin was also synthesized at this time but appears not to have been among the harassing agents used in the hostilities. It began to be industrially manufactured at the U.S. military's Edgewood Arsenal facility in the early 1920s but was quickly superseded in 1928 by the development of a British substance that came to be known as CS gas. As a result, capsaicin lay dormant as a weapon for several decades until the refinement in the 1970s of a method of extracting an active resin, a reddish brown oily compound called oleoresin capsicum (OC), from chili peppers. This in turn began to supplant the use of CS gas in incidents of civil disorder. Pepper sprays used by the police may be up to 15 percent capsaicin and its related natural compounds, while the devices sold for personal use are restricted to no more than a nonetheless pretty effective 1 percent. Aimed directly into the eyes or face of an assailant, OC has an instant, incapacitating effect, causing acute irritation to the eyes and nose on impact, and to the lungs and gastrointestinal tract on inhalation and ingestion, as well as inflammation of the skin, because capsaicin tricks the body into inflaming itself. Any severe irritation of the eyes causes them to close up tight, effectively blinding the recipient, and a prolonged choking cough, making speech impossible, ensues. The body's recovery from this will take at least forty-five minutes, and can take up to several hours. There are very few cases of fatalities caused by use of OC spray, and where there are, there may have been other aggravating medical factors. It is obviously particularly noxious to people with debilitating respiratory conditions.

Since the 1990s, pepper sprays for personal use have been big business in many countries, while remaining illegal in others, including the United Kingdom and much of mainland Europe. Not only are they used by women to ward off potential physical assaults, but workers in the United States Postal Service are licensed to use them against their ancestral enemy, hostile dogs, and forest campers against bears. By contrast, they are now forbidden, as are all riot control agents, from use in warfare, under article I:5 of the Chemical Weapons Convention of 1997. This has been both signed and ratified by all nations with the exception of North

Korea, South Sudan, and Egypt. Israel has signed it but not ratified it.

In 2010, the Defense Research and Development Organization of India announced that it had developed a chili grenade for use in terrorist incidents and counterinsurgency operations. It contains a preparation of bhut jolokia, the so-called ghost chili (then the hottest variety in the world, but since overtaken several times), and phosphorus in an 81mm missile. As well as being fitted for use as a hand grenade, it is also being mounted on tanks, from which it can create an instantaneous smokescreen that is effective up to ninety meters away, preventing attackers from using night-vision technology and thermal imaging. It is expected to be particularly successful at forcing insurgents out of their hideouts, and has already been deployed against militants in the fractious Kashmir region. Officially classified as nonlethal, it has nonetheless been blamed by medical authorities for several deaths since its introduction. Somehow inevitably, its potential target base has been expanded creatively, too. In September 2017, chili grenades were launched by Indian armed forces against Rohingya refugee people fleeing persecution in Myanmar via Bangladesh in an aggressive attempt to stop them at the border.

Weapons-grade chili may not be the happiest aspect of the centuries-long interaction between humans and capsaicin, but it represents an anthropological form of primitive imitation. If the hot pepper had never bared its chemical fangs at humanity in the first place, members of the world's most destructive species would never have learned to turn its fire on one another.

14

Superhots and Chiliheads— The Cult of Chili

The rise of the superhot movement in the United States particularly, and more generally throughout the English-speaking world, constitutes an unprecedented cultural phenomenon. There have been moments throughout food history when certain ingredients and commodities became passionately sought after. One has only to point to the wider spectrum of spices to discover a magnificent obsession that drove international trading relations to a remarkable degree in the late medieval and early modern period. Eastern spices such as peppercorns, nutmeg, mace, cinnamon, and ginger were avidly consumed for their perceived exoticism, their aura of mystical distant lands of which even educated Europeans knew very little, and the social status they conferred through their value and the logistical complexity of importing them. In this respect, as we saw in part 2, chili broke the mold, because although it seemed exotic enough, it required only adequate protection from frost and it would more or less grow anywhere.

Some food trends had more obvious dietetic under-pinnings, as was the case during the seventeenth century in the American craze for sassafras. Native to the eastern seaboard from Canada to central Florida, the deciduous tree had a number of culinary as well as medicinal uses. Its roots and leaves were used in traditional root beer and sassafras tea (banned in commercial products by the Food and Drug Administration in 1960 over concerns about the carcinogenic potential of its essential oil), and it was used as a herb in Louisiana Creole cooking for seasoning dishes such as gumbo. Its leaves and flowers found their way into salad bowls and into formulas for curing meats, and its dried root bark was an ingredient in the purgative tonic sarsaparilla. It had been used by the Choctaw people of the southern states for centuries; they dried and powdered it for medicinal applications, and also added it to their cooking. The effect of this example on white settlers was such that sassafras became an essential standby of both the domestic larder and the medicine cupboard. Indeed, it was mistakenly believed that it was efficacious against syphilis. Its popularity was so great that, as the seventeenth century progressed, it became Virginia's second most lucrative cash crop behind tobacco. These days, it still exists in the form of filé powder, made from the leaves, for seasoning and thickening the filé gumbo immortalized by the great Hank Williams in his 1952 song "Jambalaya (On The Bayou)." Otherwise, the sassafras craze has long passed.

There was a hazily defined historical point late in the nineteenth century at which oysters stopped being the food of the poor and became the must-have appetite-whetter of the well-to-do. Oysters Rockefeller, draped in enough anise-laced green herb butter to suggest the crinkling of greenbacks, was a typical restaurant dish of the transition period, formulated to a secret recipe at Antoine's in New Orleans in 1899. In early Victorian London, nothing could have been further from opulent luxury, as Sam Weller puts it to his employer on a tour through one of the shabbier purlieus of the capital in Dickens' first novel, *The Pickwick Papers* (1837). "'It's a wery remarkable circumstance, Sir,' said Sam, "that poverty and oysters always seem to go together. . . . [T]he poorer a place is, the greater call there seems to be for oysters. . . . [H]ere's a oyster-stall to every half-dozen houses. The street's lined vith 'em. Blessed if I don't think that ven a man's wery poor, he rushes out of his lodgings, and eats oysters in reg'lar desperation.'"[1] What turned oysters into recherché fashion items on both sides of the Atlantic was precisely their previous popularity. As the industrial cities filled with laborers, they snaffled most of them up, and waters polluted with industrial effluent did the rest. Their increased rarity, and the need to ensure they came from pristine marine environments, then inflated their market value, leading restaurants such as Antoine's to create suitably high-toned recipes for them, transforming the oyster from an everyday standby to an exclusive ornament of the most plutocratic tables.

The chili movement is another creature altogether. It is not about luxury, is only tenuously about exoticism, especially when most of the chilies and chili products consumed at a chili festival are likely to have been grown locally, and it is not particularly about rarity. The very hottest pepper varieties may be unusual enough items, and not seen on the general market, but the seeds are available to anybody with dirt in which to grow them. What the chiliheads' obsession seems to be about is a combination of gourmet devotion to a particular taste and a single-minded urge to self-fashioning through food. Driven by events such as the Hot Sauce Expo in New York, the annual Fiery Foods Show in Albuquerque, and the year-round network of festivals large and small that comprise the chili calendar in the United Kingdom, superhot peppers and their sauces are now big business. There is in the chili movement something of the connoisseurship attached to the markets for fine wines, specialty craft beers and upscale whiskeys, allied to the cultish feel of such fringe enthusiasms as model aircraft clubs, in which initiates swap tips and cherished memories in online forums, in between attending convocations of the like-minded. Tastings, sales, cookery demonstrations, eating competitions and, very often, as much mariachi music as you can handle, are the backdrop to a shared passion that, far from being a niche peculiarity, is out and proud. It has been concentrated mainly in the United States, Great Britain, and Australia, but Scandinavians are now getting in on the act, too, with Finland's Chilifest and Denmark's Chilifan Chilifestival among the annual events that bring an inner glow to frozen northerners.

Professor Paul Bosland, who founded and oversees the Chile Pepper Institute at the University of New Mexico, emphasizes the generational aspect of the superhot movement. "When I first started the Institute," he reports, "I was asked many times, 'Do you think chili peppers are a fad or a trend?' Thirty years later, I am not asked that any more. One of the reasons for the current popularity is that young people love spicy foods. The young generation has embraced the culture of hot foods."[2] This makes obvious sense, in that it has tended to be the rising generation in all eras that establishes new trends that older generations may (or may not) later pick up on. Certainly, the risk element, and the difficulty in calculating it, is also emblematic of a youthfully ardent thirst for new experiences. The intriguing aspect of this is that, unlike death metal, it is not a taste that wears thin with age. Once the predilection for chili has taken root, it sticks.

It is also the case that there are more opportunities these days to learn about aspects of food than ever before. To anybody even minimally interested in cooking food, the sources available, at all levels of technical proficiency, are legion. More cookbooks are published every year now than has ever been the case in seven centuries of printed recipe collections, and they are able to presume an unprecedented range of resources in the average urban reader. Even if you don't make it to a chili festival or a chili farm, the wealth of published and broadcast material on this and other hot topics is greater than it was for previous generations. "The popularity of television food shows has given many more people a chance to learn about chili peppers and how to use them," notes Bosland. Nothing quite matches hearing or reading about something to make you want to experience it firsthand, and in this way, the chili movement has enjoyed a particularly widespread dissemination through media outlets.

This is a point echoed by Ed Currie of the Pucker-Butt Pepper Company in South Carolina. "I honestly don't believe it's a last-few-years thing. Hot sauce and salsa overtook ketchup, mustard and mayonnaise as the number one and two condiments in the U.S. back in 2004 and worldwide in 2006. What I think it is, is that the media has finally caught on and is looking for new and exciting things. A producer from CNN told me that before I did the PBS thing in 2011 [a film about his chili business in which Currie talked about his original motivation to research the use of chilies for their medicinal properties], there was an average of two stories a year about peppers nationally. I've been on TV over 200 times since then and in over 10,000 media outlets worldwide. There are stories all the time now about the medicinal benefits, and the popularity of the YouTube personal channels just added to it, especially when they started monetizing ads."[3] The news media loves nothing better than a trend, and frequently feeds off its own confirmation of a trend. Something that has become a widespread cultural preoccupation, and starts to receive ubiquitous coverage and analysis, very often arose as a media creation in the first place. This does not necessarily mean it is something absurd or malevolent, although much is, but it can also be a way of disseminating taste on a scale that rapidly becomes normative. In some matters, the media has done nothing more than pick up on something that was already happening, but by the sustained attention and the spectacularized framing to which it is subjected, it becomes a whole new phenomenon.

In the case of chili, Currie is surely right. There was already a thriving market for hot pepper sauces, salsas, powders, and whole peppers themselves, supported here and there by articles in specialist food magazines and niche cookbooks with small print runs, before the broadcast and print media picked up on it. That in turn has led to the YouTube videos of people making hot sauces, recording their flushing and gasping and vomiting reactions to eating hot peppers, and—in more than one enterprising case—immersing themselves in bathtubs filled with a hundred liters of chili sauce, screaming blue murder for the edification of a world of online gawkers. The resulting hoopla has helped generate a festival circuit, thriving Internet businesses, online forums, and a coterie of informed opinion. In consequence, it has all ascended far above a simple food predilection and been transformed into a community of interest and expertise, united by an index of cultural self-identification. The chilihead, as we shall see in greater detail in the next chapter, is not just a straightforward enthusiast, but a recognized psychological type.

There is one decisive aspect to any food craze, though, that in most cases towers above all others. It's one thing to want to be the new kid on the block with a particular product, but make a bold and fundamental health claim about it, and people will flock to the market to buy it. This has been a long and enduring tradition throughout the world, especially with regard to new foods when they are still relatively unfamiliar to the masses. If new foods were not perceived as dangerous toxins, or as the decadent recourse of the idle rich, or as the savage provender of uncivilized tribes somewhere, they were advertised and promoted as health-giving elixirs. Sometimes a single ingredient passed through more than one of these stages, as did the potato on its arrival in Europe. Many commentators viewed it as pestilential, a possible cause of leprosy or fatal fever. Once those myths were put to flight, it was grudgingly approved by authorities such as the great French encyclopedist Denis Diderot, who noted that it caused flatulence and was starchy and tasteless when cooked, but might do well enough for the robust peasantry, those who didn't mind what form their sustenance came in as long as they had plenty and were not especially punctilious about succumbing to farting. In France, the potato's PR campaign was mounted most effectively by the pharmacist Antoine-Augustin Parmentier, who in the 1770s formulated a potato bread recipe for hungry Parisians, but who also staged opulent society spectaculars in which potato dishes formed the pièces de résistance, and at which Benjamin Franklin was among the honored guests. Parmentier sent bouquets of delicate mauve potato blossoms to Louis XVI and Marie Antoinette and arranged for a spurious armed guard to surround the potato patch in his own gardens, to give the impression that the mysterious tubers were worth purloining.

In eighteenth-century England, the potato was distrusted as a harbinger of Catholicism, which had been finally officially scuttled out of the national constitution by the settlement of 1688 but was forever ready to seep insidiously back in through the back door. To the cry of "No popery!" in the political agitation of the era was added the equally stern injunction "No potatoes!" By the following century, British cooks would be setting them around the roasting joint and pounding them to mash in the workers' eel and pie shops of industrial London. The potato was too productive to ignore, disastrously so in the famine caused by the crop failures of the Irish monoculture in the 1840s. In all European contexts, though, what helped the potato to a general assimilation into the everyday diet was that it was nourishing. It could sustain the manual laborer through the aching hours of toil of the long working day, its nutritional value undergirded by the satiety it provided at very modest outlay.

The medicinal benefits now being claimed for chili peppers outdo anything ever claimed on behalf of the potato. A food that can prolong life; guard against cancer, heart disease, and diabetes; promote the burning of fat and lead to weight loss; lower high blood pressure; reduce bad cholesterol; regenerate cells; soothe intestinal turmoil; counteract inflammatory conditions; keep skin healthy; relieve sinus congestion; fight migraine; and generally make you feel good about yourself has got to have something going for it, even if only some of these claims are substantiated. Remedies that promise better health and happiness go back to North America's pioneering days. In the hardscrabble lives of families on the trail during America's great push west, anything that sounded like a cure-all found a ready audience. Traveling doctors selling miraculous panaceas from the backs of covered wagons, often with the choreographed aid of an assistant in the crowd who claimed to have been rescued from death's threshold by the miracle tonic, were guaranteed a responsive hearing, even after many such enterprises had been exposed for the charlatanism they undoubtedly were. There is nothing particularly illogical about wanting to find vital sustenance in what we consume, and while the focus may have shifted in the present day from proprietary formulas to the dietary supplements of health stores, and the eye-catching claims made on behalf of this or that natural ingredient in the diet, the impulse to find the golden key to long life through the simple act of consumption remains as strong as ever—stronger now that coronary heart disease, strokes, and obesity stalk our affluent lands more virulently than ever before.

The research currently being undertaken with regard to the therapeutic potential of capsaicin is often very exciting, but it remains important to keep perspective. Any nutritional value from eating peppers should be interpreted in the light of the relatively small amounts that most people eat at any one time. A single chili pepper added to a salad or a stir-fry is not going to make a whole heap of difference to the day's nutritional intake. The most promising results, as found in the Chinese study cited in part 1, are recorded among populations who eat chili-rich dishes and condiments pretty much every day. While the taste for superhot sauces has spread like the wildfire it undoubtedly is, even the most dedicated chiliheads are outpaced for average daily consumption by the Bhutanese, Sichuanese, Indians, and Thais for whom chili has become as inevitable and indispensable as salt in the daily diet. You could take a daily capsaicin supplement for the concentrated hit it delivers, but dietary supplements and the claims made for them occupy a liminal zone between nutrition and medication.

When all is said and done, a daily tablet, very possibly on top of the range of other daily tablets you are already taking, seems a boring commitment, even with the chimerical promise of longer life, contentment, and clearer skin that it offers.

Chilies and their products are a much more enticing way of receiving whatever health benefits capsaicin confers. The problem for many people, of course, is the ferocious burn with which chilis attack the palate and the possible digestive calamities that follow—and to which some people never become comfortably habituated. That, more than anything, is why chili in the Western world has become, at its most dedicated, the preserve of a particular psychological and emotional attitude. A liking for chili is not just a food preference. It has become an achievement, one that appears to embrace the very opposite of a concern for health and well-being.

Meanwhile, a healthy dose of skepticism is often an effective tonic against the wilder claims of the peripheral health industry. Snake oil never prolonged anybody's life, but a balanced and conscientious approach to nutrition indisputably will. The trick is to find the gold amid the dross. In May 1916, the United States attorney for Rhode Island issued a legal determination against one Clark Stanley, a Providence cowboy who styled himself the "Rattlesnake King," freelance purveyor of a snake-oil liniment that, he claimed, could relieve pain and lameness, soothe the symptoms of rheumatism, neuralgia, sciatica, sore throat, and toothache, and act as an antidote to the toxic bites and stings of animals, insects, and reptiles—all for a mere fifty cents a bottle. Analysis of a sample of Stanley's product by the Bureau of Chemistry on behalf of the district court had established that it contained no snake-derived product whatsoever. The accused entered a guilty plea and was fined $20 for misbranding. Whether the product had any medical value or not was beside the point. It simply wasn't what Stanley claimed it was. What it was found to comprise was light petroleum oil mixed with a dash of beef fat, traces of camphor and turpentine, perhaps for their apothecarial aromas, and chili pepper.[4] The case may have helped fix the reputation of snake oil as the permanent symbol of a quack remedy, the stock-in-trade of grifters of all stripes from spurious self-appointed doctors to multinational retailers, but Stanley's liniment was more or less the same thing as modern capsaicin cream.

15

Man Food—How Chili Became a Guy Thing

What the rise of the superhot movement, and the competitive breeding of ever-hotter chilies, have demonstrated beyond doubt is that the taste for red-hot spice is an overwhelmingly male preoccupation. Not many cultural phenomena of which that can be said have survived into the twenty-first century with their dignity intact, but eating searingly hot food is one of them, not least because it leaves its devotees, despite all the mythologizing talk of the sexiness of chili, pretty much incapacitated for anything else for quite a while afterward. As Rudyard Kipling nearly said, if you can eat a bowl of flaming Texas red and keep your head, while all about you are losing theirs and hosing themselves down with milk, then you'll be a man, my son.

In several senses, this is hardly surprising. Chili eating pushes all the buttons for what might be seen as alpha male behavior. It involves serious risk. The consequences for some participants in chili competitions have been anything but pleasant. Vomiting may be only the start of it, and if the potential hazards include an acutely inflamed esophagus, this is an activity that can be put on a par with those extreme sports in which the danger of a life-changing injury is courted with wild abandon. People serving in the armed forces frequently put themselves in harm's way in the course of carrying out their duties in war zones and violently unstable regions, but there is a sense of necessity to that. Willingly incurring pointless risk takes courage to a whole other level, which some would see as foolhardy. The diehard chili eater laughs in the face of danger. He is prepared to take on whatever capsaicin can throw at him and live to tell the tale—at least after the soft tissue of his mouth has calmed down enough to make speech a viable proposition once more. Inside the breast of every chilihead beats the heart of a daredevil.

The second important aspect is competitiveness. It is simply not enough to demonstrate that you can swallow a Carolina Reaper. You have to be able to do it more quickly than anybody else, in greater quantities than anybody else, and when everybody else has given up. Any kind of behavior that involves exemplary risk taking carries the implication that it is worth measuring who can take the biggest risks, and for the longest time. In Britain, the same prerogative once applied to young men eating in Indian restaurants, often after an evening's heroic intake of beer. The menus that graded the sauces in dishes according to their level of fieriness— starting at very gently spiced creamy korma, and ascending through rogan josh and madras to the palate-scorching realms of vindaloo and phal—were not entirely in the business of gastronomic education, but acted as templates for those who wanted to take their ability to withstand hot spice to the next level. Half the pleasure of eating vindaloo was the awestruck shudders it evoked in those around you who were having difficulties enough with the lime pickle. The same is true of today's chili competitions. There can be no more satisfying experience than eating something you wholeheartedly enjoy while at the same time impressing everybody around you that you are managing to eat it at all. If you come away from it with a trophy or a certificate in your hand, all the better.

Above and beyond the factors of risk and competitiveness, there is also something about the sheer gratuitousness of eating chilies that is specifically male. For all that chilies are supremely nutritious, there is nothing to be gained from eating hotter and hotter manifestations. The nutrients could much more easily be found in other foods, or in milder chilies for that matter. There is a sublimely nonfunctional aspect to chili eating. It recalls the celebrated response of the British mountaineer George Mallory when asked, in an interview for *The New York Times* in 1923, tellingly entitled "Climbing Mount Everest is work for supermen," why he wanted to scale the world's highest peak. "Because it's there," he replied.[1] The following year, he was to perish on its north face in the course of another attempt.

Despite the admiration to be gained from being the first to do something, or from winning a prize for doing it, there is nothing in itself to recommend engaging in a hazardous activity when there is no need to do so. The mere fact of doing it is thrilling, to be sure, but it is entirely self-justifying in its raison d'être. Each successive new entry for the hottest chili in *Guinness World Records* is daring diehard chiliheads to eat it.

Of course, there is nothing about any of these aspects of chili eating that should not apply to women equally well. Certainly, the self-sacrifice that chili consumption seems to summon in its most dedicated exponents is hardly an unknown quantity in women's lives, and women distinguish themselves continually in circumstances that demand courage and in the competitive field of sports. There must be particular reasons then for the overwhelmingly male-dominated nature of the superhot movement. The most obvious of these would point to the mixture of evolutionary psychology and cultural expectation that has valorized competitive risk taking, and gratuitous risk taking at that, among males throughout history. In primordial times, such behavior would have established efficient hierarchies among bands of hunters, whose activities helped keep their entire social cohort alive. It was also a means of competitively deciding which ones would make the best breeding material. The physically strongest could afford to be the bravest, and the more likely to produce offspring strong enough to survive. These factors are still seen throughout the natural world, and although humans diverged a very long time ago along the path of socialization and cultural complexity, so that they are not as subject to nature's dictates as all other species on earth, they nonetheless retain the genetic imprint of their ancient influence. Despite all the efforts of sexual politics in the postwar era, archetypal gender definitions have remained stubbornly resistant to being demolished, not least on the male side, because they seem to the unreconstructed male to deliver so many benefits.

Another facet of this debate is raised by the eternally vexed question of the relative ability of the two sexes to deal with pain. Are there simply more male chiliheads because they can handle the burn better than women can? Although popular belief widely holds that the pronounced torment of childbirth has fitted women to cope with pain better than men do, and helped generate the myth of male oversusceptibility to even the most trivial of everyday illnesses, the evidence is generally in the opposing direction. There are two factors at work in this: the threshold at which pain is felt and the tolerance for it. It remains a difficult experience to measure in experimental conditions because it mainly relies on subjective reporting of pain, in which the cultural pressure mentioned above may well lead men to appear to be able to endure it for the sake of preserving their masculinity. That in itself, however, raises the question of whether pretending to endure pain helps you actually to endure it. The only way around the subjectivity

of it all, though, is to build in a motivation factor, as
was tried during experiments by a team at the University of Florida in 2017. Subjects were asked to keep one
hand in a container of freezing-cold water for up to five
minutes, some of them being offered a dollar if they
made it, while others were offered $20. For the women,
the extra cash incentive made no difference, but the
men who were offered more lasted longer in the ordeal
than those who were offered less. This would suggest
that even motivated women are less well equipped to
deal with pain than motivated men, although the leader
of the research, Dr. Roger Fillingim, concedes that the
experiment could simply show that money is the wrong
motivator for women.[2]

Women's ability to tolerate pain is governed to a large
extent by the hormone estrogen, meaning that during
the low-estrogen phase of the menstrual cycle, they
are more susceptible to it. Then again, male laboratory animals injected with estrogen, in the kinds of experiments nobody really wants to think about, display
lower tolerance for pain than the untreated males, while
those females dosed with testosterone become better
able to handle it. By the same token, females deprived
of estrogen display stress responses similar to those of
the males. The function of the female hormone in this
regard may not after all be to dull sensitivity to pain,
but to switch on the body's recognition of it in the first
place. This seems to explain why certain opioid pain-

killers work better for women than for men, and may lead eventually to gender-specific medical pain relief.[3]

Ed Currie, chili breeder and hot sauce producer, adds a little firsthand perspective on this tendency from direct interaction with his clients. He believes it is necessary to separate the ability to tolerate heat from the need to demonstrate it competitively. "I believe it has nothing to do with machismo. Women make up about 60 percent of our customers and can usually handle heat better, owing to a number of physiological factors. In the contest, yes, it is a man thing, because women aren't ego-driven idiots like we are, but overall, the love of heat knows no gender."[4]

The competitive chili scene is the prerogative of people who are driven to extremes of sensation-seeking. Much research has been undertaken since the 1970s to understand what motivates this type of behavior. Sensation-seeking (SS) individuals crave intensity, novelty, variety, and complexity in the experiences they have, and are prepared to incur personal and social risk in order to achieve them. These may include participation in dangerous contact sports, use of psychoactive substances, risky sexual behaviors, hazardous driving, pathological gambling, and, of course, a predisposition to very spicy food. What impels such people is the activation of reward responses in the brain, particularly those triggering release of the neurotransmitter dopamine, one of the body's principal natural chemicals for making us feel good. The sensual relief afforded by drinking a glass of cold water on a very hot day is a function of the brain's encouragement system to do something that is ultimately good for the organism as a whole. For some people, though, the reward system is activated by more adventurous behavior. To them, the glass of water is just a glass of water, and some way short of a sensual roller coaster. Add in a little hang gliding, followed by a session at the roulette table, and then a red-hot Thai banquet, and now you're talking. Interestingly, this may be because they already have elevated natural levels of dopamine in their system, so the reward system for them is always starting from a higher base. As Agnes Norbury and Masud Husein, authors of a 2015 paper in the journal *Behavioral Brain Research*, explain, evidence from recent studies "suggests that individuals higher in SS personality may exhibit both higher endogenous dopamine levels and greater dopaminergic responses to cues of upcoming reward."[5]

How does this relate to gender, though? Norbury and Husein note that one of the reasons that some SS individuals seek substances such as amphetamine and cocaine, which have a directly stimulant effect on the dopamine receptors, is that they show increased responses to these materials above and beyond the expected psychoactive impact. This also holds true for psychoactives that do not directly target the dopamine response, such as painkillers, tranquilizers, and alcohol. Although the proscribed stimulants have been shown to trigger higher levels of dopamine in women than in men, there is more of a correlation between its release and cognitive effects like sensation-seeking in men, seemingly because of the hormonal modulation that dopamine transmission undergoes in the presence of testosterone in the male body. Put very simply, women may be getting more dopamine than men from pleasurable stimulation, but men's bodies are doing more with the smaller quantity they get. It's the difference between simply feeling a sensation and actually positively enjoying it. Obviously, capsaicin is not amphetamine, but there is a final common pathway among all such stimulations that results in dopamine release, and the positive correlation between that response and subjectively reported feelings of elation, exhilaration, and sensual satisfaction is, so far at least, found to be specifically male.[6]

That said, Norbury, a research associate in cognitive neuroscience at Cambridge University, cautions against tying the susceptibility to sensation seeking too obviously to any physical differences between male and female subjects. "There is no strong evidence for a physiological or other biological difference being the basis of the differences in questionnaire scores. It would be important to discount the undoubted strong effects of social conditioning on gender differences in sensation-seeking behaviors, such as chili-eating, in teenagers and adults before thinking about some kind of innate biological difference."[7] In other words, nobody should run off with the idea that there are more men than women in competitive chili consumption because the female palate has a harder time handling it. Besides which, as Currie puts it, sounding a philosophical note: "As far as pleasure versus pain is concerned, doesn't everything that's good in our lives cause us both?"

The last plank in our attempt to explain why chili seems to be predominantly man food is the most speculative and least measurable postulate of all. It is the apparent readiness of men to engage in activities that are essentially silly, a willingness to make fools of themselves that might begin with frat-boy antics, run through initiation ceremonies that scale every height of physical hazard and plumb every depth of tastelessness, and rise at their most impressive to overblown romantic gestures in pursuit of the love of their lives. A recent quasi-scientific paradigm known as Male Idiot Theory (MIT) suggests that no fewer than 90 percent of avoidable grisly deaths from incautious behavior are met by men. Hitching a shopping cart to the back of a train to get a free ride home or cutting the steel hawser of an elevator in an attempt to steal it—while standing in the elevator itself—are only two of the enterprising ways that men have found to wade out of the vale of tears before their time. If there is an established gender divide in ordinary risk-taking behavior, there is an even more pronounced one, seemingly, when it comes to incurring idiotic and unnecessary risk. The authors of a paper on

MIT published in the *British Medical Journal* in 2014, wrote:

> *Idiotic risks are defined as senseless risks, where the apparent payoff is negligible or nonexistent, and the outcome is often extremely negative and often final. According to male idiot theory, many of the differences in risk-seeking behavior, emergency department admissions, and mortality may be explained by the observation that men are idiots and idiots do stupid things.*

One of the factors in these spectacularly catastrophic behaviors may be alcohol, which is not to say that men who drink necessarily always drink more than women, but that their response to it may embolden them to do stupider things than women would ever contemplate. This results in stories that are too tragic to be funny, such as the trio of men who played a game of Russian roulette that involved alternately slugging liquor shots and stamping on an unexploded Cambodian land mine. Eventually, the mine blew up, taking all three of them and the bar itself with it. Some of these people are nominated, many posthumously, for Darwin Awards, which are predicated on the idea that, in order to ensure the survival of the fittest of the species, congenital idiots eliminate themselves from the human gene pool by their inability to calculate risk meaningfully. In 2014, men constituted 88.7 percent of the award nominees, a finding of striking statistical significance. To some extent, risk taking is accounted for by external factors. Men are more likely to be employed in high-risk occupations and more likely to engage in rough contact sports, but these cannot be the only explanations, as the authors of the *BMJ* article note. "[S]ex differences in risk-seeking behavior have been reported from an early age, raising questions about the extent to which these behaviors can be attributed purely to social and cultural differences." It's also important to differentiate between types of risk. "[T]here is a class of risk—the idiotic risk—that is qualitatively different from those associated with, say, contact sports or adventure pursuits such as parachuting."[8]

The question is then: Where does chili fit along this spectrum? Can eating superhots, too, be construed as classic male idiot behavior? A coauthor of the *BMJ* paper, Ben Lendrem, comments:

In the case of competitive chili consumption, the presence of risk is undeniable, with vomiting at its least, and death at its worst. As it is a predominantly male sport and there is a present risk, I believe it would come under that category. It could be argued that the risk is not idiotic as some, in that winning the competition would garner some respect and possibly a prize, but that would vary from competition to competition.[9]

While the worldwide culinary taste for chili itself is obviously gender-neutral, the activity of competitive chili eating is anything but. If there is out-and-out idiotic risk, and there is also the kind of finely calibrated survival risk that soldiers take in battle zones, somewhere between the two lies a type of risk that is not remotely necessary but is nonetheless rewarding, not quite accurately calculable and yet gratifying. It appears to form an overlap between pursuits such as extreme sports with all their associated daredevilry and the category of idiotic risk that the *BMJ* authors identify. The forty-seven-year-old man who entered a contest to eat Indian bhut jolokia, the infamous ghost pepper, in 2016, and ended with an inch-wide tear in his esophagus was very lucky to escape with his life, following an intensive period of hospitalization over three weeks.[10] I have no wish to apply such a harsh designation in this particular case, but given that it received widespread publicity and that any future sufferer from the same effect could well end as a fatality, would you not have to be an idiot, and very probably a male idiot at that, to go down the same route? Yet people have and will. Where does the enjoyment of capsaicin, and the determination to prove oneself adept at tolerating its extremes, turn into possible Darwinian self-elimination?

16

The Globalization of Taste— Can Chili Save Us?

The evolution of taste in the postmodern world has been informed by a gigantic paradox. It consists in the fact that the range of the everyday diet in the developed world is more broadly based now than it has ever been in human history. People have a spectrum of options available to them that would have baffled their parents in their youth, and been entirely uncharted territory to their grandparents. One can proceed day by day from Chinese food to Indian to Mexican to Moroccan to Greek to Thai to Italian and back again, and even if many of these cuisines are experienced only in the form of fast food or supermarket ready meals, they command a degree of reference that has only been gradually learned by the most recent generations. Restaurants of divergent ethnicities, and no ethnicity at all, have always existed, but they are not generally where taste is formed, more where it is confirmed, at least at the upper end of the scale.

At the same time, despite this proliferating diversity and forming a slightly unstable counterbalance to it, is the relentless homogenization of taste. There may be tamales and foo young, jalfrezi, and stifado, but what overwhelmingly constitutes the international diet is the uniform pabulum of burgers and fries, pizza, fried chicken, sandwiches, tacos, doughnuts, ice cream, and chocolate. This is the hegemonic Western regimen that has successfully colonized more or less every region of the earth, and is readily taken up by younger people in the developing world as a luxurious alternative to the very indigenous food styles in which more aspirational Westerners have painstakingly schooled themselves. That the largest burger chain on the face of the planet could achieve its most extensive European penetration in France, world citadel of gastronomy since the Enlightenment, at the cost of little more than a momentary flurry of violent dissent among farmers in the Languedoc, is a massive indicator not just of the transmutation of taste but of cultural upheaval, too.

Food writers may righteously bewail this state of affairs, and many countervailing movements have sprung up to try to offset its global power. The world's various systems for protecting designations of origin for particular foods; the locavore movement that may mean eating only produce that has been grown in one of these protected designations, or only eating food grown a little way up the road from where you live; the slow food movement that would like us to take as long over eating, and thinking about food, as our leisured ancestors used to; eating only food that has been grown in conjunction with phases of the moon, or at the very least organically; the various subtraction diets that aim to rebalance planetary ecology, as well as the individual human body, by cutting out meat, fish, dairy products, cooked food, processed food, solid food, anything containing ingredients your grandparents would not have heard of, anything that would have been unavailable to our paleolithic forebears as they scraped a bare existence on the African grasslands of prehistory: all are attempts to avoid the straitjacket of corporately influenced eating that has the rest of the affluent world bound fast in its restraints. And yet the overall effect of them is minuscule in the context of the globalized diet. Indeed, in some quarters, these movements have spawned defiant countercurrents in the form of so-called dirty eating and guilty eating. If you've eaten a bowl of porridge for breakfast or shaved a little carrot into your sandwich, you are free to go nuts later on with gourmet burgers, pulled pork, and loaded stuffed-crust pizza.

In and against this homogenizing context, the influence of chili has been an instructive development. Its incorporation into the global diet has in one sense been inevitable. Chili burgers and chili dogs have been with us long enough to have seeped into the Western eating repertoire, spicier versions of bland everyday foods. The osmosis of Mexican food into its Tex-Mex and less illustrious fast-food variants has taken chilies with it. It could hardly have done otherwise. Chili con carne, whatever its origins, has been an American dish since the nineteenth century, while pizza has long since been cast adrift from its Neapolitan moorings and become the neutral vehicle for virtually anything that can be sliced and scattered on top of it. Chilies have been one of the more prominent options, and indeed one that can claim more of a culinary heritage in Campania pizza blitzed with peperoncini, cherry tomatoes, and buffalo mozzarella than many a pineapple-topped Anglophone mutant. In much of this tendency, however, there is little more than a blameless impulse to make the seasoning a little sharper. Paul Bosland of the Chile Pepper Institute makes this point: "One can look at chili pepper heat as one would salt. It enhances a dish. However, as with salt, too much and the dish is ruined."[1] Vigorous seasoning of savory food is the first and easiest recourse against blandness. Overuse of salt, its primal form, has now ascended to the level of a health alert across the Western world, but has quite often been accompanied by energetic peppering, too. Chili—whether in the form of paprika, cayenne pepper, chili powder, or hot sauce—is a means of turning up the volume on that tingling edge still further. Bosland is indubitably right, though, to stress the benefit of striking a balance.

What the chili movement has demonstrated is that there is a deeper potential to the interest in hot flavor, or more accurately the hot *effect* that its products leave in the mouth and perhaps even throughout the whole organism. Chili confers another status on food alto-gether. No longer does it simply satiate, gratify the taste buds, and beguile the senses. It also transforms the body for a time and, in its most radical manifestations, alters the consumer's state of mind. Its mordant burn inverts our relationship to food, making it much harder to overeat, and turning the act of eating from some-thing that one might do all but mindlessly while talking with friends or watching TV into an activity that draws attention to itself. You can't binge on chilies. You can barely even snack on them. There are other categories of taste that might have similar effects on consumption. It would be hard for most people to eat a lot of very sour food—pickles, sharp citrus fruits—or much of anything with a bitter aftertaste, such as balsam pear or fresh arti-choke hearts. But those effects are restricted to taste alone, whereas chili is about much more than taste. By alerting the trigeminal nervous system that something in-cendiary is happening to the body's vulnerable tissues, it triggers a series of sympathetic responses that, as we have seen, go beyond simply being left with a fiery mouth.

Assuming that we can lay aside the notion of chili addictiveness, which started out as speculative science but has morphed into little more than a piece of popu-lar food ideology, the taste for chili in the Western world requires other explanations. After all, our excursion through the history of this ingredient has shown that it has been adopted throughout Africa and Asia as an everyday dietary staple, and a highly prized one at that,

without engendering single-minded movements of en-
thusiasts like the gastronomic storm chasers of the
English-speaking world. The plant breeding of ever hotter varieties, and the vigorously pullulating hot sauce
market, are answering another kind of need altogether,
one that appears to have its own anthropological under-
girding in affluent societies.

As I argued in the opening chapter of part 3, a significant aspect of the appeal of chilies to the most
hardcore is the lure of the forbidden. In today's climate
of unprecedented health anxiety, much of it securely
grounded in just cause, worries over the potential long-
term costs to well-being of what we eat and drink have
come to a sharp point. If saturated fats and trans fats,
too much salt, too much sugar, and too much alcohol
strew their casualties across the medical wards of hos-
pitals all over the first world, nobody needs to look too
far to find an example of food that, if not actually forbidden, is a matter for strong caution, and in medical
extremis, may well end up being forbidden to us, too.
Against this baleful backdrop, chili constitutes a whole
different kind of forbidden, a mostly positively benign
one. In this case, it is nature itself that seems to be forbidding this food to human beings, who have nonetheless sufficiently overcome their natural aversion to
it to make it a worldwide fundamental ingredient. What
this allows diehard chiliheads to feel, especially with
the most incandescent examples of chili, is that they
are venturing into areas where only the most intrepid

dare go. How much more enlightening, and less zombi-
fying, this feels than loading your protesting digestion
with thirty-two ounces of rump steak. It's risk that might
well earn you respect, rather than shudders of distaste,
and will not, if you're careful, incur any lasting damage.

Sooner or later, though, one would expect this com-
pulsion to wear off. The fact is that chilies are not, like
other mood-altering substances, prohibited. Unless you
are one of the community of heat-seekers who is permanently in search of setting new records of endurance,
chili just becomes an ordinary part of the diet. Might it
be, then, that its appeal lies precisely in its role of enlivening that bland, homogenized food culture we just
anatomized? Its adoption in centuries gone by was most
eagerly enacted exactly where grain-based subsistence
diets with little variation were the norm, so that their
everyday fodder was constructively transformed into
something more appealing. Now the pattern has been
reversed. In centuries past, the Western regimen
spanned the moral and economic range in the industri-
alizing countries between the sustenance of unadorned
piety and the Lucullan exorbitances of haute cuisine,
but has now languished into the sort of deathless uniformity with which people living under rationing re-
gimes are familiar, and so has needed something to make
it seem more interesting. Proliferating variations on the
standard models are one recourse—hello to chicken
curry pizza and Thai peanut butter burgers—but there
are only so many twists on the basic model that any

food will take before desperation and a slew of bad ideas set in. Chili-ing everything up was an alternative approach. It doesn't have to depend on the ceaseless churn of innovation, and it works every time. No matter how many chili meatball subs you may have eaten in the past, the palate impact of that first bite remains a jolt to the senses.

That experience has hardly ever been available from food, even in the largely stomach-turning annals of competitive eating. It is a marker of self-definition, and self-definition has been one of the signal impulses of individuals living in conflicted late modernity. In a gastronomic and cultural universe that is hungry for new sensation—or indeed for any sensation at all—chili peppers have become a modern life-giving elixir, an invigorating, potentially risk-laden antidote to the disconnected and anomic human condition. If the key to unraveling a globalized world and its homogenizing food culture is to emerge from within globalization itself, then the chili pepper, the world's most widely cultivated spice crop, with around twenty-five million tons produced annually, and therefore a truly global ingredient par excellence, might just be the magic bullet that helps the human palate resist its surrender to bland standardization.

The salient point in all this is that it depends on what cultural vantage point you are starting from. When nearly all food is expected to be hotly spicy, as in India and much of southern and Southeast Asia, the experience of hotness is part and parcel of what it means to eat.

Recall the Bhutanese woman saying that eating without chili would be the last word in boredom, hardly like eating at all. Where it remains one of the options, even if an increasingly pervasive one, as in the economically dominant Western world, it maintains its status as a diverting gastronomic experience. Indeed, it is precisely because of that status that it has engendered a fanatical band of camp followers permanently in search of the next life-changing encounter on their way to an infernal capsaicin heaven. In this light, chili looks to have become a way of overemphasizing food through hotness, of creating another kind of uniformity at a much more elevated level. It is often argued that the bland junk-food diet of the Western world has now produced several generations of passive and atrophied consumers who scarcely care for the achievements of high culture or the state of the environment. To the contrary, it looks rather more like the other way around. A hypnotized junk culture of mindless entertainment and industrially manufactured celebrity has engendered a suitably unchallenging diet to go with it. If chili is the antidote to this, it has in one sense already been degraded by the association, but in another, it does little more than repeat the pattern of homogenized consumption but with the addition of a little—or a lot of—oral scorching to remind that you are after all eating something rather than mechanically ingesting it. It alters the glutton's relation to surfeit, because while even the greediest can reach a point where he cannot stuff in even one more potato chip, it isn't possible to fill up on chili in the same way, only arrive at a stage where his oral tissue won't take any more fire.

At the personal level, something about the apparent negativity of the experience of eating very hot food that irritates the organism is key. Paul Rozin and his team of research psychologists, reporting in the journal *Judgment and Decision Making* in July 2013, investigated this theme in the light of Rozin's established theory of benign masochism, applying it to a whole range of aversive triggers from pungently malodorous cheeses to fairground thrill rides, painful deep-tissue massage and hot chili. The culturally acquired liking for phenomena that arouse negative emotions is at least as old as classical tragedy and survives in rude health today in the widespread attachment to tear-jerking melodrama and sad music, and to the choking desolation of contestants who are voted off TV talent shows. Huge numbers of people enjoy the deceptively lethal fear aroused by insanely fast and high roller coasters. When it comes to taste, pungency and bitterness have their legions of followers in aficionados of unpasteurized soft or blue cheeses, fermented herring, and Chinese preserved egg. The level of habitual exposure and the cultural context in which benign masochism takes place play a strong role in these last predispositions, as the authors acknowledge: "[W]e are confident that enjoyment of the burn of chili pepper is more common and more extreme in Mexico than in the United States."[2]

What seems to be happening is that consumers of very hot foods actually enjoy the body's defensive responses to something that is inherently harmless as much as they enjoy the burning sensation itself, and the enjoyment is characteristically predicated on the level of pain experienced being just within the threshold that each individual feels he or she can handle. One or two SHU units more and it would be unbearable, but finding one's limits and just disporting oneself on that borderline provides the optimal level of enjoyable hedonic reversal. Not all negative responses can be mined for their pleasurable potentials. Rozin and others point out that physical nausea is not a noticeably enjoyed sensation. Nor, we might add, is boredom, even though huge numbers of people may have had to develop at least a tolerance for featureless ennui in their lives.

Where Rozin and his associates pinpoint the explanation for benign masochism is in the interface between perceived and actual threat. "Benign masochism refers to enjoying initially negative experiences that the body (brain) falsely interprets as threatening. This realization that the body has been fooled, and that there is no real danger, leads to pleasure derived from 'mind over body.' This can also be framed as a type of mastery."[3] In other words, we know the hot pepper sauce is not actually physically burning our mouths, and that knowledge is exactly what allows us to enjoy the sensation that it is doing harm. Rational knowledge has achieved ascendancy over the body's susceptibility to deception. This is undoubtedly true in the case of those among the cohort of respondents who took part in the experimental research for this paper who positively enjoy spicy food. For those who find it hard to believe that their organism is not being damaged by an onslaught of capsaicin, that moment of hedonic reversal does not occur. Spicy food will never be enjoyable for them. At the heart of this, however, I suspect there is a deeper level still that would make for interesting future exploration. Many people enjoy masochistic experiences not so much because they appreciate the safely controlled way in which they are delivered to them, but because they feel they somehow deserve them. They are an objective external indicator of their own emotional state, as in the classic definition of the psychological type of victim defined by Ofer Zur in a 2008 paper: "[V]ictims harbor feelings of self-inefficacy, of not being successful in affecting one's environment or one's life. Consistent with the above characteristics, victims are likely to attribute the outcome of their behavior to situational or external forces rather than to dispositional forces within themselves." As long as the benefits of being a victim outweigh the costs, individuals so disposed will cling to archetypal behaviors such as feeling "the right to empathy or pity, the lack of responsibility or accountability, righteousness, or even relief as the bad self is punished."[4] It may well be that a liking for painfully hot spice, especially as it is manifested in those who push themselves further and further along the Scoville spectrum with the release of each successive record-breaking pepper, are unconsciously punishing themselves for some unspecified deep-rooted failing. If weepy TV drama speaks to the unhappy social condition in which its devotees are marooned, and who may well constitute the bulk of contemporary society, food that hurts to eat it is saying something to its consumers about the passivity to which a homogenized gastronomy has reduced them. It is the revenge of food for Western humanity's disconnection from the principles of rational and natural nutrition. This is not the Bhutanese or Nahuatl Mexican experience, by and large, but it could well become so when burgers and pizza rule their worlds, too.

Chili peppers have undertaken an extraordinary cultural itinerary from their original wild shrubs in the tropical zones of the Americas to the rows of multicolored pepper sauces on the shelves of first world specialist retailers, via the voyages of colonial enterprise that began to make the world into one vast market in the sixteenth century. They have bestowed their forceful personality on cuisines in all corners of the earth, brought excitement and nutrition to zones where the diet was sorely deficient in those elements, and engendered one of the strangest gastronomic fetishes in the gargantuan complexity of food history. Which is pretty good going for a little fruit that was only telling human beings that it didn't want to be eaten.

Acknowledgments

The cultural diffusion of chili peppers in the most recent era has seen the study of them extend across a wide spectrum of disciplines, and I have benefited in this book from instructive exchanges with some of the foremost authorities in many fields. Chili as a subject looks set to continue developing into some very surprising and unexpected areas, which, I suspect, will teach us more about our relationship to food in general in this troubled century. We need to go on thinking productively about it. Meanwhile, perhaps as a result of my work on this book, my chili con carne is gradually becoming something to be proud of.

In particular, I would like to thank the following people for generously sharing their research, their thoughts, and their time with me: Dr. Paul Bosland of the Chile Pepper Institute at New Mexico State

University; Chilli Dave of the Clifton Chilli Club, the United Kingdom's largest hot pepper association; Ed Currie, chili breeder extraordinaire at the PuckerButt Pepper Company in Fort Mill, South Carolina; food historian Rachel Laudan at the Institute for Historical Studies, University of Texas at Austin; Ben Lendrem, intrepid researcher in the protean field of male idiocy; Dr. Agnes Norbury, research associate in cognitive neuroscience at Cambridge University; Professor Paul Rozin of the psychology department of the University of Pennsylvania, whose multidisciplinary work in the psychology of sensation and emotion has been a richly suggestive contemporary resource; and Robb Walsh, Texas food historian, restaurateur, and all-round chili authority.

For everything from editorial guidance to shared intelligence, and not forgetting the initial inspiration for the whole project, I'd also like to express my gratitude to my editor, Daniela Rapp, for her scrupulous attentions to the manuscript, as well as to Ryan Harrington and Lucas Hunt.

Thanks also to those of my family, friends, and colleagues who have sustained me during the writing of the book, especially Houman Barekat, Elizabeth Garner, Rochelle Venables, Sheila Walton, and Tim Winter.

Notes

Introduction

1. The Dragon's Breath chili pepper, bred in Wales by Mike Smith, almost certainly overtook the Carolina Reaper in 2017, but before it could be ratified, Ed Currie announced that he now had a chili that was twice as hot as the Reaper, named for the time being Pepper X. It currently awaits ratification by *Guinness World Records*.
2. Steven Leckart, "In Search of the World's Spiciest Pepper," *Maxim*, October 29, 2013, maxim.com/entertainment/search -worlds-spiciest-pepper.
3. Thomas J. Ibach, "The *Temascal* and Humoral Medicine in Santa Cruz Mixtepec, Juxtlahuaca, Oaxaca, Mexico." Master's thesis, University of Tennessee, 1981.
4. Zeynep Yenisey, "Hot and Spicy Condoms Now Exist, and We're Really Not Sure Why," *Maxim*, August 9, 2017, maxim .com/maxim-man/spicy-condoms-2017-8.

PART ONE: BIOLOGY

1. Our Favorite Spice

1. Joshua J. Tewksbury et al., "Evolutionary Ecology of Pungency in Wild Chilies," *PNAS*, August 19, 2008, pnas.org/content/105/33/11808.full.
2. Jun Lu, Lu Qi, et al., "Consumption of Spicy Foods and Total and Cause Specific Mortality," *BMJ*, August 4, 2015, bmj.com/content/351/bmj.h3942.
3. Parvati Shallow, "Chili Peppers May Fire Up Weight Loss," CBS News, February 9, 2015, cbsnews.com/news/chili-peppers-may-fire-up-weight-loss/.
4. Heather Lyu et al., "Overtreatment in the United States, *PLOS ONE*, September 6, 2017, journals.plos.org/plosone/article?id=10.1371/journal.pone.0135892.
5. Yin Tong Liang et al., "Capsaicinoids Lower Plasma Cholesterol and Improve Endothelial Function in Hamsters, *European Journal of Nutrition*, March 31, 2012, link.springer.com/article/10.1007%2Fs00394-012-0344-2.
6. Mustafa Chopan and Benjamin Littenberg, "The Association of Hot Red Chili Pepper Consumption and Mortality," *PLOS One*, January 9, 2017, journals.plos.org/plosone/article?id=10.1371/journal.pone.0169876.
7. Ann M. Bode and Zigang Dong, "The Two Faces of Capsaicin," *Cancer Research*, April 2011, cancerres.aacrjournals.org/content/71/8/2809.
8. A. Akagiz et al., "Non-carcinogenicity of Capsaicinoids in B6C3F1 Mice, *Food and Chemical Toxicology*, sciencedirect.com/science/article/pii/S0278691598000775.

PART TWO: HISTORY

3. Spice of America

1. Bruce D. Smith, "Reassessing Coxcatlan Cave and the Early History of Domesticated Plants in Mesoamerica," *PNAS*, July 5, 2005, www.pnas.org/content/102/27/9438.

2. Linda Perry and Kent V. Flannery, "Precolumbian Use of Chili Peppers in the Valley of Oaxaca, Mexico," *PNAS*, July 17, 2007, pnas.org/content/104/29/11905.full.
3. Cited in Andrew Dalby, *Dangerous Tastes: The Story of Spices* (Berkeley: University of California Press, 2000), p. 149 (translation modified).

4. Three Ships Come Sailing
1. Translated by A. M. Fernandez de Ybarra, New York, 1906, available at ncbi.nlm.nih.gov/pmc/articles/PMC1692411/pdf /medlibhistj00007-0022.pdf.
2. Translated by A. M. Fernandez de Ybarra, New York, 1906, available at repository.si.edu/bitstream/handle/10088/26153 /SMC_48_Chanca%28Tr.Ybarra%29_1907_27_428-457.pdf ?sequence=1&isAllowed=y.
3. Jack Turner, *Spice: The History of a Temptation* (London: Harper Perennial, 2005), p. 49.
4. Translated by Richard Eden, cited in Jean Andrews, *Peppers: The Domesticated Capsicums* (Austin: University of Texas Press, 1995), p. 4.
5. Lizzie Collingham, *Curry: A Tale of Cooks and Conquerors* (London: Vintage, 2006), p. 50.

5. Blazing a Trail
1. Angela Garbes, *The Everything Hot Sauce Book* (Avon Mass.: Adams Media, 2012), p. 6.
2. W. H. Eshbaugh, "The Genus *Capsicum* (Solanaceae) in Africa," *Bothalia* 14, 3 & 4, 1983, pp. 845–48.
3. Rachel Laudan, *Cuisine and Empire: Cooking in World History* (Berkeley: University of California Press, 2013), p. 202.
4. Heather Arndt Anderson, *Chillies: A Global History* (London: Reaktion Books, 2016), p. 69.
5. Gayatri Parameswaran, "Bhutan's Tears of Joy Over Chillies," September 9, 2012, aljazeera.com/indepth/features/2012/09 /201299102918142658.html.

6. "Red and Incredibly Beautiful"

1. E. N. Anderson, *The Food of China* (New Haven, Conn.: Yale University Press, 1988), p. xx.
2. Charles Perry, "Middle Eastern Food History," in Paul Freedman, Joyce E. Chaplin, and Ken Albala, *Food in Time and Place: The American Historical Association Companion to Food History* (Oakland: University of California Press, 2014), pp. 107–19.
3. Ho Ping-ti, "The Introduction of American Food Plants into China," *American Anthropologist* 57:2 (May 1955), pp. 191–201.
4. Caroline Reeves, "How the Chili Pepper Got to China," *World History Bulletin* XXIV:1, (Spring 2008), pp. 18–19.
5. Yang Xuanzhang and Li Piao, translated by Nick Angiers, "Hot Peppers in China," *China Scenic*, 2014, available at chinascenic.com/magazine/hot-peppers-in-china-273.htm.

7. From Piri Piri to Paprika

1. Ken Albala, *Eating Right in the Renaissance* (Berkeley: University of California Press), 2002, p. 240.
2. Cited in Amit Krishna De, ed., *Capsicum: The Genus Capsicum* (London and New York: Taylor and Francis), 2003, p. 147.
3. Joanne Sasvari, *Paprika: A Spicy Memoir from Hungary* (Toronto: CanWest Books, 2005), pp. 59–60.
4. Dave DeWitt, *Precious Cargo: How Foods from the Americas Changed the World* (Berkeley, Calif.: Counterpoint, 2014), p. 86.
5. Changzoo Song, "Kimchi, Seaweed, and Seasoned Carrot in the Soviet Culinary Culture: The Spread of Korean Food in the Soviet Union and Korean Diaspora," *Journal of Ethnic Foods* 3: 1 (March 2016), p. 80.

8. Bowls o' Red and Chili Queens

1. William Kitchiner, M.D., *The Cooks Oracle; and Housekeeper's Manual* (New York: J and J Harper, 1830). Available at archive.org/details/cooksoracleandh00kitcgoog.
2. "History," penderys.com/history.htm.
3. Laudan, p. 202.

4. Robb Walsh, *The Chili Cookbook* (New York: Ten Speed Press, 2015).

5. Rebecca Rupp, "To Bean or Not to Bean: Jumping into the Chili Debate," nationalgeographic.com, February 5, 2015, theplate .nationalgeographic.com/2015/02/05/the-great-chili-debate/.

6. Anderson, p. 41.

7. S. Compton Smith, *Chile con Carne; or, the Camp and the Field* (New York: Miller and Curtis, 1857), p. 99.

8. Andrew F. Smith, *Eating History: 30 Turning Points in the Making of American Cuisine* (New York: Columbia University Press, 2009), p. 50.

9. Charles Winterfield, "Adventures on the Frontiers of Texas and Mexico," *The American Whig Review*, 2: 4 (October 1845), p. 368.

10. Francisco J. Santamaría, *Diccionario General de Americanismos* (Mexico City: Pedro Robredo, 1942).

11. Edward King, "Glimpses of Texas I: A Visit to San Antonio," in *Scribner's Monthly* (January 1874), pp. 306–308.

12. John Nova Lomax, "The Bloody San Antonio Origins of Chili Con Carne," August 10, 2017, texasmonthly.com/food/bloody -san-antonio-origins-chili-con-carne/.

9. Pepper Sauce

1. Cited in Denver Nicks, *Hot Sauce Nation: America's Burning Obsession* (Chicago Review Press, 2017), p. 44.

2. Jennifer Trainer Thompson, *Hot Sauce!* (North Adams, Mass.: Storey Publishing, 2012), pp. 15–16.

10. Taste and Touch

1. Pamela Dalton and Nadia Byrnes, "Psychology of Chemesthesis—Why Would Anyone Want to Be in Pain?," in Shane T. McDonald, David A. Bolliet and John E. Hayes, eds., *Chemesthesis: Chemical Touch in Food and Eating* (Oxford: Wiley-Blackwell, 2016), p. 25.

2. Paul Rozin, "Getting to Like the Burn of Chili Pepper: Biological, Psychological, and Cultural Perspectives," in Barry G. Green, J. Russell Mason, and Morley R. Kare, eds., *Chemical*

Senses Volume 2: Irritation (New York and Basel: Marcel Dekker, 1990), p. 239.

3. Paul Rozin, "Preadaptation and the Puzzles and Properties of Pleasure," in Daniel Kahneman, Ed Diener, and Norbert Schwarz, *Well-Being: The Foundations of Hedonic Psychology* (New York: Russell Sage Foundation, 2003), p. 125.
4. Ibid., p. 127.
5. Paul Rozin, email message to author, 10 December 2017.

PART THREE: CULTURE

11. The Devil's Dinner

1. Alan Davidson, ed., *The Oxford Companion to Food* (Oxford University Press, 1999), p. 248.
2. Charles Dickens, *David Copperfield* (London: Bradbury and Evans, 1850).
3. Eneas Sweetland Dallas, *Kettner's Book of the Table, a Manual of Cookery, Practical, Theoretical, Historical* (London: Dulau and Company, 1877), p. 157.
4. Ibid.
5. Charles Lever, *O'Malley, the Irish Dragoon*, Volume 2 (Tucson, Ariz.: Fireship Press, 2008), p. 134.
6. Edgar Allan Poe, *The Complete Works of Edgar Allan Poe, Vol. VII: Criticisms* (New York: Cosimo Classics, 2009), p. 265.
7. Anthony Trollope, *The Warden* (London: Longman, Brown, Green, and Longmans, 1855).
8. Lauren Collins, "Fire-Eaters," *The New Yorker*, November 4, 2013, newyorker.com/magazine/2013/11/04/fire-eaters.
9. nationalgeographic.com/travel/destinations/south-america /bolivia/bolivia-hot-sauce/.
10. Leigh Dayton, "Spicy Food Eaters Are Addicted to Pain," *New Scientist*, newscientist.com/article/mg13418172-800-science -spicy-food-eaters-are-addicted-to-pain/.
11. Stephanie Butler, "The Natural High of Intoxicating Foods," history.com/news/hungry-history/the-natural-high-of -intoxicating-food.

12. Earth Erowid and Fire Erowid, "Hot Chiles: Surfing the Burn," November 2004, erowid.org/plants/capsicum/capsicum _article1.shtml#fer.

13. fatalii.net/FG_Jigsaw . . . boards.straightdope.com/sdmb /archive/index.php/t-248653.html . . . thehotpepper.com/topic /37166-best-tasting-superhot/.

14. Chris Kilham, "Hell Fire in Your Mouth," n.d., medicinehunter .com/psychoactives.

12. Hot Stuff

1. "Spice It Up!" *Amy Reiley's Eat Something Sexy,* n.d., eatsome thingsexy.com/aphrodisiac-foods/chile-pepper/.

2. Maria Paz Moreno, *Madrid: A Culinary History* (Lanham Md.: Rowman & Littlefield, 2017), p. 45.

3. Turner, p. 215.

4. Sylvester Graham, *A Lecture to Young Men on Chastity* (Boston: GW Light, 1838), p. 47.

5. Laurent Bègue et al., "Some Like It Hot: Testosterone Predicts Laboratory Eating Behavior of Spicy Food," *Physiology and Behavior* 139 (1), February 2015, p. 375, available at researchgate.net/publication/268978579_Some_like_it_hot _Testosterone_predicts_laboratory_eating_behavior_of_spicy _food.

6. Waguih William IsHak, ed., *The Textbook of Clinical Sexual Medicine* (San Francisco: Springer, 2017), p. 417.

7. Rita Strakosha, "Modern Diet and Stress Cause Homosexuality: A Hypothesis and a Potential Therapy," April 9, 2017, psikolog1.wordpress.com/2017/04/09/modern-diet-and -stress-cause-homosexuality-a-hypothesis-and-a-potential -therapy/.

8. Andrews, p. 113.

9. John McQuaid, *Tasty: The Art and Science of What We Eat* (New York: Scribner, 2016), p. 176.

10. Bjeldbak, Gitte, Patent application: "Method for Attaining Erection of the Human Sexual Organs," September 8, 1998, google.com/patents/US6039951.

11. M. Lazzeri et al., "Intraurethrally Infused Capsaicin Induces Penile Erection in Humans," *Scandinavian Journal of Urology and Nephrology*, 28 (4), December 1994, pp. 409–12.

13. Fighting Talk

1. Frances F. Berdan and Patricia Rieff Anawalt, eds., *The Essential Codex Mendoza* (Berkeley: University of California Press, 1997), p. 123.
2. Ibid., p. 161.

14. Superhots and Chiliheads

1. Charles Dickens, *The Pickwick Papers* (London: Chapman and Hall, 1837)
2. Paul Bosland, personal email correspondence with the author, November 30, 2017.
3. Ed Currie, personal email correspondence with the author, December 6, 2017.
4. Joe Nickell, "Peddling Snake Oil," *Skeptical Inquirer*, December 1998, csicop.org/sb/show/peddling_snake_oil.

15. Man Food

1. "Climbing Mount Everest Is Work for Supermen," *The New York Times*, March 18, 1923.
2. Lee Dye, "Studies Suggest Men Handle Pain Better," April 17, 2016, ABCNews.com, abcnews.go.com/Technology/story?id=97662&page=1.
3. "Chronic Pain Conditions,"n.d., webmd.com/pain-management/chronic-pain-conditions#1.
4. Ed Currie, personal email correspondence with the author, December 6, 2017.
5. Agnes Norbury and Masud Husein, "Sensation-seeking: dopaminergic modulation and risk for psychopathology," *Behavioral Brain Research* 288, July 15, 2015, pp. 79–93.
6. Patricia Riccardi, David Zaid, et al., "Sex Differences in Amphetamine-Induced Displacement of Fallypride in Striatal and Extrastriatal Regions," *The American Journal of Psychia-*

try, 1 September 2006, ajp.psychiatryonline.org/doi/full/10
.1176/ajp.2006.163.9.1639.

7. Dr. Agnes Norbury, personal email correspondence with the
author, December 3, 2017.

8. Ben Lendrem et al., "The Darwin Awards: Sex Differences in
Idiotic Behavior," *British Medical Journal,* December 11, 2014,
bmj.com/content/349/bmj.g7094.

9. Ben Lendrem, personal email correspondence with the author, November 29, 2017.

10. "Ghost Pepper—Eating Contest Leaves Man with a Hole in
His Esophagus, CBSNews.com, October 18, 2016, cbsnews
.com/news/ghost-pepper-sends-man-to-hospital-hole-in
-esophagus/.

16. The Globalization of Taste

1. Paul Bosland, personal email correspondence with the author,
November 30, 2017.

2. Paul Rozin, Lily Guillot, Katrina Fincher, Alexander Rozin,
and Eli Tsukayama, "Glad to Be Sad, and Other Examples of
Benign Masochism," in *Judgment and Decision Making* 8:4,
July 2013, pp. 439–447.

3. Ibid.

4. Ofer Zur, "Rethinking 'Don't Blame the Victim:' The Psychology of Victimhood," *Journal of Couples Therapy* 4: 3–4, October 2008, pp. 15–36, available at zurinstitute.com/victimhood
.html.

Select Bibliography

Albala, Ken. *Eating Right in the Renaissance*. Berkeley: University of California Press, 2002.

Anderson, E. N. *The Food of China*. New Haven, Conn.: Yale University Press, 1988.

Anderson, Heather Arndt. *Chillies: A Global History*. London: Reaktion Books, 2016.

Andrews, Jean. *Peppers: The Domesticated Capsicums*. Austin: University of Texas Press, 1995.

Berdan, Frances F., and Patricia Rieff Anawalt, eds. *The Essential Codex Mendoza*. Berkeley: University of California Press, 1997.

Campbell, James D. *Mr. Chilehead: Adventures in the Taste of Pain*. Toronto: ECW Press, 2003.

Collingham, Lizzie. *Curry: A Tale of Cooks and Conquerors*. London: Vintage, 2006.

Dalby, Andrew. *Dangerous Tastes: The Story of Spices*. Berkeley: University of California Press, 2000.

Dallas, Eneas Sweetland. *Kettner's Book of the Table: A Manual of Cookery, Practical, Theoretical, Historical*. London: Dulau and Company, 1877.

Davidson, Alan, ed. *The Oxford Companion to Food*. Oxford: Oxford University Press, 1999.

De, Amit Krishna. *Capsicum: The Genus Capsicum*. London and New York: Taylor and Francis, 2003.

DeWitt, Dave. *Precious Cargo: How Foods from the Americas Changed the World*. Berkeley, Calif.: Counterpoint Press, 2014.

DeWitt, Dave, and Paul W. Bosland. *The Complete Chile Pepper Book*. Portland Ore.: Timber Press, 2009.

Dickens, Charles. *David Copperfield*. London: Bradbury and Evans, 1850.

———. *The Pickwick Papers*. London: Chapman and Hall, 1837.

Floyd, David. *The Hot Book of Chillies*. London: New Holland, 2006.

Foster, Nelson, and Linda S. Cordell, eds. *Chilies to Chocolate: Food the Americas Gave the World*. Tucson: University of Arizona Press, 1992.

Freedman, Paul, Joyce E. Chaplin, and Ken Albala, eds. *Food in Time and Place: The American Historical Association Companion to Food History*. Oakland: University of California Press, 2014.

Garbes, Angela. *The Everything Hot Sauce Book*. Avon, Mass.: Adams Media, 2012.

Graham, Sylvester. *A Lecture to Young Men, on Chastity*. Boston: G. W. Light, 1838.

Green, Barry G., J. Russell Mason, and Morley R. Kare, eds. *Chemical Senses*, Volume 2: *Irritation*. New York and Basel: Marcel Dekker, 1990.

Hildebrand, Caz. *The Grammar of Spice*. London: Thames and Hudson, 2017.

IsHak, Waguih William, ed. *The Textbook of Clinical Sexual Medicine*. San Francisco: Springer, 2017.

Kahneman, Daniel, Ed Diener, and Norbert Schwarz, eds. *Well-Being: The Foundations of Hedonic Psychology*. New York: Russell Sage Foundation, 2003.

Keay, John. *The Spice Route: A History*. Berkeley: University of California Press, 2006.

Laudan, Rachel. *Cuisine and Empire: Cooking in World History*. Berkeley: University of California Press, 2013.

Lever, Charles. *O'Malley, the Irish Dragoon,* Volume 2. Tucson, Ariz: Fireship Press, 2008.

May, Dan. *The Red Hot Chilli Cookbook.* London: Ryland Peters and Small, 2012.

McDonald, Shane T., David E. Bolliet, and John E. Hayes, eds. *Chemesthesis: Chemical Touch in Food and Eating.* Oxford: John Wiley and Sons, 2016.

McQuaid, John. *Tasty: The Art and Science of What We Eat.* New York: Scribner, 2016.

Moreno, Maria Paz. *Madrid: A Culinary History.* Lanham, Md.: Rowman & Littlefield, 2017.

Naj, Amal. *Peppers: A Story of Hot Pursuits.* New York: Alfred A. Knopf, 1992.

Nicks, Denver. *Hot Sauce Nation: America's Burning Obsession.* Chicago: Chicago Review Press, 2017.

Poe, Edgar Allan. *The Complete Works of Edgar Allan Poe,* Vol 7: *Criticisms.* New York: Cosimo Classics, 2009.

Santamaría, Francisco J. *Diccionario General de Americanismos.* Mexico City: Pedro Robledo, 1942.

Sasvari, Joanne. *Paprika: A Spicy Memoir from Hungary.* Toronto: CanWest Books, 2005.

Smith, Andrew F. *Eating History: 30 Turning Points in the Making of American Cuisine.* New York: Columbia University Press, 2009.

Smith, S. Compton, *Chili Con Carne: or, The Camp and the Field.* New York: Miller and Curtis, 1857.

Thompson, Jennifer Trainer. *Hot Sauce!* North Adams, Mass.: Storey Publishing, 2012.

Trollope, Anthony. *The Warden.* London: Longman, Brown, Green and Longmans, 1855.

Turner, Jack. *Spice: The History of a Temptation.* London: Harper Perennial, 2005.

Walsh, Robb. *The Chili Cookbook.* New York: Ten Speed Press, 2015.

Woellert, Dann. *The Authentic History of Cincinnati Chili.* Charleston, S.C.: The History Press, 2013.

Index

A

Acosta, José de, 216
Adjuma, 59
African Birdeye, 56
African cooking, 103, 105–7
African Devil, 56, 204
aji, 6, 93
Aji Amarillo, 67
Aji Cereza, 33
Aji Dulce, 59
Aji Limo, 60
Aji Limon, 67
Aji Pinguita de Mono, 33
Aleppo (Halaby), 33
alpha male behavior, 245
Alvarez Chanca, Diego, 95
American Spice Trade Association (ASTA), 20
Americas
    discovery of, 91–93, 99–102
    pre-Columbian diet, 11
Ammazzo (Joe's Round), 34
Anaheim, 34
Ancho, 34
Andrews, Jean, 102
Anghiera, Pietro Martire d', 99

Apache F1, 35
Apache people, 227
aphrodisiacs, 214–15, 222–23
Arabian people, 118
Arawak people, 8
Asian cooking, 103, 124–26
ASTA unit, 20
Austria, xvi, 146
Aztecs, xviii, 8, 83–85, 225, 226–27

B

Bacio di Satana, 35
Bangalore Torpedo, 56
Barbados, 181
Bartholomew the Englishman, 217
Basque cooking, xix, 142
Baumer's Crystal Hot Sauce, 177
beer, chili-flavored, 183
Beeton, Isabella, 150
Bellissimo, Teressa, 177
bell peppers, x, xvii, 135
Bertrand steamboat wreck, 172–73
B. F. Trappey and Sons, 176–77
Bhutan, xiii–xiv, 118–21, 242
Bhut jolokia, xi, 6, 57
Big Jim, 35

Birdeye (Piri Piri), 36
"bird pepper," 40
Bird Pepper Sauce, 172
birds
    and dispersal of chili seeds, 4–5, 13
    not sensitive to chilies, 13
bishop's hat, 68
black pepper, 97, 110–11
Bola, 37
Boldog, 36
Bolivia, 6, 13, 78, 206–7
Bonnet peppers, 6
Bosland, Paul, 236, 261
bottled hot sauces, 171–84
Brazil, 4, 100, 225
Brazilian Starfish, 6, 68
bread, as chili antidote, 23
Brillat-Savarin, Jean-Anthelme, 193
Britain
    bottled hot sauces, 171
    chili beer, 183
    chili movement in, xi, 235, 246–47
    cookbooks, 152–53
    cuisine, 149–51, 198–201
    slave trade, 106
British Virgin Islands, 181
Bruce family of Louisiana, 177
Bucholz, Christian, 16
Buffalo chicken wing sauce, 177
Bulgarian Carrot, 36
Burma, route to China, 123
Butch T Scorpion, 66–67
Byzantine empire, 137

C

Cabai rawit, 6
cacao, 77
Calabria, 143
canario, 69
cancer, 29–30
Cape Verde, 202
Capónes, 37
capsaicin, 15–18
    biological effect of, 12, 21–24, 222
    measuring SHU value of, 18–20
    name of, 16
    pure alkaloid, banned as food
        additive in EU, xii, 17–18
capsaicin liniment, 223, 244

capsaicinoids, 15, 16
Capsicum annuum, xvi, 5–6, 106–7
    domestication of, 73
    varieties, 33–56
Capsicum baccatum, 6, 86–87, 88
    domestication of, 73–74
    varieties, 67–69
Capsicum chinense, 6, 86–87, 133
    domestication of, 73–74
    varieties, 59–67
Capsicum frutescens, 6, 106–7
    domestication of, 73
    varieties, 56–59
Capsicum pubescens, 6–7, 69, 88
    domestication of, 73
Caribbean cooking, 6, 180–82, 225
Caribbean hot pepper sauce, xix
Caribbee Hot Sauce, 181
Carolina Reaper, xv, 60, 209, 211
Casabella, 37
Cascabel, 37
casein, 22
Catholics, 216
Cayenne, 5, 37–38
cayenne sauce, 154, 171
Central America, 4
central Asian republics, 147
Cerrado region of Brazil, 4
Charleston Hot, 38
chemesthesis, 186–87
chemical warfare, 225–27
Chemical Weapons Convention of
        1997, 229–30
Cheongyang, 38, 116–17
Cherry Bomb F1, 38–39
chiles rellenos, 155–56
Chilhuacle Amarillo, 39
Chilhuacle Negro, 39
Chilhuacle Rojo, 39
chili
    acquiring a taste for, 190–91
    addiction to, xiii, 207–8
    antidotes to distress from, 22–24
    antimicrobial properties of,
        15, 27
    as aphrodisiac, 214–15, 222–23
    archaeological findings, 7, 77
    bland diet enlivened by, 187–88
    boon to poor people, 133

chemesthetic (haptic) properties
of, 186–87
cookbooks on, 152–55, 237
feel of, in the mouth, xx
first European description of,
95–96
forbiddenness of, as lure, 263
globalization of, xv, 170–71, 260–61
health benefits claimed, 30, 160,
239–43
hot effect of, 12–13, 261–62
many uses of, in the Americas,
89–90
media exposure of, 237–39
and mood, effect on, 189
name and spelling of, xxiii, 8
no direct tissue damage from, 21
overconsumption of, 29–31
pain from, xi–xii, 22–24
in pith not seeds, 17
reasons for the taste for, 262–70
sense of alertness from, 221–22
similarity to illegal drugs, 206,
210–12
unique properties of, 186–92
warming or chilling effect of, in
extreme climates, 188–89
chili bricks, 160–61
chili burgers and dogs, 260
chili chocolate, 183
chili con carne ("chili"), 160–69, 261
guidelines for making and
ingredients to omit, 168–69
name of, 163–64
chili-eating competitions, xiv–xv
dangers of, 245–46, 256–57
men vs. women in, 251, 254,
256–57
chili festivals and expos, 235–36
chiliheads (users), 211–12, 235–39
chili high, 23–24
chili parlors, 166–67
Chili Pepper Company, 63
chili peppers
as aphrodisiacs, 214–15
bombs and grenades made from,
94–95, 225, 230
burning of, 119, 202, 225–27
chopping seeds and all, 16–17

as a currency, 10
essential ingredient in
Mesoamerica, 81
hotness of various kinds, 9
nutrients in, 7, 25
race to breed the hottest, 211, 248
rarely found in stores, x
slow to be adopted in Europe, 135,
142–51
trading in, 5–6, 78, 155
varieties of, 32–69
warding off evil spirits with, 202–3
weaponized, 224–31
why humans became attracted to,
14–15
chili plants
botanical description of, 3
as decorative, 126–27, 155
domestication of, 8, 73–77
names of, satanic, 203–4
origins in America, 5, 73, 111
taken to Europe, 100–101
chili powder, 157–60
chili products, with diabolical
names, 204–5
Chili Queens of San Antonio,
165–66, 167
chili smoke, 81–82
as chemical warfare, 225–27
disciplining kids with, 82, 226–27
purgative and exorcizing function
of, 119, 202
Chiltepin, 9, 40, 155, 172
Chiltomaline, 158
Chimayo, 40
China, 122–34, 242
routes of chili trade, 122–26
Chinese cooking, 6
modern changes in, 133–34
taste categories in, 127
Chipotle, 40–41
chocolate drinks, 77–78, 80, 139
Choctaw people, 233
Cholula brand, 179
Choricero, 41
Christianity, 137, 201
Christmas Bell, 68
Christmas peppers, 52
Cincinnati chili, 165

Civil War (American), 174
coffee, 117, 139
color of foods, xvii
Columbian Exchange, 91, 104
Columbian Exposition (Chicago, 1893), 168
Columbus, Christopher, 91–99
competitiveness, male, 246–49
Congo Basin, 106
controlled substances, with diabolical names, 205
corno talisman, 203
Cortés, Hernán, 76
Costeño Amarillo, 41
cowboys, 155
Criolla Sella, 68
crowd control, capsaicin used for, 228–29
CS gas, 228
cumin, 157, 161
Currie, Ed, xv, 60, 64, 211, 237–38, 251, 254
Cyklon, 41

D

da Gama, Vasco, 108
Dagger Pod, 42
Dallas, Eneas Sweetland (pseudonym Kettner), 199–200
Darling, Stephen Foster, 16
Darwin Awards, 255–56
Datil, 60–61
De Arbol, 42
Deggi Mirch, 42
Demon Red, 204
Denmark, chili movement in, 236
depression, 189
dermatitis, 22
designation of origin, 259
Devil, his dinner in Hell, 197
"deviled" dishes, 146, 197–201
Devil's Brew, 204
Devil's Tongue, 203–4
Dickens, Charles, 198–99, 234
Diderot, Denis, 239–40
diet
    bland, enlivened by chili, 11, 187–88, 261, 264–66
    human, evolution of, 31

digestive system, effect of chili
    improved digestion, 189–90
    vomiting and diarrhea, 11, 22, 29–30, 208
dirty eating movement, 260
diseases, European, 86
dopamine, 24, 189, 251–53
Dorset naga, 63
Dragon's Breath, 61, 211
dressings, chili in, 80–81
Duo lajiao, 128

E

Eagle Brand Chili Powder, 157–58
Ecuador, 74, 78
édesnemes, 144
Edgewood Arsenal (U.S.), 228
elites
    chili reserved for, 10, 76
    food of, 81, 104
    vs. mass tastes, xvii
endorphins, 23–24, 189, 207, 215
    and libido, 220–23
Erica's, 181
erös, 144
Escoffier, Georges-Auguste, 145
Espelette, 43, 142
Estilette, Adam, 177
estrogen, 250
ethnic cuisines, globalized, 258
Europe
    chili cultivation in, xvi–xvii
    cuisines of, 135–51
European Union, xii, 17
evil eye (*malocchio*), 203
extreme sports, 246

F

Facing Heaven, 43
fasting from salt and chilies, 83, 87
Fatalii, 61–62
Feathered Serpent, 80
Fer (psychonaut), 209–10
fiber, dietary, 25
Fiery Foods Show (Albuquerque), 235
filé powder, 233–34
Filius Blue, 43
Finland, chili movement in, 236
Finnriver Cider Company, 183–84

Firecracker, 44
Fire Foods, 63
Fish pepper, 44
food
    globalization of, 104–5
    plain and simple, 140–41, 216
    senses involved in consumption
        (smell, taste, haptic), 186
    trends and fads, 232–39
Fowler, Gerald, xv, 63
Frank, Jacob, 177
Frank's RedHot, 177
French cooking, xvii, 140
    classic, 142, 198
French Enlightenment, 140
Fresno, 44–45
Fujian, 124–25
fumigation, by chili smoke, 7
fungi on chilies, 13–14

G

Galen, 136
Garden Salsa F1, 45
Garner family, Carolinas, 178
gateway theory of drug use,
    208
Gebhardt, William, 157–58
General Tso's chicken, 129–30
Georgia Flame, 45
Germany, 146
Ghost pepper, 57
Glasse, Hannah, 152
global diet (Western), 258–61
    blandness of, 264
    countervailing movements to,
        259–60
    link with junk culture, 266
Goa, 108, 109–10, 113–14
Goat Horn, 45
gochujang, 115–16
gongbao (kung pao) chicken, 131–32
goulash, 144
Graham, Sylvester, 218–19
Grenadines, 181
guaiwei, 131
guajillo, 48
Guangzhou, 124–25
Guindilla, 45–46
Gujin Xiaoshuo, 214

H

Habanero, 6, 62
Hainan Yellow Lantern, 62
Haiti, 182
Halaby pepper, 33
halászlé (fisherman's soup), 145–46
hallucinogenic effects of chili,
    209–10
"hawk pepper," 55
health effects of chili, 25–31,
    120–21, 160, 239–43
Hell, thirst of sinners in, 197
herbal medicine, 137
Hippocrates, 136
Hoffmansegg, Count von, 145
Hong Man-seon, 116
horticulture of chili, 101–2
hot (sexual meaning), 213–14
hot pepper movement, x–xii
Hot Sauce Expo (New York), 235
House of Chilli, 183
huang deng long jiao, 62
humans
    evolution of diet, 31
    intelligent enough to ignore pain
        of capsaicin, 21
humoral theory, xviii, 136–39,
    216–18
Hunan, 123–26
    cuisine (Xiang), 128–30
Hunan hand syndrome, 22
Hungarian paprika, 36
Hungarian Yellow Wax, 46
Hungarian Yellow Wax (Hot), 46
Hungary, cooking, 143–46
Huy Fong Sriracha Hot Chili Sauce,
    182–83

I

Ibach, Thomas J., xviii
Inca Empire, 85–89, 225
Inca Garcilaso de la Vega, 87
India, xiii, 6, 242
    capsaicin-based chemical
        weaponry, 230
    cooking, 109–11, 141–42, 159, 265
    overland route to China, 123
    warding off car accidents with
        chili, 202–3

Indian cooking, 246–47
Indonesia, 6, 108
Inferno F1, 46
Infinity, 63
initiation ceremonies, 88–89
insects, feeding on chilies, 13–14
intoxication from chili, xi
Italy, xvii
  cooking, 142–43, 198
  corno talisman worn in, 203

J

Jacquin, Nikolaus von, 6, 133
Jalapeño, 5, 40, 46–47
Jaloro, 47
Jamaica, 180–81
Jamaican Hot Chocolate, 63
Japan
  cuisine, 114
  trade with Portugal, 113–14
Japones, 57
J. McCollick & Co, 172
Joe's Long, 47
Joe's Round, 34
José Cuervo tequila manufacturer, 179
Joya de Cerén volcano, 82–83
Jwala, 47–48

K

Kahlúa, 183
Kambuzi, 6, 58
Kashmir militancy, 230
Khorasan, 123–24
Kilham, Chris, 212
kimchi, 116
Kiradjieff brothers, 165
Kitchiner, William, 153–54
Korea, cuisine, 115–17, 148
Kristang culinary tradition, 201

L

Last Dab hot sauce, 64
lavanderas, 161, 167
Lea & Perrins, 171
Leckart, Steven, xv
Lemon drop, 6
Lever, Charles, 200
life expectancy, chili consumption
  and, 26–28

liquid chromatography, 20, 32
liquor, chili-flavored, xvi, 148–49,
  183–84
llajwa, 206–7
Llewellyn's, 181
locavore movement, 259
locoto, 6, 69
Lottie's Barbados Hot Pepper Sauce,
  181
Louisiana, 173–76, 177–78
Louisiana Hot Sauce, 177
Lucifer's Dream, 204

M

Macao, 108, 113, 114–15, 122, 124
Madame Jeanette, 65–66
maize, 79–80
ma la gan guo, 130
Malagueta, 6, 58, 98
Malawi, 6
Male Idiot Theory (MIT), 254–57
Mallory, George, 247
mammals, deterred by chili, 12
mano and *metate* method, 74
manzano, 7, 69
Mao shi hongshao rou, 129
Mao Zedong, 129
masochism, 191–92, 267–70
Massachusetts, bottled hot sauces,
  171–72
masturbation, 218–19
Matouk's Trinidad Scorpion Pepper
  Sauce, 180
Mayan civilization, 82–83, 225
McIlhenny, Edmund, 173–77
McIlhenny's Tabasco pepper sauce,
  59
medical claims for chili, 99
medicinal systems
  humoral theory, 135–39
  Islamic, 137
  non-Western, xviii
melegueta pepper, 58, 97, 106
men, in chili movement, 245–57
Mesoamerica
  cooking styles of, 79–80
  food trinity of (maize, beans,
    squash), 79
  pharmacopoeia of, 7

Mexico
  ancient, 4, 73–77
  bottled hot sauces, 178–80
  chile cultivation, 6, 73–77
  chili introduced to U.S. from, 155
  cooking, 108–9, 156–57, 191, 202, 260
  warding off evil spirits with chili, 202
Micko, Karl, 16
Middle East, cuisines, 117
milk, as chili antidote, 22, 164
minerals in chili, 7, 25
Mirasol, 48
Miss Anna's, 182
Mixe-Zoque people, 76
mold on chilies, 13–14
mole, 39, 108–9
Moruga scorpion, 6, 180
Mrs. Greaux Hot Pepper Sauce, 181
Mulato, 48
mythologies, chili in, 11, 86–87, 119

N

Naga jolokia, 57
Naga Morich, 63
Nagasaki, 114
Naga Viper, xv, 63
Nahautl language, xxiii, 8
Nahua peoples, xviii
nam phrik, 112–13
Native Americans (of U.S.)
  adoption of chilies, 155
  use of chilies in war, 227
Nazca people, 87
Near East, 117
Nelson, E. K., 16
neurotransmitters, 24
Nevis, 181
New England dishes, 153
new foods from America
  not fitting into the humoral system, 138–39
  not readily absorbed by European elites, 138–39, 215–16
  as ornamentals in European botanical gardens, 139
  perceived as both dangerous and health-giving, 239–41

New Mexico No. 9, 48–49
New Mexico Sandia, 49
New Mexico State University, xi
New York City, bottled hot sauces, 172
North African cuisine, 118
North American cooking, 152–69
novels and other writings, chili in, 198–201
NuMex Big Jim, 35
NuMex Twilight, 49

O

Oaxaca, 76
obesity, chili as preventive, 27
OC (oleoresin capsicum), 228–29
offerings to the gods, 80
Ogeer, Wahid, 66
Olmec people, 76, 79–82
opiates, 23
opioids, 250–51
Orozco, 49
Ottoman Empire, 117
Oviedo y Valdés, Gonzalo Fernández de, 101
oysters, 234–35

P

pain
  enjoyment of, 191–92, 267–70
  men vs. women in dealing with, 249–51
palate, desensitized, 19–20, 207
paleolithic diet, 260
Paper Lantern, 64
paprika, 143–48
Parmentier, Antoine-Augustin, 240
Pasado, 50
Pasilla, 50
Pasilla de Oaxaca, 50
Peking duck, 134
Pendery, DeWitt Clinton, 158–59
penis
  enlargement of, 217, 223
  a pepper resembling, 221
Peperoncino, 50, 142

Peppadew, 68–69
pepper (black), 97, 110–11
pepper sauce, 170–84
pepper sprays, 228–29
pepper vodka, 149
Pepper X, 61, 64, 211
peptic ulcers, 120
Pequin, 51
Perón, 69
Perry, Linda, 5, 78
Persian cuisine, 118
perspiration, 188
Peru, 6, 78, 85
Peter I the Great, 148
Peter Pepper, 51, 221
Philippines, 108
Pickapeppa Hot Pepper Sauce, 181
Pickapeppa Sauce, 181
pimentón, 143
Pimiento, 51
Pimiento de Padrón, 52
Piri Piri, 6, 36, 56, 58
Pizarro, Francisco, 85–86
pizza, 261
Poblano, 5, 48, 52
Poe, Edgar Allan, 200
Poland, 149
police, capsaicin use by,
    228–29
Portugal/Portuguese
    in Africa, 106
    in Americas, 99–102
    in Asia, 124–26, 201–2
    colonization, 107–15
    cooking/cuisine, 101–2, 109–10,
    142
    slave trade, 105
potatoes, 86, 239–41
Prairie Fire, 52–53
Protestant theology, 140, 216
psychoactive substances,
    252–53
PuckerButt Pepper Company, ix, xv,
    60, 61, 64, 237
puya, 179

Q

qixingjiao ("facing heaven pepper"),
    132

R

red color of foods, xvii, 126
Red Devil, 204
Red Habanero, 204
Red Hot Chili Peppers (a rock band),
    213
Red Savina, 65
reward response, 251–53
Riot, 53
risk taking, 246–49
    pointless (gratuitous), 247–49
    pointless (idiotic), 254–57
rocoto, 6, 69, 88–89
rocoto longo, 69
rocot uchu, 87
Rohingya people, 230
Romania, 146
root-knot nematode, 38
Russia, 147–48

S

Saavedra, Jose-Luis Sr., 179
Sahagún, Bernardino de, 77, 84–85
Saint Kitts, 181
St. Louis, 173
Salsa Tamazula, 179
San Antonio, 165–68
Santa Fe Grande, 53
Santaka, 53
Santamaría, Francisco, 164–65
sarsaparilla, 233
sassafras, 233–34
Satan's Kiss, 204
sauces, 141, 153–54
Scandinavia, 147
Scotch Bonnet, 6, 65
Scoville, Wilbur Lincoln, 18
Scoville heat unit (SHU), ix
seasoning, chili as, 11, 74, 80
Sebes, 53–54
Seidler, Kamilla, 207
self-defense, capsaicin used for,
    228
sensation-seeking (SS) individuals,
    251–53
sensory neurons, 21
sepen, 187
Serpent, 63
Serrano, 54

sex
    aids for newlyweds, 217
    chili and, xviii, 213–23
sex differences
    in chili eating, 248–54
    in dealing with pain, 248–51
shamanic medicine, xviii
Shishito, 54
shizhuyu, 128
SHU readings, ix, 19–20, 32
Sichuan, 123–26, 242
    cuisine, 130–32
Sichuan peppercorns, 127, 131
signatures doctrine, 220–21
Siling Labuyo, 58–59
Silk Road, 123
Simmons, Amelia, 153
The Simpsons, 208–9
skin creams, capsaicin-based, 29
slave trade, xvi, 100, 105–6
slow food movement, 259
Smith, Eliza, 152
Smith, Mike, 61
Smith, S. Compton, 163
Smokin' Ed's Carolina Reaper, ix–x
snake oil, 243–44
Solonaceae family, 3
Song of Songs (Bible), 214, 217
Sos (Sauce) Ti-Malice, 182
South America, 4
Southeast Asia, taste for chili in, 191,
    201, 265
South Pacific, Chinese in, 125
Southwest (U.S.), cuisine, 155–69
Soyer, Alexis, 198
Spain/Spanish
    in Africa, 106
    in Americas, 83, 85–90, 99–102, 225
    cooking, 142, 143
    trade and colonization, 107–8
Späth, Ernst, 16
Spice Islands (Moluccas), 108
spices
    accused of provoking temper and
        concupiscence, 188
    medical uses of, in humoral theory,
        137–38
    mystique of, 232
    suspicion of, by Europeans, 216–17

spice trade, 92–93, 96–98, 137–38,
    139–40, 232–33
spicy hot taste (China), 127
Sri Lanka, 201
sriracha, 113, 183
Stanley, Clark, 243–44
subtraction diets, 260
sugar, xv–xvi, 100
sugo all'arrabbiata, 143
Super Chili F1, 54
superhot movement, 232–44
    men (males) in, 245–57
    younger generation in, 236
Suriname Red, 65
Suriname Yellow, 59, 65–66
Szentesi Semihot, 55

T

Tabasco, 6, 59, 173
Tabasco hot sauce, 173–76
Taino people, 94–95, 225
Takanotsume, 55
Tang Xianzu, 126–27
Tapatío Hot Sauce, 179
tastes, five, in Chinese gastronomy, 127
Taylor, Butch, 66
tea, 139
Tears of Fire, 55
Tehuacán Valley, 75
Terry, Marshall, 209
testosterone, 250
Tewksbury, Joshua, 13–15
Texas, 160, 163–69
Texas Pete Hot Sauce, 178
Tex-Mex cuisine, 156–57, 260
"Thai chili," 36
Thai Dragon F1, 55
Thailand, xiii, 242
    cuisine, 112–13
Thai pepper, 6
Thresh, John Clough, 16
Tibetan cooking, 187–88
Tobin, William, 167
togarashi, 114
Tokyo Hot F1, 56
tomatoes, 154–55
Tran, David, 182–83
transient receptor potential (TRP)
    channel, 12, 21

Trappey, Bernard, 176
Trappey's Louisiana-Style,
    176–77
Treaty of Tordesillas, 99–100
"tree chili," 42
Trinidad and Tobago, 6, 180
Trinidad Moruga Scorpion, 66
Trinidad Scorpion Butch T, 66–67
Trollope, Anthony, 200–201
Turner, Jack, 97

U

Ubatuba Cambuci, 68
uchu (chili), 87
Ukraine, 146, 149
umami, 127, 153
Underwood Deviled Ham Spread,
    197–98
United States
    bottled hot sauces, 171–78
    cookbooks, 153–55
    hot pepper movement in, x
    Westward expansion, 241
U.S. Virgin Islands, 182

V

Valentina, 179
Venetian Republic, 117
Veracruz, 76
Victorian cookery, 200–201
vindaloo, 110, 247
vitamins in chili, 7, 25
vodka, chili-flavored, 148–49

W

war, chili used in, 224–31
warding off evil spirits with chili,
    202–3
water, not a chili antidote, 23
West Africa, 100, 202
Western cuisine, xiv, 16–17, 120
Western Spice Mills, 173
White, Maunsel, 173
wild bird pepper, 5–6
wild chili
    domestication of, 73
    evolution of, 3–4
    gathering of, 9
women, and chili, xiv–xv,
    248–54
Woods, Nick, 63
Worcestershire sauce, 171

X

Xiaomila, 6

Y

Yellow lantern, 6
Yi Yin, 127
young people, and chili, 236
Yunnan, 6
yuxiang, 131

Z

Zenker, F. G., 147
zhitianjiao, 43
Zunsheng Bajian, 126

31901064532791